To The Good People of Gaza

To The Good People of Gaza

THEATRE FOR YOUNG PEOPLE BY JACKIE LUBECK AND THEATRE DAY PRODUCTIONS

Edited and with an introduction by
SAMER AL-SABER

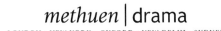

LONDON • NEW YORK • OXFORD • NEW DELHI • SYDNEY

METHUEN DRAMA
Bloomsbury Publishing Plc
50 Bedford Square, London, WC1B 3DP, UK
1385 Broadway, New York, NY 10018, USA
29 Earlsfort Terrace, Dublin 2, Ireland

BLOOMSBURY, METHUEN DRAMA and the Methuen Drama logo are trademarks of Bloomsbury Publishing Plc

First published in Great Britain 2022

Plays copyright © Jackie Lubeck, 2022
Introduction copyright © Samer Al-Saber, 2022
Afterword copyright © Jan Willems, 2022

Jackie Lubeck has asserted her right under the Copyright, Designs and Patents Act, 1988, to be identified as author of this work.

Saber Al-Samer has asserted his right under the Copyright, Designs and Patents Act, 1988, to be identified as editor of this work.

Cover design: Jess Stevens

All rights reserved. No part of this publication may be reproduced or transmitted in any form or by any means, electronic or mechanical, including photocopying, recording, or any information storage or retrieval system, without prior permission in writing from the publishers.

Bloomsbury Publishing Plc does not have any control over, or responsibility for, any third-party websites referred to or in this book. All internet addresses given in this book were correct at the time of going to press. The author and publisher regret any inconvenience caused if addresses have changed or sites have ceased to exist, but can accept no responsibility for any such changes.

No rights in incidental music or songs contained in the work are hereby granted and performance rights for any performance/presentation whatsoever must be obtained from the respective copyright owners.

All rights whatsoever in this play are strictly reserved and application for performance etc. should be made before rehearsals by professionals and by amateurs to the respective copyright holders

No performance may be given unless a licence has been obtained.

A catalogue record for this book is available from the British Library.

A catalog record for this book is available from the Library of Congress.

ISBN:	HB:	978-1-3502-6182-2
	PB:	978-1-3502-6181-5
	ePDF:	978-1-3502-6183-9
	eBook:	978-1-3502-6184-6

Typeset by RefineCatch Limited, Bungay, Suffolk

To find out more about our authors and books visit www.bloomsbury.com and sign up for our newsletters.

Contents

Preface *Jackie Lubeck* vii

Introduction *Samer Al-Saber* 1

1: To The Good People of Gaza (2010)
  Play #1: The Blue Play 9
  Play #2: The Red Play 23
  Play #3: The White Play 37

2: Entanglement (2011)
  Play #1: The Grandfathers 51
  Play #2: The Mothers 65
  Play #3: The Brothers 75
  Play #4: The Sisters 87

3: A Human Writes (2012)
  Play #1: The Weavers 99
  Play #2: The Electricians 117
  Play #3: The Cooks 131

4: Lost and Found (2013)
  Play #1: The Room 153
  Play #2: The Shop 165
  Play #3: The School 179
  Play #4: The Brother 195
  Play #5: The Tree 207

5: Thirteen Ways of Looking at a Blackbird (2015)
  Play #1: One Thousand Questions 223
  Play #2: The Snow Trip 237
  Play #3: The Boys in the Mirror 251
  Play #4: The Boys Who Can't Sit Still 263

Afterword *Jan Willems* 277
Vernacular glossary 281

Preface

What would happen if I wrote the word 'blue', I asked myself after we signed the agreement with United Nations Refugee and Works Agency (UNRWA) in Gaza to provide 200,000 school children with a theatre day during the summer programme of 2010. With blue coloured text, I typed *The Blue Play* and began with the description of the costumes and sets. When the first character spoke, it was a boy on the telephone, talking to our theatre in Gaza City. He was asking if the next play could be about him, his friend, and the boy they both saved. He knew that Theatre Day Productions told stories and he had one.

As the boys in the blue play began to make decisions, lines were deleted as soon as they were written, and I noticed how fed up we all were with our complaints about ourselves and the dire political situation in the Gaza Strip. Misery was becoming boring. There were good people in Gaza. We worked and played with them every day. They were the school boys and girls, the mothers and drivers, the excited teachers, the shopkeepers and fruit-sellers, those who regularly baked birthday cakes, and who sided against pain and disappointment. What about them? What about the good and regular people of Gaza with their thoughtful and sometimes utopian reactions to the most horrible events. Written in 2010, the four colour-coded plays were worked around the smartest and kindest impulses of people in Gaza under the most cruel of circumstances.

The tone of this collection stayed with me during the daily and expected routine horrors that took place in the Gaza Strip and over the five years that I wrote plays for the summer programme. It was almost unbearable to think of these characters and the people they represent during the deadly bombardments in 2009, 2012, and 2014. All of them, under the rain of bombs, still baking birthday cakes while defending their young.

Dust settles. The people come out. Stories are told.

As the boys in the blue play began to make decisions, lines were deleted as soon as they were written, and I noticed how fed up we all were with our complaints about ourselves and the dire political situation in the Gaza Strip. Misery was becoming boring. There were good people in Gaza. We worked and played with them every day. They were the school boys and girls, the mothers and drivers, the excited teachers, the shopkeepers and fruit-sellers, those who regularly baked birthday cakes, and who sided against pain and disappointment. What about them? What about the good and regular people of Gaza with their thoughtful and sometimes utopian reactions to the most horrible events. Written in 2010, the four colour-coded plays were worked around the smartest and kindest impulses of people in Gaza under the most cruel of circumstances.

When relative calm falls over Gaza, a question mark shows. Families are tense and households are entangled with each other and with the military authority that both lets people live and regularly tries to kill them. Grandfathers dwell in the memories of a homeland long gone, a solution never to be found in their life-times, and mothers, brothers, and sisters take their places in the hierarchal way of life lived by most Palestinians. The four 'entanglement' plays bring sixteen related people to the stage, on one day in a hot summer. Grandfathers, mothers, brothers, and sisters, each live in a world of their own, barely connected to each other, examining life from their specific perspectives, and bringing the audience four versions of existence.

The plays of 2012 began life as a never-produced five-act play. *Three Sisters* brought a young modern leader – the new king – to power. He is watched over by the old and corrupt Wazir of his father's reign. Our good king Mazen tries to get things done in a practical and reasonable way while the old values stop him at every corner. As the mammoth play was never produced, I broke it up into *The Weavers*, *The Cooks* and *The Electricians* with the *Money Changers* still waiting to be written, all characters from the main play. In a land where Mercedes are horse-drawn carriages and email is hand-delivered, our king walks among the people listening and coming to solutions on issues from water, health and of course electricity (not working since 2008).

The year 2014 would be a short year before the skies opened up for fifty-two days of black deadly rain during the month of Ramadan. Summer was cancelled for war but the school year did come and we were asked to prepare a programme for both teachers and kids before the year started. I looked at what was lost. All that is precious: house, shop, tree, school and people. I wrote six plays, each with three players, three for girls, three for boys, because that's what the UNRWA programme needed. I found six stories and the series is called *Lost and Found*.

If there were 'Thirteen Ways of Looking at a Blackbird' certainly there were thirteen ways to explain the Gaza Strip. The last plays I wrote were an attempt to do just this. What are the thirteen images of this place that bring so many into such confusion? Why is Gaza Gaza? Siege, religion, family, sand, prison, birds, noise, sandwiches, depression, sea, heat, smiles and phones. Thirteen words that regularly circle overhead for residents of Gaza. To these qualities, I add a stubborn desire to hope, to go on, and to assume that something might one day change. These six plays were written and inspired by a Wallace Stevens poem of the same title.

Here they are. The last plays I wrote for Theatre Day Productions in Gaza. What makes these plays different from those preceding them is that no one improvised for me. Unlike the plays of prior years, there were no rehearsals for research. The plays were written in Jerusalem after I was banned from Gaza. I have never seen them nor heard them in the Arabic, for which they were written. Maybe they are the 'exile' plays. Maybe that's what happens when you cannot go where you want to be.

Jackie Lubeck
Jerusalem 2021 – Lockdown

Introduction
Samer Al-Saber

To The Good People of Gaza is an anthology of plays written for Gaza by Jackie Lubeck, an American who arrived in Palestine in 1972, then never left. Few questions arise from our encounter with these plays, and thankfully immense answers live in their words, dialogues, characters, plots, and more expressively, staged experience. This introduction serves as a guide for reading and producing these plays by way of reflecting on the answerable questions and highlighting the embedded answers that may easily go unnoticed. But before we delve into the joys, light, ingenuity and darkness that make up this anthology, we must contend with the perception that these plays are not written by a Palestinian. This imperative is a product of today's considerations of the politics of identity, not a necessity for the context of the plays or the playwright. Who is Jackie Lubeck? What does this anthology say about the critical identity politics of today? Where does Theatre Day Productions fit in the unique and unprecedented recent history of Palestine in one respect, but also in the contemporary realities of Gaza?

Playwright Jackie Lubeck

For nearly five decades, Lubeck worked in Palestinian theatre across occupied Palestinian territories, first operating lights and stage managing for her partner, the late director Francois Abu Salem, then becoming a crucial founding member of Jerusalem's El-Hakawati Theatre Company from 1977 until they disbanded in 1990. In the early nineties, Lubeck worked with Edward Muallem and Iman Aoun in Ashtar Theatre, which operated in both Jerusalem, Ramallah, and Gaza. In 1995, with her Dutch husband Jan Willems, she founded Theatre Day Productions, a company that can be described today as a twenty-five-year young theatrical odyssey. Lubeck's persistence and durability can be exceeded by few figures in contemporary Palestinian theatre. Undoubtedly, in terms of cultural institution building in Palestine, the size, scope and continuity of Lubeck's contributions can only be compared to the journeys of Al-Kasaba's George Ibrahim, Sanabel Theatre's Ahmad Abu Sal'oum and Ashtar's Edward Muallem who was her compatriot from the days of El-Hakawati. Leading women such as Iman Aoun, Raeda Ghazaleh and Marina Barham, among many, have created prolific lives in contemporary Palestinian theatre, all constructing their own uniquely different paths, albeit witnessing Lubeck's near half century-long achievements in Palestinian cultural production.

This playwright's early days in theatre were coincidental. She worked as a stagehand and production assistant on Sunduq Al-'ajab's production of *Lamma Injanina* (*When We Went Crazy*). Her minor contribution to the production led to her becoming François Abu Salem's premier theatrical confidante and protégé in addition to being a romantic partner. From Abu Salem, she learned the power of collaboration, stepping in for missing actors and supporting production in technical roles. Before long, in every sense of the word, they were creative partners. Not even Lubeck can determine the degree of his influence on her or hers on Abu Salem's recognized artistic contributions. But it is clear that Abu Salem's years with Lubeck were his most productive, adventurous, worldly, and perhaps, aesthetically generative. In those years, 1977–90, as a husband-and-wife duo, with their partners in El-Hakawati, they created theatre that rivalled world-class theatrical experiences of the ilk of the Grotowski company and Theatre de Soleil. During this period, Lubeck grew into a theatre artist, professional ensemble member, co-founder, improvisor, actor, playwright, designer, producer, fundraiser and accomplished creator.

Theatre Day Productions (TDP) can be seen as the culmination of Lubeck's successes and failures during her years at El-Hakawati 'university', where much of her work was improvised and often in reaction to or in support of fellow ensemble members and her primary collaborators, including François Abu Salem, Edward Muallem and Radi Shehadeh. In TDP, she successfully co-created an institution that is undeniably hers. Her fundraising approach developed into an artform. While she wrote one play for El-Hakawati, she conceived of and wrote ten for TDP. By comparison, her considered and considerable experience in the establishing, funding and running of TDP far outweighs her contributions as a singular leading member of El-Hakawati. François' naive love-struck Jackie of the mid 1970s may bear resemblance to Jackie's 1980s theatrical dynamo worker-bee in El-Hakawati, but certainly pales in comparison to the mature businesswoman, playwright and artist, who manifested a million-dollar theatrical institution into existence in the early twenty-first century.

Identity politics: What's a Palestinian?

How long does it take to become a Palestinian? If one is born to Palestinian parents, it takes about nine months of pregnancy and a successful birth. Who is more Palestinian, a baby just born to a Palestinian parent or the American-born Lubeck after five decades of working in Palestinian theatre? Her marriages to a Frenchman, who adopted Palestinian culture and dialect as his own and a Dutch citizen, who worked with her in Palestine as an equal, did not facilitate her assimilation into Palestinian society. Although she adopted the nuances of Palestinian politics, she never became a Palestinian in the familial sense. But can Lubeck write an American play or television script with as much expertise as her work in Palestinian theatre? Her plays are culturally Palestinian. They exhibit familiar everyday concerns in Gaza, whether they are dealing with recent war times, children's fantasies, quality of life, the Nakba, the occupation, health, dreams, money, destruction, gender, or family structure. They are also decidedly influenced by a world heritage of popular cultural production in the way Palestinian playwrights adapt tropes and formulas that are familiar to Western readers and theatre-makers.

The greatest challenge of identity politics is the constantly changing rules of engagement according to each context and set of power relations. A Palestinian immigrant in America fights to be recognized as both a citizen and a Palestinian, even at times, refusing assimilation in favour of a hyphenated identity or one that equally and discretely claims both identities. Can an American maintain their identity while adopting a partial Palestinian one? Is Jackie Lubeck a Palestinian playwright? Is she a playwright of/in Palestinian theatre? Is she an American playwright who writes Palestinian plays? How necessary are these categorizations to the reading of these plays? These questions are premised on essentialized characteristics of who and what is Palestinian. They suggest that identity is acquired by birth, not experience. Yet, the experience of the Palestinian people is itself a counterpoint to the idea that historical belonging is simply a question of birthright. The State of Israel buttresses its claim to a population of world Jewry by amplifying the value of the birthright essentialism. The most salient Palestinian critique to this claim is one of lived experience: Palestinians live under occupation, have no citizenship rights and ultimately live without prospects of self-determination. While the state aims to grow its population on an essentialism, Palestinians demand human rights that are premised on lived experience. In the end, the impasse is one of access: despite the existence of many exceptions, the State of Israel sees Palestinians as essentially not Israeli, nor Jewish, therefore, not potential citizens for assimilation into Hebrew culture. If Palestinians truly are a pluralistic society that rejects the logic of the occupying state, should not their identity be flexible, definitively anti-essentializing and possible to be adopted? Casting meaning and motives upon State logics and identity politics is a futile exercise, but this deconstruction makes for a more reasonable understanding of Lubeck's personal subject position and professional choices.

The premise of contemporary identity politics as Stacy Abrams once put it in *Foreign Affairs* is that it equalizes the playing field. But this function of the phenomenon assumes a set of power relations where an oppressed population resists forces such as colonialism or patriarchy. How must individuals like Jackie Lubeck be seen when their lineage aligns with American empire and the Israeli project in the Middle East, but their politics, practices and actions align with the Palestinian struggle? The contemporary tendency to evaluate her and her record based on a common set of labels must be resisted. An analysis of her positionality is more appropriate because identity is in the details. She is more than an ally because she dedicated a lifetime to practicing Palestinian theatre as a professional pursuit. She has not adopted Palestinian family life through marriage and was not adopted into a Palestinian family, therefore, she is not assimilated into Palestinian society and its familial structures. In Palestine, both in the West Bank and Gaza, she has long-standing professional relationships, personal friendships, influential connections, social networks and artistic associations that are far deeper than those of an expatriate or a foreigner. Lubeck is fully embedded in Palestine. The necessary question is: can one be a Palestinian theatre professional without being of Palestinian lineage? Of course!

In her long commitment to Palestinian theatre, Lubeck has rejected basic essentialisms. When asked about her lineage, Lubeck said: 'One could say – like with the ear of Van Gogh in one of the books "let's get this out of the way". I was born to two Jewish parents who likened religion to a culinary experience. I have learned to trade chicken soup and potato pancakes for mansaf and mjadara with ease.' This description adopts the informality of Palestinian culture, insisting on the significance of lived experience and emphasizing her relationship with the people and the place. This approach exists similarly in her plays, which examine how human beings encounter living conditions, not the essentialisms constructed to control them. In this sense, Lubeck and her work carry the same identity: a lived experience in Palestine under harsh conditions that she has shared in real time with her colleagues, neighbours, co-workers and friends. Her life is not heroic in the manner of foreigners who pretend to conquer another culture, but it is distinctive in her unwavering commitment to Palestine and its theatre. As far as the politics of identity is concerned, although fifty years of living in a place may not change one's lineage or genetic makeup, it does present the undeniable reality that identity is a fluid idea. Just as I, a Palestinian theatre-maker, can write and grow into a Canadian or American playwright or scholar while proudly maintaining my ongoing commitment to my practiced, historical and familial Palestinian identity, a young woman from Brooklyn may carry memories and perspectives from her early life, then grow into a maker of Palestinian theatre and provide deep insights into the lives of people under siege in Gaza. As a point of departure, I will not fetishize her identity and neither should you. Instead, let us focus on the plays.

Reading Lubeck's plays

Jackie Lubeck wrote the plays in this anthology for Theatre Day Productions' partnership with the United Nations Relief and Work Agency (UNRWA). Performed by and for Palestinian refugee youth during a yearly event called *The Summer Games*, these plays represent five years of the most active theatrical enterprise in Gaza from 2010 to 2015. The UNRWA wanted to create activities for their students who were normally on summer vacation. The usual activities were in the areas of sports, painting, sculpture, music and other creative pursuits, but at the time they did not include the theatre. When approached to create such a programme for tens of thousands of Gazan youth, Willems and Lubeck initially did not believe it would be possible. How can the live and personal creative practice of theatre reach tens of thousands of children in one summer? Swimming, acrobatics and soccer could function like summer camps because all they needed were coaches and appropriate common facilities. By contrast, performed plays need theatrical spaces, scripts, costumes, music, directors, actors, rehearsals, audiences and long periods of preparation. The negotiations between UNRWA and TDP led to the development of a programme that included the creation of these plays and a remarkable method for producing youth theatre.

The programme is a miraculous exercise in theatre management and practice. To understand it, one must consider consider some of the realities of education in Gaza. One of UNRWA's key resources for Palestinian refugees is its schools, which are a limited resource as real estate and supply of participating populations. Many of the school buildings functioned in scheduled shifts to accommodate more students. For example, in one building, a school has a particular population attending from 7:30am until noon. Upon their departure, another set of students arrives, but these students are an entirely different school that has a different name, attending from 12:30 to 5pm. Each school had its own set of employees, teachers, cleaning staff and guards. Inspired by this idea of shift schools, TDP created its own discrete sets of teachers who worked in shifts for each school. Just as a school changes their population, the TDP teaching team would repeat the morning programme in the afternoon, thus reaching a second school while working in the same building. Simultaneously, this effort would occur in other school buildings across the Gaza Strip, multiplying limited resources through this practice. By having multiple teams working the same programme across the UNRWA system simultaneously and technically in repertory, TDP was able to reach tens of thousands of youths each summer. The entire programme typically ran for a period of ten to sixteen weeks, depending on various factors including political conditions, safety from Israeli bombardments and whether Ramadan occurred in the summer. Consider the magnitude of this effort: in a series that has four plays, all plays are performed by three teams each, twice a day, for 200 to 250 children per show, six days a week for several weeks.

To envision or produce these plays effectively, a reader must take the production context into account. While the plays were produced through intimate work by small teaching teams with a small number of students, they were also produced for large schools that often have enrollments of a thousand students or more. Moreover, they were systematically rehearsed and mounted in each school by teaching teams and students who were aware of other teaching teams and students attempting to create the same endeavour. In effect, imprinted within these plays is a culture of theatre-making and a codified system of production in and for UNRWA in Gaza. The pattern of production is simple but emotionally draining and labour intensive: small teaching teams, minimal set requirements, locally recognizable costumes, few characters that often do not exceed five, specific local settings and culturally Palestinian content that acknowledges the harsh realities in Gaza, while providing a template for the youth to think and dream beyond the context of siege, war and destruction. Unsurprisingly, the template of production demonstrates a deep understanding of Gazan realities. None of the plays demand conditions that do not already exist in the schools. Characters are separated by gender. The stories abide by the tenets of Gazan traditions. Most pertinent to reading the plays is Lubeck's embeddedness in Palestine for nearly fifty years and thus the emergence of the plays from local life and concerns.

Each set of plays contains two contradicting forces that mirror Gazan realities: a desire for levity and freedom on one hand, and an intensely predominant reality of destruction and death on the other. In the aftermath of the bombardments of 2010, *To The Good People of Gaza* celebrates families and children who help each other out in times of distress: sewing a wedding dress, collaborating to collectively succeed, and bringing familial warmth in the absence of treatment for a dying child. After the 2011 destruction, *Entanglement* nurtures cohesion within Palestinian society as political parties divide and see no hope of unity. We see Palestinian grandfathers proudly recounting their stories to a census officer, while brothers work together to defend their neighbourhood, sisters fight stunted customs, and mothers struggle to save their families. In the dire conditions of siege in 2012, *A Human Writes* revels in the ingenuity of Gazan life, where a young king communicates with his people. The electricians' genius makes a computer work from nothing, the weavers combine forces to create cloth and the cooks inspire a life of equality. In 2013, still reeling from Israel's 'Pillar of Defense' operation in the previous year, Lubeck focused the next set of plays on the aftermath of destruction. *Lost and Found* told stories of living in a destroyed room, shop, and school. In effect, admiring young people's resilience as they live, study, work and commune in the rubbles of these spaces. The war on Gaza in 2014 prevented the summer games from happening, but in 2015, Lubeck's *Thirteen Ways of Looking at a Blackbird*, inspired by a Wallace Stevens poem, articulated stories and voices that emerged from unanswered question and posttraumatic circumstances. How might a Gazan child feel about snow in Jerusalem? Might learning the value of a single great memory help young boys fall asleep? Is it possible for all of one's selves to co-exist after collective trauma?

To read or perform these plays is an expression of walking in the shoes of Gazan youth, who have previously performed them. In the process, a relinquishing of privilege must be exercised and aspired to. How might one feel if they were part of a society under siege? What might being a refugee or a descendent from refugees be like? Is there a way to understand one's life through the complications, joys, and struggles of youth who do not have basic rights and privileges that most young people should have? Each play provides an opportunity for deep insight and a joyful game. Conceptually, Lubeck plants playful rhythms and actions in each play. Whether old men are playing a local version of backgammon, boys in the midst of a spelling game, or girls whispering into a box, the actions of the characters tend to take place in an alternate reality that, perhaps, can only happen in Gaza. Structurally, the author opens the play by introducing a situation that develops into a quirky dramatic action, and most often closes with a surprising revelation. The dialogue is dynamic: fully capitalized words in the plays don't always indicate shouting. They suggest potential variations, such as concern, provocation, and sometimes, shouting. All the actions and the situations are familiar to the youth, resulting in easy involvement, mimicry, and performance.

As theatres, artists, schools, universities, teachers and students consider producing these plays, Palestinian realities that motivated these works continue to exist on the ground. Gaza and its people continue to survive against extreme odds. Their ingenuity and creativity generate inspiration to Palestinians and allies across the world. Theatre Day Productions continues to function under duress and despite unrelenting political instability. These realities are deeply embedded in the plays, even when they are not explicitly stated. The profound connection – between the energy of the youth in the stories and in performance, and the horrific violence experienced in living conditions, siege and war – cannot be underestimated in production. While the stories may effortlessly generate laughter in rehearsal and before the audience, they cannot become an anthropological experiment of visiting a war zone. As 'The Summer Games' was a magnificent effort to heal wounds by opening up possibilities through imagination, the experience of staging and watching these plays must nurture the impulse to be involved in bettering the lives of the people of Palestine, particularly in Gaza. The actions resulting from this impulse invariably inspire all involved to grow into the individuals they have always aspired to become.

I enthusiastically recommend that you read, produce, and perform these plays.

1: To The Good People of Gaza (2010)

Play #1: The Blue Play

Characters

Boy One, *a good kid.*
Boy Two, *can't read.*
Boy Three, *a not so good kid.*
Boy Four, *can't talk.*

Everything is variations of blue. Jeans, light blue shirts, striped blue shirts. **Boy One** and **Boy Two** *are on stage. They look at the mobile phone that* **Boy One** *is holding.*

Prologue: Calling the theatre. Kareem is on the phone (*happens off set*)

Boy One   I'm going to call him.

Boy Two   Call. Call.

Boy One *hesitates and then finally calls.* **Boy Two** *stands there. During the phone call,* **Boy Two** *loses all concentration: he ties his shoes, unties them, ties them, and they become untied. He moves around, can't stand still. He takes a bag of smashed chips from his pocket and starts to eat them.* **Boy One** *is trying to keep him by his side.* **Boy Two** *tries to listen on the phone. He tries to talk. He generally bothers* **Boy One**.

Boy One   Kareem? Hi, how are you doing? (*Listening.*) Oh. I am the boy from (*name of school*). I was in the summer games last year and you were the teacher. I am Mohammed from Gaza School B and I was the one who told the story about the stupidest kid in the world and then we made a scene that was really funny and everyone was laughing. (*Listening.*) You remember me! (*Listening.*) I'm fine. Everything is fine. I found your phone number in the flyer. I kept the flyer. I hope I'm not bothering you. (*Listening.*) No, everything is fine. About that story . . . that was a real story. The boy is my neighbour. His father wants to pull him out of school. The teachers are trying to help him but you know how that goes. (*Pause.*) I was wondering if you have any ideas of how I can teach him. Kareem, he doesn't know how to read. It's really a problem. (*Pause.*) OK. I'm listening. (*Listening.*) A game? (*Listening.*) I can do that. (*Listening.*) Ah, ah, ah, I remember that game. (*Listening.*) OK. (*Listening.*) OK. (*Listening.*) OK. (*Listening.*) OK. (*Listening.*) OK. (*Listening.*) I'll try it out. (*Listening.*) Thursday. (*Listening.*) At three. Great. Thanks. Thanks a whole lot. It would be funny if it works. Thank you. Assalamu Alaykum.

Boy One (*to* **Boy Two**)   What's the matter with you? Can't you stand still for a second?

Boy Two   No. What'd he say? What about Thursday? What about three? Thursday is a bad day. I can't do anything on Thursday. I have to work for my father on Thursday.

Boy One   Calm. I'm going to meet him on Thursday. You . . . don't do anything. Tie your shoes.

Boy Two   They keep coming undone.

Boy One   Because you're doing it wrong. Look. (*He shows him.*) Now you. (**Boy Two** *doesn't do it right.*) Together. This here, and this here, and cross, and no, no, cross, and over, and through. From the beginning. (*They continue.*) If you can't tie your shoes, how are you going to learn how to read?

Boy Two   I don't wanna read. Who needs reading? No one in the whole family can read. I don't even know what a book looks like. I'm hungry. Let's go catch rats.

Boy One   Fine. Let's go catch rats. Where?

Boy Two   Near the port. That's where they're fat and big.

Near the port. Water blue, big blue garbage bags, blue garbage, water garbage, bright blue, faded blue, grey-blue, black-blue, mix of sea and blue. Even some green-blue, turquoise blue. Costumes blue.

Boy Two   We have to sit quietly before they start moving. They already heard us come so now they are hiding. Shshshsh.

Boy One   Rat. (*Spelling it out in letters.*) R-A-T.

Boy Two   What?

Boy One   R-A-T.

Boy Two   R-A-T.

Boy One   Rat.

Boy Two   Good.

Boy One   How do you catch a rat?

Boy Two   You don't know how to catch a R-A-T? Everyone knows how to do that.

Boy One   Show me.

Boy Two   OK. So we're sitting, right, real quiet. (*They sit.*) No. You moved. You can't move because that makes noise. (*They sit even more still.*) Good. That's better.

Boy One   Now what?

Boy Two   Listen, you hear that.

Boy One   Listen. L-I-S-T-E-N.

Boy Two   L-I-S-T-E-N. Listen, you hear.

Boy One   What?

Boy Two   Listen carefully. (*They listen with concentration.*)

Boy One   Yeah, I hear it.

Boy Two   That's a rat moving.

Boy One   Do you know how to spell 'moving'? M-O-V-I-N-G.

Boy Two   Moving. M-O-V-I-N-G. Now, when a R-A-T is M-O-V-I-N-G we cannot make a sound.

Boy One   Sound. S-O-U-N-D.

Boy Two   S-O-U-N-D. And without a S-O-U-N-D you take off your shoe.

Boy One   S-H-O-E.

Boy Two   And you wait until the R-A-T appears.

Boy One Appears. A-P-P-E-A-R-S.

Boy Two And when the R-A-T A-P-P-E-A-R-S – you take your S-H-O-E and hit him on the head with all your strength.

Boy One Head. H-E-A-D. Strength. S-T-R-E-N-G-T-H.

Boy Two If you don't hit the R-A-T on the H-E-A-D with all your S-T-R-E-N-G-T-H he will run away and we don't have the R-A-T. We really have to catch all the rats.

Boy One We catch. C-A-T-C-H.

Boy Two Are you ready to C-A-T-C-H your first R-A-T?

Boy One Absolutely. Let's do it. We sit silently.

Boy Two But if I can't read it, what's the use of it?

Boy One It's a game. That's what Kareem called it.

Boy Two Yeah, it's a game. Who's Kareem?

Boy One A guy. And there's another game . . . The next game I show you what each of the letters look like. Even more fun. And we will do this every day and, at the same time, we will catch all the rats.

Boy Two If we get bored of catching rats, can we also catch birds.

Boy One Absolutely. Birds. B-I-R-D-S.

Enter **Boy Three**.

Boy Three What are you doing?

Boy Two Catching R-A-T.

Boy One R-A-T-S-S-S-S. Rats. It's plural.

Boy Three Great. I'm playing with you.

Boy Two You know how to catch rats? Since when?

Boy Three Everyone knows how to catch rats.

Boy One E-V-E-R-Y-O-N-E. Everyone.

Boy Three What are you doing?

Boy Two Catching rats.

Boy Three No, with the E-V-E-R-Y-O-N-E?

Boy Two Nothing. It's part of something.

Boy One Something. S-O-M-E-T-H-I-N-G.

Boy Two S-O-M-E-T-H-I-N-G.

Boy Three Stop. You'll scare the rats.

Boy One   Scare. S-C-A-R-E.

Boy Three   You're both idiots.

Boy Two   Wait. Listen. (*To the rat.*) I hear you. I hear you Mr Dirty Rat.

Boy One   Dirty. D-I-R-T-Y.

Boy Two   Shshshshshshsh.

Silence. The boys silently take off their shoes. They all raise a shoe high and POW . . . they kill the first rat.

Boy Two   Excellent. (*Waiting.*) Excellent. (*Waiting.*) I said excellent.

Boy One (*surprised by the dead rat*)   Excellent. E-X-C-E-L-L-E-N-T.

They sit.

Boy Two   E-X-C-E-L-L-E-N-T.

Boy Three   If you two don't stop that, I'm leaving.

Boy Two   We're C-A-T-C-H-I-N-G R-A-T-S.

Boy Three   Shut up, you idiot. I'm going.

Boy One   Idiot. I-D-I-O-T.

Boy Two   That's an important one. (*To* **Boy Three**.) I-D-I-O-T.

Boy Three   I said shut up and you will N-E-V-E-R L-E-A-R-N T-O R-E-A-D because you are finished.

Boy One   F-I-N-I-S-H-E-D. Finished.

Boy Two   What did he say? What did he spell?

Boy One   Forget it. It's not worth it. (*To* **Boy Three**.) Go home.

Boy Three   I'm going. But if you keep making all that noise, the rats will never come out. (*He stays.*)

They catch another rat.

Boy Three   Oh great God forgive me for this mess. Astaghfirullah Al Adheem.

Boy Two   Spell.

Boy One *tries to spell* Astaghfirullah Al Adheem *and keeps getting stuck.* **Boy Three** *also tries. Finally, they all have this sentence worked out and they all do it, not in unison, but each one in his own time. They catch another rat.*

Boy Two   How many words are there?

Boy One   Words. W-O-R-D-S. I say there are a million. M-I-L-L-I-O-N.

Boy Two   That's a lot of words.

Boy Three   And that's a lot of rats. There aren't enough rats.

Boy Two   We're also going for birds. B-I-R-D-S.

Boy Three   I'm really good at catching birds. Actually, I'm the best.

Boy Two   Everyone knows how to catch birds. Why aren't you going home?

Boy Three   I am.

Boy Two   Shshshshshsh. Listen.

They catch another rat. And then another.

Boy Three (*to* **Boy Two**)   I heard your father is not letting you go back to school. That you're going to work in the market.

Boy One   Market. M-A-R-K-E-T.

Boy Two   M-A-R-K-E-T.

Boy Three   Because you're too old and you're too stupid. That's what I heard. Everyone on the street heard it. Everyone heard the story of that Mohammed. It's called 'The Stupidest Boy in the World'. He told it last summer.

Boy One (*angry*)   It was a make believe story. Shut up. Story. S-T-O-R-Y.

Boy Two   What S-T-O-R-Y?

Boy Three   About the stupidest kid in the word. And it sounded exactly like you. Even your name.

Boy Two (*to* **Boy One**)   What story?

Boy One   I'm telling you, it was pretend. Everyone was talking about everyone. They even talked about me and how I think I'm so smart. It was all pretend.

Boy Two   But you are smart.

Boy One   And you don't know how to read and that's no good. Read. R-E-A-D.

Boy Two   So it's true!

Boy One   It's halfway true.

Boy Three   You see. You're the stupidest kid in the world. W-O-R-L-D.

Silence.

Boy Two   I'm going home. I'm gonna to start collecting all the vegetables that fall off the other stands, the ones that are still good to eat. That's what my father said. I'm not with him in the stand but running after the vegetables. That's what he wants. Vegetables. V-E-G-E-T-A-B-L-E-S.

Boy One   You just spelled vegetables! All by yourself.

Boy Three   He's a real genius now.

Boy One   Will you shut up or I swear I'll hit until you die.

Boy Three   Fight. Fight. F-I-G-H-T.

Boy One   I'm not fighting.

Boy Three   Coward. C-O-W-A-R-D!

Boy Two (*to* **Boy Three**)   G-O H-O-M-E! (*Pause, to himself.*) I can spell? (*To* **Boy One**.) I'm really angry with you . . . but something is telling me I shouldn't be. So be careful. (*He hears something.*) Shshshshshsh.

They all hear a new noise.

Boy One   What's that?

Boy Two   I don't know. Shshshsh. I'm going to look.

Boy One   Careful. C-A-R-E-F-U-L

Boy Three   Will you stop that nonsense. Shshshsh.

Boy One   What is it?

Boy Two *finds* **Boy Four** *under the garbage. They pull him out. He is covered with junk and blue paint and looking ratty and miserable. Silence.*

Boy Two   What is this?

Boy One   It's a boy.

Boy Two   What kind of boy?

Boy Three   A rat boy.

Boy Four   Grggrgrgrgrgrgrgrgrgrgr.

Boy One (*to* **Boy Three**)   Why are you like that? Look what we found. A human boy. (*To* **Boy Four**.) Are you OK? Who are you?

Boy Two   Who is your father? F-A-T-H-E-R.

Boy Four   Blah wa blah ma. (*He cannot talk. He only makes sounds.*)

Boy Three   He's an idiot.

Boy Two   I-D-I-O-T. What do we do with him?

Boy Four   Blahahahahahahahah.

Boy Three   Hit him on the head. Hit him hard. Then he'll talk.

Boy One (*to* **Boy Four**)   Can you talk?

Boy Four   Blah wa blah ma.

Boy Two (*shouting loudly*)   Talk. Can you talk? Talk. T-A-L-K. Maybe he can spell.

Boy Four   Blah wa blah ma.

Boy Three   I know him. He can't talk. He's the biggest idiot in the world.

Boy Two   What are we gonna do with him? (*Pause. To* **Boy Four**.) R-A-T. Rat.

Boy Four   Blah wa blah ma.

Boy Two   No no no. R R R.

Boy Four   Blah Waawaaa blah.

Boy Three   I tell you he's an idiot.

Boy Two   Stop saying idiot . . .

Boy Four   Aaaaaaaaaah!

Boy One   He understands?

Boy Two   Why is he in the garbage? (*Shouting very loud to* **Boy Four**.) Why are you in the garbage?

Boy Three   He's not deaf, stop shouting. His parents don't want him around the house.

Boy Four   Ughghghg.

Boy One   He understand us. (*To* **Boy Four**.) Can you understand us?

Boy Four   Aaaaah.

Boy One   We have to help him. Help. H-E-L-P.

Boy Two   How? (*Thinking.*) H-O-W.

Boy Three   Forget it. There's no helping him. He's not good for spelling, not for the market, not for nothing. Only the garbage.

Boy Four   Grrrrrrrrrrrrrrrrrrrrrrrrrrrrr.

Boy One   He disagrees with you.

Boy Four   Aaaah.

Boy Three   So what?

Boy Four   Grrrrrrrrrrrrrrrrrrrrrrrrrrrrr.

Boy One   Look. He already doesn't like you. No one likes you.

Boy Three   Shut up.

Boy Two   He's right. No one likes you. You're the most hated kid in the world.

Boy One   It's true. No one likes you.

Boy Three   Shut up. Just both of you shut up.

Boy One   And they also told a story about you . . . or did you forget that?

Boy Three   I hope you both die . . . all three of you! (*He again pretends to leave.*)

Boy Two (*to* **Boy Four**)   Say 'rat'.

Boy Four   Trtrtrtrtrtr.

18   Play #1: The Blue Play

Boy Two   No. Rat. Rat. (*Shouting.*) Rat.

Boy One   Don't yell at him.

Boy Three   Very funny. The one who can't read is teaching the one who can't talk. God save us.

Boy One   I thought you were going home. Why don't you go home?

Boy Two   Because no one likes him at home. No one at all. (*To* **Boy Four**.) Say 'you'. Yoooooooo.

Boy Four   Ooooooo.

Boy One   Not bad. Again.

Boy Four   Oooooo. Trtrtrtrtrtrtr.

Boy Two   Again. YYYYou.

Boy Four (*desperately trying*)   Ooooo. Yooooooo.

Boy One   Right! Yes! Good. Good. G-O-O-D.

Boy Three   Hit him on the back.

Boy One   Go home.

Boy Three   Hit him on the back.

Boy Two   Go home.

Boy Two *and* **Boy One** *think.*

Boy One   Hit him gently.

Boy Two *hits* **Boy Four** *on the back.*

Boy Four (*to* **Boy Three**)   Yoooou Raaaaat!

Silence.

Boy Two   That's the best first sentence in the world. Let's try another one. (*To* **Boy Three**.) You rat!

Boy One   Yeah, you rat! (*Fast pause.*) How did you know that?

Boy Three   Just a guess.

Boy One (*to* **Boy Four**)   Mohammed. Mmmmhaaaammmmeddddd. M-O-H-A-M-M-E-D.

Boy Four   Mmmmmmmmmmm.

Boy Two   No. Mooohhhaaammmmeddddd.

Boy Four   Mmmmmmmmm.

Boy Three   Hit him.

Boy One   I'm not hitting him again. Go home. (*To* **Boy Two**.) Hit him again.

Boy Four   Mhmd.

Boy One   He almost said it.

Boy Two   Mohammed. Mohammed.

Boy Four   Mmmmmmm.

Boy One   Hit him again.

Boy Two *hits him again.*

Boy Four   Mhamed.

Silence.

Boy Two   He can talk.

Boy One   We can't just keep hitting him. He needs a doctor.

Boy Three   His parents don't want to go to the doctor. They have no money. They just ignore him.

Boy One   How do you know?

Boy Three   His family is really mean. Nobody likes them.

Boy Two   Family. F-A-M-I-L-Y. How do you know all this?

Boy Three   Just a guess.

Boy Two   Nobody likes them . . . and nobody likes you . . . so maybe you're related.

Boy One   Just a guess? Hey, you creep, do you know this boy?

Boy Three (*long pause*)   He's my cousin.

Boy One *and* **Boy Two**   WHAT . . . you know him, he's your cousin. WHAT IS WRONG WITH YOU PEOPLE? WHAT IS WRONG WITH ALL OF YOU?

Boy Four   Grrrrrrrrrrrrrrrrrrrrrrrrrrrrrrrr. Grrrrrrrrrrrrrrrrrr. Blah waaaah. Oooooooooooooooo. Trtrtrtrtrtrtrt. Blaaha grrrrrrr waaaaah.

Boy One   Calm. Calm down. Wait. Shshshshshshsh. Everyone sit down.

Boy Four *goes to his garbage and gets a bottle of water. They drink.*

Boy One   This is so not good. This is completely terrible. This is absolutely not possible.

Silence.

Boy Four   Mmmmmmmmmm.

Boy One   What.

Boy Four   Mnnnnnnnnnn.

Boy Three It means 'money'. There is no money.

Boy Two You really are the most hated boy in the world.

Boy Three It's better than being the most stupid boy in the world.

Boy One STOP. Everyone be quiet.

Boy Four (*sighing*) Huuuuuuuuuuuu.

Silence.

Boy Two Any ideas?

Boy Three About what?

Boy Four Ughghghg.

Boy One About us.

Silence.

Boy Two What about us?

Boy One You can't read, he can't talk, and him . . . (*To* **Boy Three**.) You really are mean. This is your cousin.

Boy Three We're not allowed to talk to him or play with him or anything. They just threw him away.

Boy Two What a life. L-I-F-E.

Boy One It's crazy, it's wrong. W-R-O-N-G.

Boy Three It's driving me crazy.

Boy One What?

Boy Four Ughghghghghgh.

Boy Two (*to* **Boy Four**) What? (*To* **Boy Three**.) No, you can't speak?

Boy Three Shut up! I can speak. It's my father, my brothers, my uncles. They don't like anyone but themselves. They want to own the neighbourhood. They don't want me to have any friends. They want me to leave school. And I want to stay in school. They want me to carry a gun.

Boy Four Aaaahhhhhhhhhhhhh!

Boy Two A gun? Why?

Boy Three To shoot people they don't like.

Boy One But you're only a boy.

Boy Three I have to be a man.

Boy One And your cousin?

Boy Three Like I said, they threw him away. He's not allowed to come home.

Boy One So you come here?

Boy Three Sometimes. To bring him stuff.

Boy Four Grgrgrgrgrgrgrgrgrgr.

Boy Three But not enough and he gets hungry and sad.

Boy Two Well now you're the most hated boy in the world AND the stupidest boy in the world.

Boy One I'm taking him home. (*To* **Boy Four**.) Do you want to come home with me?

Boy Four Ahahahahahahahahaha.

Boy Three They'll kill you.

Boy Two Then I'll take him home with me.

Boy Three They'll kill you too.

Silence.

Boy Two It's getting late.

Boy One Yeah. We can't just leave him here.

Boy Three He lives here.

Boy Four Ughghghg. Blaahala walalal.

Boy One He's not happy about that.

Boy Two Why don't we just stay here. Eventually, everyone will get worried and they'll come look for us. And we can tell them the story. And someone will take care of this boy.

Boy Three They'll kill them.

Boy One They can't kill everyone. (*Pause*.) So we stay?

Boy Two (*pause*) We stay.

Boy Three (*pause*) We stay. And hope they don't kill us.

Boy Two And we play another game.

Boy Three You want to play?

Boy Two Did you ever hear the story of the nicest boy in the world?

Boy Three No such thing.

Boy Two Listen. There was this boy who met this other boy who was really the stupidest boy in the world. And he taught him how to spell.

Boy Four Aaaaaaaaahhhhhh.

Boy Two Shshshshsh. Listen. I hear another rat.

All four boys have their shoes in their hands, held high, ready to get the rat. Freeze! End.

Play #2: The Red Play

(Boys Version)

Characters

A **Poet**, *fifteen years old.*
A **Father**, *Abu Issa.*
A **Mother**, *Im Issa.*
A little brother, **Noor**, *five to seven years old.*
Khaled, *a neighbour, adult.*
Teacher
Grandfather

There are ten flip charts on the scene. The **Poet** *has the six colours that come in the set of permanent markers, however, he always starts with red. The* **Poet** *and his little brother,* **Noor***, are on stage.*

The **Poet**   Today is a nice day. Maybe it's a little hot. We can live with hot. I hope it's a nice day for everyone. But I doubt it. Right now someone in the world is dying. (*Short pause.*) And now he is dead. Rest in peace whoever you are. (*Pause.*) Today is a nice day. A little hot but we can live with hot. Hot is good. (*Pause.*) Of course the rain is better. But then the rain makes a mess and we're all busy cleaning mud. Then we get yelled at because our shoes are dirty. I don't like all that yelling. It's a noisy world. (*Pause.*) Today is a nice hot day and. . . . Clouds are the best. It means rain is coming but it's not yet here. (*Pause.*) Yesterday, I looked at the bad things. That was a waste of time since I already know them. Today I want to look at the good things. It's a mysterious game I play . . . looking at things. (*Short pause.*) Nothing here is really a pure mystery . . . but so far no one knows about my mysterious game.

Noor   Except me!

Poet   Right. Except you. (*Short pause.*) The first good thing is . . . (*He goes to the first flip chart and writes 'one' on it. Shouting.*) There is nothing good. I am making a fool of myself. There are no mysteries and there is nothing good. We are all unhappy. The whole family. Mother, father, brothers, mother's sisters, mother's brother's, father's sisters, father's brothers, grandmothers, and grandfather. Thank God one grandfather died. He's the only one who's happy.

Father (*offstage*)   Are you playing that game again?

Poet   No mysteries!

Mother (*offstage*)   Is your brother with you?

Noor   Yes, yamma, I'm here. I'm watching him play his game. He's going to draw any minute now.

Poet   No mysteries.

Noor   Tell me your last poem. And then draw. Come on. Do it.

Poet   My brother Noor. He wants to hear poems. (*Draws a little simple boy.*) Alright.

> The day is a circle in which
> We are turning all the time
> It starts with the hope of light
> It ends with dark confusion
> We turn and turn and turn
> Turning makes us dizzy
> At once we are light and confused
> Full of hope and dark
> Caught between hits and hurts
> Dreaming of silence
> We turn and turn and turn

We ask when and what and where and why
We get 'no' and 'never'
We are told to be silent
We are silent
But it is so loud we cannot hear or think.
We turn and turn and turn
Like that carousel at the beach
It turns but children cry
It looks like a carousel
But it only keeps us turning
To be continued . . .

Noor   I like it. That's why I'm dizzy. From turning and turning and turning . . .

Poet   Sit down. Stop turning.

Mother (*offstage*)   Ya Noor, come in.

Noor   Soon, yamma, soon.

Mother   Not soon. Now.

Father (*offstage and to the* **Mother**)   Let him stay outside. It's a nice day. Play, yabba, play. I'm going to sleep for half an hour.

Noor   He's drawing again.

Poet *draws on Board Two the number two in red. He draws a mother and a father. This drawing brings in red and a second colour.*

Poet   It is good when people are sleeping. When all people are sleeping, nothing bad can happen.

Mother *enters.*

Mother   We have to take out the garbage and go get water. Get the cart because there is a lot of garbage. Come on you two. There are things that need doing. This house doesn't run by itself. Noor, yamma, do you want to help me arrange your toys?

Poet   Yamma, do you know that if everyone would sleep nothing bad would happen.

Mother   And nothing would get done either. Are you going to take the garbage and bring the water today or tomorrow. Get the cart. (*Seeing drawing one.*) Who is that?

Poet   My brother. He is one nice thing that happened to me today. (*To* **Noor**.) Poems.

Noor   Poems and drawings.

Mother   Yes, he is very nice. And handsome. Tell me your last poem.

Poet   It's not really a poem. It's a story. It's about a boy who is chosen. One day the angels saw him walking to the first grade with his new school bag. One look . . . and they decided to walk with him every day . . . until they decided that they wanted him with them. The next day, the angels went to heaven. Do you know there is a great carousel in heaven . . . very big, and all red, and you sit on horses and gazelles and even in giant coffee cups. (*The brother laughs.*) But this carousel didn't go round and round. No. It carried the boy around the skies that were lit with small stars that twinkled and he went throughout heaven and the world was happy.

Noor   And he ate ice-cream and corn. And he learned adding.

Mother   Ice-cream and corn?

Noor   Of course, and you learn to add . . . (*To* **Poet**.) Right?

Poet   Of course. Heaven has everything.

Mother   That's a nice story. (*Pause.*) Now let's pull that cart. There isn't a drop of water to drink. (*As she passes Board One she blows it a kiss.*) How are you doing in school? Did you finish your homework?

Poet   Everything is fine.

Mother   Good.

Mother *and* **Poet** *start to exit. A neighbour,* **Khaled***, meets them.*

Khaled   Good evening, Im Issa. Salam ya Poet. What did the doctor say?

Poet   The same as he always says.

Khaled   God keep him. (*To* **Noor**.) Hey Noor, I just got a motorcycle, one and a half horses. I'm putting it together. Why don't you come and help me. I need you to hand me the tools. What do you say?

Noor   Can I, yamma?

Mother   Of course . . . you can go later with your brother. (*To* **Khaled**.) Thank you.

The **Poet** *and the* **Mother** *and* **Khaled** *exit. The* **Father** *enters.*

Father   Your brother is putting silly ideas in your head. He should have friends of his own and you should have friends of your own. Come sit here with me, little man. (*Pause.*) God chooses the best for you.

Noor   God chooses the best for everyone.

Father   Right. But he chooses the best for you faster than for the others.

Noor   How do you know?

Father   I had a dream.

Noor   I had a dream, too. That I got one hundred per cent in adding. What was your dream about?

Father   You were in school and together with your friends you were playing 'police and thief'. When you finished that game, you played football. Then you ate cookies. Lots of them. And then – from God – you all started running in every direction. You know how dreams are sometimes strange. A hundred boys all running in circles. In my dream I was watching and I got so dizzy I woke up.

Noor We were running from the headmaster. (*He laughs. Pause.*) When can I go back to school and play with my friends?

Father I don't know.

Noor I think I'm not going back to school, right yabba. (*Silence.*)

Father This is the will of God. The angels love you and they want to make sure you can do everything that you wish for. (*He takes some money from his pocket.*) I am giving this money to your mother. Anything you want – within reason – she will buy for you.

Noor You're giving me money? I love you, yabba. But what about my brother the Poet, and Mother, and grandmother and grandfather?

Father We all agreed. This is money for you. So when your mother comes back with the Poet, we will give it to her and you go buy what you want.

Noor Thank you, yabba . . . but why?

Father Because . . . that's the way things are.

Silence.

Noor Can we go to the carousel later?

Father Yes. All of us together will go to the carousel. And I will eat the biggest ice-cream.

Noor *laughs. The* **Mother** *and the* **Poet** *return. The four are together. They prepare the meal. Needless to say it is all variations of red/pink/dark red. No hot pink. While they are preparing the meal . . . during the next scene the* **Poet** *is drawing a carousel and/or big ice-cream on Board Three. There is a knock on the door.*

Teacher It's the Teacher Mahmoud coming to visit.

Noor Teacher Mahmoud! Come in, come in.

Mother Welcome. Join us. Sit.

Teacher How are you, big boy?

Noor Good. How are you? How is the school yard? How are my friends?

Teacher They all say hello to you and everything is the same as it was. Look what I brought you. The adding books from the second grade! I think you can do them. Have a look.

Noor I will try.

Teacher You can't come to school so the school comes to you.

Mother That is so kind of you. Thank you so much.

Noor The school comes to me. Poet, look, the school comes to me.

Mother (*to* **Teacher**) Sit. Please.

Teacher Enjoy your meal and I must go. (*To* **Noor**.) I will come back in a few days to check your work. How is that?

Noor I will solve them. And I will solve all of them. Thank you.

Mother Thank you. Thank you very much.

Teacher Goodbye all.

Noor Teacher Mahmoud likes me.

Mother And the angels like you, too.

Noor Yamma, I want to buy a red car with a remote and a red football uniform. I want to be a football player in a red car. Nice, huh?

Father Very nice. That's what we'll buy you.

Poet And you can wear the uniform every day. Like in the World Cup.

Noor And I am the attacking mid-fielder. Number sixteen. I have a team of eleven players. Messi, Ronaldo, Rooney, Kaka, Xavi, Iniesta, Ribery, Eto'o, Casillas, Henry, Alves . . . and Yabba.

Poet And what about me?

Noor There is only one of you. You can tell the poems at the start of the games.

Father What? And there are twenty of me?

Noor Yabba, you know what I mean. There is really only one of him. And you know that no one tells poems anymore.

Mother And no one tells a good story either.

Father My father tells good stories.

Noor But they are all about wars and they are about what happened one hundred years ago.

They eat watermelon.

Mother So who has a story for this meal.

Silence. During the story the **Poet** *draws on Board Four. He draws an electric plant with a man lying down and other men around and an ambulance coming and two small babies. He adds to the drawing as the facts are made known.*

Mother I have one. Once there was a man who worked in the electric company. One day, he touched a live wire and he got a big shock. It was so big that he fell down and fainted. All the other workers came to see what they could do. They yelled and called his name. They called the ambulance. The man could hear and see what was going on. But he forgot how to speak. He tried to speak but his tongue didn't work. On the way to the hospital, he made a plan. He would stay the way he was and would never speak again. When he got home, his wife who was a teacher, gave him a board so he could write down whatever he wanted. And that's how they lived for many years until the wife had a baby. A boy. And when the man saw his first son, he said God is Great. And he continued to speak to his son and from then on he spoke once again.

Poet   That's because it's a noisy world and he didn't want to make it any noisier.

Mother   I suppose so.

Noor   So he really loved his son.

Mother   Yes and then they had a second son.

Noor   And?

Mother   The man talked even more and more and he began to sing.

Noor   So the second son made him sing?

Father   Oh yes, the second son made him sing.

Poet   That's a good story.

Father   And that's a good drawing.

Noor   Yamma . . . (*Pause.*) I'm getting so tired.

Mother   Come. (*To* **Poet** *and* **Father**.) You two clean up. (*To* **Noor**.) Let's give you a small bath and then you stay in your room and rest a little.

Poet *and* **Father**.

Poet   We have to pray harder.

Father   I am.

Poet   Does he understand? (*Pause.*) Yes. Somewhere he understands.

Father   I don't want to talk about this. It is written. It is God's will.

Silence.

Poet   You can't save him with money and presents.

Father   God forgive you, I'm not trying to. But I can make him happy.

Poet   Yes. (*Pause. Thinking.*) Yabba, we should have a party.

Father   A party? Are you crazy?

Poet   No, we should have a party. We will bring cakes and all the family, everyone, and all the boys in his school, and in the school next to his, and the neighbours, and all the teachers and all the headmasters. We'll bring the whole ministry of education! A party is the best thing we can do for him, yabba. A party where he is the knight . . . in a football uniform.

Father   A knight in a football uniform?

Poet *goes to Board Five – he writes 'Party'. He draws: cakes, people, dancing, smiling faces, he writes 'Friends, Neighbours, Aunts, Uncles, Teachers'.*

Father A party!

Poet Listen.

> Everywhere you look you see sadness and grief
> Everywhere you look you see pain and sorrow
> Everywhere you look you see black and darkness
> Everywhere you look you see barriers and borders
> Here in *this* home we do what we want
> Here in *this* home we change the world
> Here in *this* home we laugh and celebrate
> Here in *this* home we have a party
> We have to look at what is good.
> We have to look at what is beautiful
> We have to look at what we have
> We have to look for new beginnings

Father A party!

Poet We have to.

The **Grandfather** *enters.*

Grandfather Peace on this house.

Father Good afternoon, Haj.

Grandfather How are you, yabba? You have to keep strong. (*To* **Poet**.) And you too.

Poet We are having a party for Noor.

Mother (*entering*) A party?

Father A party!

Grandfather (*pause*) Good for you. That little man deserves a party. Listen, I want him in my qumbaz, with a hattah and the agal. I will dress the same. And so will the two of you. He likes when the men wear that. I'll get them from the souk. (*Pause.*) What did the doctor say?

Father The same as he always says.

Grandfather And we will dance with sticks. He has to learn that. I will teach him. We will dance together with sticks for all who come. Don't you worry, I will soon be with him in heaven. I'm going to the souk.

The Party Scene. All characters and the audience are at this party. Actors, with make up palettes, will draw smiles on the faces of audience members. **Noor** *is wearing a red football uniform. The* **Grandfather** *is wearing traditional dress only in red.*

Poet I have a poem.

Mother We've never seen you looking so happy and like the brother of the groom.

Grandfather We've never seen you stand so strong before us all.

Khaled We've never seen this many people dance with sticks

Teacher We've never seen such a player in all his form

Mother We've never seen so many people together

Father We've never seen the smile that comes to your face

Poet Oh knight of the happy football players . . .

Grandfather Oh knight of the happy stick dancers . . .

Poet Oh knight of our hearts . . .

Poet *and* **Mother** *and* **Father**.

Poet I want to trade places with him. We have to pray more. We have to pray more.

Father I ask forgiveness from God . . . My son . . . please . . .

Poet I will die instead of him. I will go and he will stay. That's how it has to be. Pray more. I will pray more. We will all pray more.

Mother Enough. Stop. He is happy now. He loved the party. (*Pause.*) The party was a good idea.

Poet It was a terrible idea. (*He starts a drawing on Board Six – a doctor.*) We have to find another way. I want a doctor, a team of doctors, a team of international doctors, a team of international doctor specialists, the best in the world. What he has inside him, they have to take it out of him and put it in me. I already lived a long life. I'm fifteen. It's enough. He needs more time. Do you hear? It's enough and he needs more time. I go. He stays.

Father Stop! Stop this minute.

Mother You don't know what you're saying. You are not responsible. This is the will of God. This is how he was born. This is why your father started singing to him when we found out. And this is why you tell him stories and make him drawings. You are you and he is he. This is the will of God.

Poet We didn't try hard enough. We didn't take him out to best doctors.

Father We didn't get permission.

Poet We don't need permission!

Father We need permission, my boy, we need permission.

Poet We don't need permission!

Mother Habibi, we need permission.

Poet   He cannot die so young. He will become . . .

Poet *draws on Board Seven . . . an old man in a red football uniform and holding a stick.*

Poet   . . . he will become . . . a fat old Haj, like Grandfather, with one hundred grandchildren and two hundred great children.

Father   Enough! (*He smacks the* **Poet**.)

The **Poet** *cries. The following is the song 'Don't Let the Sun Catch You Crying' by Gerry Marsden. The original song should not be played for copyright purposes. The actors should simply say the lines. It is an homage.*

Mother   Don't let the sun catch you crying

Father   The night is the time for all your tears

Mother   Your heart may be broken tonight but tomorrow in the morning light.

Father   Don't let the sun catch you crying. The night-time shadows disappear

Mother   And with them go all your tears, for the morning will bring joy

Father   To every girl and boy

Mother   Don't let the sun catch you crying

Father   It may be hard to discover . . .

Mother   . . . That someone goes and not another

Father   But don't forget that life is a game

Mother   And it continues again and again

Father   Don't let the sun catch you crying

Mother   Don't let it.

The Marsden song ends here. **Poet** *draws on Board Eight a crying boy surrounded by the sunshine.* **Noor** *appears. He is not well. He is holding his football.*

Noor   I am so very, very tired.

Mother   Come. Sit with us.

Noor   Tell me a new poem.

Poet   I don't have one.

Noor   Of course you have one. You always have one.

During this story, the **Mother** *draws on Board Nine. She draws a family sitting together.*

Poet   Once there was a boy who had a little brother . . .

Noor   No. Start it . . . once there was a boy who had a big brother . . .

Poet   That's a whole other story. (*Pause.*) Alright. Once there was a boy who had a big brother. The boy liked the colour red . . .

Noor   Wait. I want to hear about the big brother.

Poet   Why?

Noor   Because it's the big brother who is going to tell everyone about the little boy because the little boy can't talk. Like the man in the electric company. He will stop talking soon and he hasn't learned to add properly so the big brother . . . it's your story . . . tell it.

Father   It sounds to me that it's your story.

Noor   I'm too tired, yabba.

Poet   Noor, tell us the story so the big brother can tell it after the boy stops talking.

Noor   Once there was a boy who liked the colour red and he had a red football uniform. He had a big brother who was always talking in poems and stories. And this boy was happy especially on the first day of school because his brother was in school. That first day was the best day of his life. All his friends and cousins were in the same class and they ate lunch together and they played games in the school yard and they ran a lot. And they jumped a lot. And on Friday, he sat with his father and the men and they ate a great meal. Like the mukhtars. He drank coffee and sometimes he even poured the coffee. And there was a war on but inside the house there wasn't a war. And the boy had a red car that he bought with his own money. And it was a beautiful car. And he drove because he loved to drive. And one night he went to sleep and he dreamed he was driving in his football uniform. He drove and he drove and in the morning . . . he didn't wake up.

Noor *puts his head on mother's lap and goes to sleep. (He dies.)* **Poet** *at Board Ten – he draws a red car driving in the sky. He writes 'Noor's Car' on the drawing. The* **Mother** *is with* **Noor***. The* **Father** *goes up to the board.*

Father   You cannot be who you are not.

Poet   You can.

Father   Not in these circumstances.

Poet   But in other circumstances?

Father   Yes. In other circumstances I think you can be whoever you want to be. (*Pause.*) And whoever you choose to be . . . you can draw, or tell, or think, or believe.

Poet   Do you believe that?

Father   Yes.

Poet   I can't believe.

Father   Fine. You cannot believe for three days, my boy, but after that you have to start believing again. Do you understand?

Poet No.

Father Yes you do.

Poet (*adding to Board Ten*)   Dream!

End.

Endnote: The Drawings on the Boards

1. A little boy.

2. A mother and father.

3. A carousel.

4. An electric plant.

5. A party.

6. All the doctors.

7. An old man dressed like Noor.

8. A crying sun with a boy.

9. A family of four (drawn by the mother).

10. A red car with 'Noor's Car' written on it.

Play #3: The White Play

Characters

Girl One, *Shireen, fourteen to fifteen years old.*
Girl Two, *Nadeen, fourteen to fifteen years old.*
Girl Three, *Raneen, fourteen to fifteen years old.*
Girl Four, *Haneen, fourteen to fifteen years old.*

Everything in the play is a version of whites except for the flowers and the yarns. Have fun with it. Curtains, stage cloth (floor), costumes, and of course hats. The scene happens in the courtyard of the house of Shireen.

Shireen Five, four, three, two, one! My birthday is February twenty-ninth so I was born in the year with the extra day. There are two hundred and fifty thousand others like me. My mother told me that when she was twenty-five she had long hair and green eyes. But her eyes are brown. How do eyes change colour? Makes no sense. Otherwise my mother is lovely. My brother didn't speak for seven years. When he turned eight, he was the first kid to reach the third step on the ladder. He waved to us like he was in the circus. He shouted 'look at me' . . .! My father is forty and fat. He says he weighs two hundred and fifty kilos which I don't really believe because yesterday he brought only two kilos of meat. And all he keeps saying is that he busted his butt working for twenty years and it's all for nothing. Now he works cleaning. My older brother just got a five CC motorcycle with the serial number three thousand seven hundred. He's a boy, you know what I mean. And my baby brother just learned that one times two equals two so he thinks he's a genius. My last brother is in class five room six and did acrobatics in school, so he says. And then he says that his class won a football game they played against class one room three with a score of twenty to zero which I also don't believe. So we are four boys and one girl. Me. I am fourteen. Together, that means five uniforms and five school bags. I need a five second break. (*Pause.*) I have three girlfriends. Together we are four smart girls. With talent. Today in school we *heard* a dabkeh on the school radio. Imagine listening to a dance. It was done by kids in class four room six. It felt like twelve hours of listening to stomping. Me and girlfriends, who sit next to each other, ate all our chips. Also today, when I came home I learned my grandfather had found fifty shekels and the house was upside down. He was saying that two halves of fifty means a twenty and a five or a seventeen and an eight. I asked my grandfather if he wanted me to help him divide the money but he said NO. That he had worked on the railway and carried ten bags of coal for twenty years and also worked in construction on the thirtieth floor and that he worked as a coffee-boy when he was twenty so he knew all he had to know about spending fifty shekels. I don't believe him either. About the fifty shekels, I asked if I could have ten and he said no and then I said five and again no and then four, and no, and then two and he said OK but divide it with your brothers. My friends are coming. Together we sound like fifty violins playing. Now you know everything.

Enter **Haneen** *with bags full of white fabric.*

Haneen Can you believe that we actually *listened* to a dabkeh.

Shireen What a waste of time.

Haneen How are you?

Shireen Good.

Haneen If you feel like talking . . .

Shireen What do you have there?

Haneen My cousin Hala is getting married. We went out looking for dresses. No one liked anything. So I thought I would make one for her . . . myself! She says she wants a special one and not all those regular puffy ones. And she wants to be comfortable. She's different, you know what I mean.

Shireen So what's in the bag? Show.

Haneen We need a clean space. Everything in this bag is white.

They get a huge sheet or piece of fabric and cover the playing area. It has to be a kind of beige so white will show up on it. Or light gray. Something light. **Haneen** *starts to take things out of the bag. All beautiful. White fabric, lace, ribbons, etc.*

Haneen (*holding up a big piece of fabric*) This is the basic fabric for the dress. And this is the lace for the edges. Here I found a way to make a new kind of strap with some strings left over from the curtains. I will have to wash them but it will be ok. And look, I found some of this (*little pieces of decorative things*) and I think I can figure out how to make small flowers that look like silk. I have no idea what to do about the shoes. I never made shoes before. That's the most difficult.

Shireen You must have twenty metres here. It's beautiful. When is the wedding?

Haneen Next month or maybe a little later. I don't have all that much time because I have to sew it by hand.

Shireen She needs to decide the exact date! I say September fifteenth. Then we have thirty days to make it.

Haneen We?

Shireen Of course. I'll make it with you. (*Thought.*) Even better . . . let's do it the four of us together. We can make the absolutely most gorgeous wedding dress ever worn in Gaza.

Haneen Where are those girls, anyway? We agreed absolutely to meet here after our homework.

Shireen Nadeen will be here in ten to twelve minutes and Raneen in six to ten.

Haneen Will you stop with all your numbers. The world doesn't work that way.

Shireen Well it should. Do you know that Raneen didn't get one hundred per cent on the exam and she wants to take it again. So her mother's sister went to the school today to the headmistress.

Haneen What did she get?

Shireen Ninety-five per cent. She was crying so be nice to her.

Haneen I'm always nice to her.

Shireen Be extra nice, OK.

Haneen There's no big difference between ninety-five and one hundred.

Shireen There most certainly is. If I owed you a hundred shekels and gave you back ninety-five would you accept?

Haneen No.

Shireen So there's a difference. She wants a hundred. Let's think about the dress. And the shoes. And the hair. And the make-up, and the presents she has to give out. Let's think of every detail for her wedding. We'll make a big project out of it and if she doesn't want it . . . one of us can use it.

Haneen Are you getting married so soon?

Shireen (*to herself*) It will be beautiful . . . (*To* **Haneen**.) No . . . I'm not getting married soon. But if it's beautiful we can make two of them . . .

Haneen . . . and we can get married together to a pair of handsome brothers.

Shireen You have anyone in mind?

Haneen Absolutely not.

They laugh! **Raneen** *comes rushing in.*

Raneen Sorry. (*Catches her breath.*) I can take the test over again.

Haneen Don't you think it's a little bit silly? I mean I know you want one hundred but ninety-five is enough.

Raneen If I owed you a hundred shekels would you accept ninety-five?

Shireen You see?

Raneen It was a silly mistake and I know the reason. It was a writing mistake. I answered question nine with the answer of eight and ten with nine making it look like one mistake. It's clear that if you move them all up, it's one hundred per cent. I don't know how I could be so stupid. (*To* **Shireen**.) How are you? How are you feeling?

Shireen (*pause*) It's all in the numbers. If everyone paid attention to all the numbers life as we know it would be different. Look. We're making a wedding dress!

Raneen I don't know how they can't see this technical mistake.

Shireen It's a mistake. It's not one hundred per cent. We're making a wedding dress.

Nadeen *comes in with her wool. It's all different colours.*

Nadeen Hello to everyone. (*To* **Shireen**.) Hi, habibti, how are you today? Did you sleep?

Shireen I slept the whole night.

Nadeen I had a fight with my mother. I didn't eat anything. Are there any chips left?

Raneen What wedding dress?

Haneen We ate them all. Why are you always fighting with her?

Nadeen She doesn't understand anything I'm doing. When I talk with my sisters and brothers about school she always tells us to be quiet and to talk about something else. She wants to talk about what we'll cook on Friday. How boring is that!

Raneen   Teach her.

Nadeen   I tried to explain the classes we take but she doesn't get it. Last week she visited the school to talk to my teacher. I showed her a computer – you all saw it – she wants nothing to do with it. I showed her some programs and even some games and she got really annoyed. She said she had to get out of the school because she had to cook dinner or my father would divorce her. At home, she didn't even mention visiting the school to anyone at all. She doesn't want to hear about school work. And she also says that my father should visit the teachers because he graduated university.

Haneen   So what's the problem?

Nadeen   He works all the time. He says it's my mother's job. No one is following my school work now. Not him. Not her.

Nadeen *opens a bag and begins to crochet.*

Nadeen   I'm making a hat . . . it calms me down.

Raneen   But it's summer.

Nadeen   I'm preparing for the winter.

Shireen   Make a wedding hat.

Raneen   What wedding dress? What hat?

Nadeen   A wedding hat? Who?

Shireen   For Haneen's strange cousin Hala. She can't find a dress.

Raneen   Ya Hala! Ya Hala. She's getting married. How old is she? Twelve?

Shireen (*to* **Haneen**)   Ignore her.

Nadeen   Tell me about the dress.

Raneen   Or fourteen . . . It happens all the time. Too many times.

Haneen   She hasn't seen all the dress shops yet . . . but if we make one that is absolutely the only one of its kind and completely gorgeous, she will wear it and everyone will ask where she got it and we'll say that we made it.

Raneen   No one sews anymore. And no one knits. That's for old women and people with nothing to do.

Nadeen   And what am I doing? Physics? It's nice to make things. Try it.

Raneen   Forget it. I am absolutely *not* going to start sewing and knitting.

Haneen (*to* **Shireen**)   'Be extra nice . . .' She's making it difficult.

Raneen   I don't know how I could be so stupid. No one talk to me. (*She takes out a book and starts reading.*)

Play #3: The White Play

So: **Nadeen** *is crocheting,* **Raneen** *is reading, and* **Shireen** *and* **Haneen** *are looking at the stuff. Starting here, the text is said, and the dress is being made until the end of the play with all girls involved.*

Haneen *has a big notebook. During the scene she and* **Shireen** *are looking at the fabric and drawing at the same time. And also holding up the fabric and thinking towards some plan . . .*

Shireen So this is the basic fabric?

Haneen Yes. Because it's pretty and it's comfortable for the bride.

Nadeen Comfortable is really important. I went to the wedding of Inas and her whole back was red from the plastic piece inside the back of the dress that keeps it up. Every time she moved you could tell it hurt.

Raneen How did she dance?

Nadeen Perfectly. But it hurt. And her feet were all red . . . and blue . . .!

Haneen I have no idea how to make shoes.

Nadeen I'm hungry.

Raneen You can't make shoes.

Shireen You can. What do you think a shoemaker is?

Raneen Someone who *fixes* shoes.

Nadeen Wrong. He can also make shoes. My grandfather made shoes a million years ago.

Raneen You see. A million years ago.

Nadeen My mother is still living like it's a million years ago.

Raneen Make her dinosaur shoes.

Shireen Very funny.

Raneen I can just see it . . . big green hairy shoes with big toenails painted red. Why is she getting married? Too stupid to stay in school?

Haneen I know you're in a really bad mood so either read and be quiet or help us. I am going to make this dress whether you help or not so get off my back. And Hala is not twelve but twenty-eight. She graduated from Al Azhar University, second in the class, and she is marrying a handsome fellow named Majd . . .

Raneen Second?

Shireen Oh, shut up! (*To* **Haneen**.) Let's continue. I'll stand and you put it around me.

Haneen Good.

Haneen *takes out some pins and sewing things. They play with fabric, try this and that, with fabric, strings, ribbons, etc. We have the start of the dress. They try many possibilities.*

Nadeen   Let me see. Try to wrap this here and that there. No. Give me a pin. We try this here and that there. (*They continue trying with the dress.*) Give me those strings. I can do something with them. I am so completely hungry. I don't know why I'm always hungry.

She takes the hat she is working on and puts it down and takes a piece of fabric, white, and begins a veil.

Raneen   You have the obsessive-compulsive sickness.

Shireen   What? She has no sickness.

Raneen   Yes she does. When you keep doing something over and over again because something is missing. Like crocheting . . . and eating. (*About* **Shireen**.) Like her and numbers. Everyone has it.

Nadeen   Like you and your test.

Raneen   That's different. It was a technical mistake.

Shireen   Sounds like the same thing to me.

Haneen (*to* **Shireen** *in the 'dress'*)   Stop moving. Hold this in place. (*Short pause.*) My mother has a sickness. The forgetting disease. She forgets what she did five minutes ago and remembers what she did when she was fifteen. It's making her crazy.

Raneen   It happens to all old people.

Haneen   She's not that old. But my brother's wife Anan is always making fun of her and yesterday . . . hold the fabric higher please . . . yesterday my brother told her to watch out how she talks to my mother. They had a fight and afterwards Anan cooked us a good meal. When my mother went to bed those two sat together watching television.

Shireen   Romance. Romance.

Raneen   Don't talk about romance. I can't stand romance. All those films you watch, they are just films. That's not real life. This is real life. Right here. And it doesn't always end happily ever after.

Shireen   Why are you so negative? Why can't you see that some people are happy?

Raneen   No one is happy. Show me someone who is happy. Show.

Shireen   We're happy.

Raneen   We are not happy.

Shireen   Well I am happy.

Silence.

Nadeen Can you believe we actually had to listen to a dabkeh in school.

Shireen Ya Allah, enough of that dabkeh.

Haneen I need someone to hold this piece.

Nadeen My hands are busy.

Shireen (*to* **Raneen**) Come help! It'll make you happy. I promise. Look how nice it is.

Raneen Fine. I don't need to study. It was just a technical mistake. They can see there was an extra answer. You'd think they would figure it out . . . an extra answer hanging off the exam.

Shireen Enough with this exam.

Haneen Stop moving.

Raneen All year I get one hundred per cent. I don't understand it. I tell you I can *teach* this math subject.

Nadeen Don't go thinking you're the smartest person on the planet. There are plenty like you.

Raneen Where . . . where are they?

Shireen The ones who didn't make a technical mistake and got a one hundred per cent. Like me.

Nadeen Me too.

Haneen I got eighty-five. It's good. Smart in math isn't everything. Smart in life . . . now that's something.

Shireen Smart in life . . . I like that!

Raneen That's the philosophy sickness . . . People who talk about 'life' all the time as if they can change it.

Haneen We can change it. How's the veil coming?

Girl Two Philosophically speaking, it's going to be an absolutely gorgeous hat. (*To* **Raneen**.) Come hold this string.

Raneen So now I'm 'hold this and hold that' person, ya'ni the assistant to this ridiculous project.

Nadeen Yes. That's exactly what you are Ms. Ninety-five Per cent. I have to eat something.

Shireen I'll fix us something to eat in a few minutes. Just let's get this part of the dress done.

Nadeen Imagine this: my father comes home, he eats with papers next to him. If it's not papers from work, it's the newspaper. I love my father . . . but he's never home and when he is home he's always working . . . and I have so many questions to ask him. I want to work in his office when I graduate. (*To* **Raneen**.) Here . . . try this on. (*She tries a kind of veil on the head of* **Raneen**.) Very, very pretty. But it's not done. Take if off.

Haneen Let me see it. Put it on Shireen.

Raneen All that's missing are the dinosaur shoes. I have the nail-polish. Bright red. I like your father, too. He's really smart.

Nadeen It doesn't do me much good.

Raneen Talk to him.

Nadeen I can never find one minute alone with him where he can listen. He's busy all the time.

Now **Nadeen**, **Raneen**, **Haneen** *are around* **Shireen** *who is looking more and more like a bride.*

Shireen I need a five second break.

They all sit down. **Shireen** *gets a tray of things to eat. While she's off stage . . .*

Raneen She has no problems. She can talk about happiness.

Nadeen She is trying.

Raneen Her brother was killed. Everyone has someone who was killed.

Haneen You are mean and that's not nice. Why are you playing like your problems are the most important ones? We're making a wedding dress. Let's make it. And be nice.

Raneen I'm just being realistic. My uncle died. My cousin died. My neighbour's son died.

Haneen It was her brother.

Nadeen Your heart is ice.

Raneen Yes. My heart is ice.

Shireen *is back with a tray of simple food. . . . Watermelon and white cheese.*

Shireen Here we are . . . eat some watermelon . . . it's as cold as your heart.

Raneen Sorry. I'm really sorry. (*Pause.*) Really.

Shireen I'm not really happy. I try to make happiness.

Raneen How do you do that?

Shireen You think about the good things. When you find yourself thinking about the bad things and you feel the sadness start coming . . . look . . . you see this rubber band on my wrist. When I feel the tears I pull the rubber band like this (*she plucks it*) and that reminds me to think of something else. My brother was a good kid. He fell off the ladder. I don't think of him laying there broken. I think of his smiling face when he got to that fourth step of the ladder. He was laughing. He made it to the fourth step. (*Pause. Again she snaps the rubber band.*) So, how about the dress? Let's continue.

Raneen   What is going to become of us?

Silence. Quietly:

Haneen   Maybe I'll end up like my mother, forgetting who I am.

Nadeen   Or I'll end up like my father, working all the time and having a heart attack.

Shireen   I could end up losing one eye like my mother.

Raneen   And I can end up dead.

Raneen   I know they are dead. (*Pause.*) When baba was killed . . . it was hard. You all remember. Then my mother. She died of sadness. (*Pause.*) I love my aunt and we are fine living with her. But I don't get to see my brothers since they moved in to my uncle's house. Now my uncle wants all four of us together, no more Friday visits, and my aunt is angry and sad. And now they are all fighting about who owns us. Can you imagine?

Silence.

Nadeen   It's such a long day . . . such a noisy night . . .

Shireen   The house is full of people… my ring tone is on your phone.

Haneen   We have to keep going, keep holding each other up.

Raneen   When we feel we are falling or just falling.

Shireen   We won't stop trying and can't give in.

Nadeen   To demands made by the others.

Haneen   But I hurt and tire and find no calm.

Shireen   Our ring tones are all on your phones.

Nadeen   I will call you and you and you.

Haneen   Answer all the calls.

Nadeen   That's womankind. Philosophically speaking.

Haneen   What about the dress?

The girls get up. **Shireen** *puts on the dress and they continue putting it together.*

Shireen   I think we are really smart and the best of friends on the planet earth.

Haneen   We should make a pact.

Raneen   What kind of pact.

Haneen   That for as long as we live we will be best friends. We will stand by each other through all the bad and all the good. And that when we are ninety years old we will sit together and talk about the day we made a wedding dress.

Raneen (*looking at* **Shireen** *in the dress*)   It looks funny.

Haneen   You think so?

Raneen   Funny. But pretty. I think people will ask who made it.

The dress is very funny and very beautiful. A clown bride. They look at her. They arrange her, they wrap more fabric on her. **Raneen** *makes some dinosaur shoes out of fabric and wraps them around the feet of* **Shireen**. *They all laugh because they have created a bride clown. Very funny costume.*

Shireen   Try not to get worried

>Let's not think of the worries
>Or dim lights or buzzing
>We are one and we are four
>And the bride is on her way
>Let's not think of classmates or
>Of those not here, not near, now gone
>We really are one and we really are four
>And tomorrow is on her way
>Think of a good time
>Surely it's coming
>Bright, and working, clean, white
>Something is definitely on the way.

End.

2: Entanglement (2011)

Play #1: The Grandfathers

Characters

Malek, *Abu Ahmad, old, mean streak, clownish, stubborn, the oldest, has energy, springs on his feet.*
Abu Ihab, *second oldest, traditional, kind, is losing his energy.*
Ashraf, *Abu Mohammed, third oldest, on the young side, confused.*
Mohammed, *Abu Ahmad, the youngest of them, and the man who counts the people.*

The 'shesh-besh' board is set up on a coffee stool. No one is really playing against anyone but every so often someone makes a move, as written. They are in a ground floor courtyard that has been turned into a 'garden' or place for them to sit. It's the result of years of things being put there including old furniture and other junk. It's not garbage. It's comfy. The men gather here because they have nothing else to do. Maybe their children live in the building or house above this space.

Scene One

Malek (*holding several pieces of paper*)   This paper is telling me that I am old.

Abu Ihab   It only tells you that you were born. You're not old. You're a little older than me.

Malek   Did I ask your opinion of anything? Did I ask you if you are older than me or me than you? Why are you talking anyway?

Abu Ihab   Why are you yelling? It's a nice day . . . who shouts in the morning?

Ashraf   Leave him alone. Let's play cards.

Malek   Yes, go waste your lives and play cards. Two geniuses, that's what I have. Play cards. I'm making a revolution. Someone gives me a paper that says my age. I say my age. Not a piece of paper.

Ashraf   Yes, sidi. You are the oldest so you are the smartest.

Abu Ihab   Bring the sheshbesh. I wonder why I didn't get a paper.

Malek   And respect your elders. (*Playing with the papers.*) This paper I know. I can't lose this paper or I won't get my flour. I have twenty years of flour since the wife died. I should have learned to bake bread.

Ashraf *and* **Abu Ihab** *play* with the shesh-besh pieces.

Abu Ihab   Ya Abu Ahmad, there are many things we should have learned.

Malek   Do I ask for a comment on every word I say? I need quiet.

Abu Ihab   What do you need quiet for? Are you planning the revolution?

Malek   Ya Abu Ahmad, don't make fun of the revolution. It will come. That suitcase in the corner is going back to Izdoud (Ashdod) and I'll carry it there myself.

Abu Ihab   I am Abu Ihab. You are Abu Ahmad.

Ashraf   Sheshbesh!

Malek   You're still alive.

Abu Ihab   Astaghfirullah Al Adheem.

Malek   But this paper is telling me that I am old and that they are sending someone over to see IF I AM ME. ALIVE. They send me a paper . . . the neighbour brought it, who is that boy who brought it? Find out who that boy is.

Ashraf   Do you want me to find out?

Malek   No, play your sheshbesh. Shoo ya'ni? We wait until the feast until you decide your move. Who's that boy?

Abu Ihab   You don't need to know. He's the son of the son of someone. That's what you need to know. The son of the son of the son of someone who lives here.

Malek   Abu Ahmad, you know I always respected you, but you . . . but I have to know who that boy is. What will happen if we stop knowing who is coming and going? (*Speech.*) What will happen if we stop knowing our neighbours and the sons of our neighbours? What will happen to us if – God protect us – Why are you playing three four like that, Abu Ahmad?

A little lost. . . . Silence by all.

Abu Ihab   Ya Abu Ahmad, you're Abu Ahmad. I'm Abu Ihab. What's wrong with you today?

Scene Two

Malek   Where is my breakfast? First you put in the salt. You have to put the salt in first and then the pepper.

Abu Ihab   Wrong. Wrong. Wrong. First a little water. Then salt.

Malek   Wrong. Play. It's your turn.

Abu Ihab   As you like. I'm not eating.

Malek   Don't eat. Starve to death. (*About Ashraf.*) Is he still alive?

Abu Ihab   No! Astaghfirullah Al Adheem.

Ashraf   Do you want me to help you, ya Abu Ahmad?

Malek   Do you know how to bake bread? I have thirty kilos of flour. How can we have breakfast without bread?

Abu Ihab   Ya zalameh, we have bread. (*Sound of lots of small bombs, nothing serious, quite regular.*) Listen. There it is. The same sound I've been hearing for a hundred years.

Abu Ihab   Boom boomtaktak-tak-taaaaak, Boom boom-boom. It's always been like that. Boom Tak and then it repeats itself and comes back like a mowwal. It was nice when the women were here. They would sing and we would dance. Who remembers that dance. Boom tak-tak, Boom tak-tak (*dabkeh rhythm*).

Malek   What is this?

Ashraf It's the paper the boy brought you this morning. The son of someone.

Malek What does it say? Read this to me. Word by word.

Ashraf Let me see.

Malek Read. Don't miss a word.

Ashraf Are you Malek Ahmad Mohammed Ibn Ahmad Malek Mohammed Ibn Mohammed Malek Ahmad Ibn Mohammed Mohammed Malek Ahmad Malek Malek?

Malek That is I.

Ashraf That's what it says on the paper.

Malek The breakfast is ready. Did you bake bread?

Scene Three

A knock.

Mohammed Is anyone home?

Malek I am here but I am not home.

Abu Ihab And I am here but I am not home!

Ashraf I am home. Tfadal. Come in.

Mohammed Oh dear . . . OK, which one of you is Malek Ahmad Mohammed Ibn Ahmad Malek Mohammed Ibn Mohammed Malek Ahmad Ibn Mohammed Mohammed Malek Ahmad Malek Malek?

Malek Which one of us is that? (*Confusion by all.*) What do you want with him?

Mohammed Which one of you is him?

Abu Ihab Come in. Sit. We'll figure it out. Abu Mohammed (*to* **Ashraf**), put up the coffee.

Malek Welcome. Sit. Abu Mohammed, put up the coffee.

Mohammed Alhamdulillah. The whole morning I am turning from house to house. No one offers coffee anymore these days.

Abu Ihab Sit. We have coffee for all. (*To* **Ashraf**.) Put up the coffee. Where did the music go? Boom. Boom boom ta tatataaaaa. Boom boomboom. You know that song. It's an old song.

Mohammed I know it well. We have the same song on our street.

Malek What street?

Mohammed It has no name. It was never a street. One day Abu Hussam built a house and then it became a street.

Malek Then it's Abu Hussam Street. Ya zalameh, we have to know where everything is. What will happen to us if we stop knowing where people are? What will happen if we get old, God protect us, and we don't know who is coming and who is going. Abu Ahmad bring juice.

Ashraf Ya Abu Ahmad, you're Abu Ahmad and I am Abu Mohammed. OK, so who are you?

Malek SHUT UP!

Ashraf (*to* **Mohammed**)   Sugar?

Abu Ihab Make it very sweet. There is a guest. Welcome. Sit. Make the coffee sweet Im Ihab.

Malek (*to* **Abu Ihab**)   Im Ihab died you fool. (*To* **Mohammed**.) He forgets everything. Welcome. Here is a pillow. Where is the breakfast?

Mohammed No. No. I had breakfast. Alhamdulillah. Ya'tikum el afieh! So which one of you is Malek Ahmad Mohammed Ibn Ahmad Malek Mohammed Ibn Mohammed Malek Ahmad Ibn Mohammed Mohammed Malek Ahmad Malek Malek?

Malek Eat! Sahtayn.

Scene Four

Mohammed He didn't answer the letters he was sent and if you don't answer the letters, yanni, if you don't go visit them, they send me here to talk to you. So which one of you is . . .

Malek . . . Welcome. Bring the board, throw the dice. Sheshbesh, inshallah.

Ashraf I am Abu Mohammed. Why didn't I get a letter?

Mohammed Wallah, I don't know. Some people get a letter, some people don't get a letter, some people get a phone call, some people don't get a phone call.

Ashraf Some people have a satellite and some people don't have a satellite.

Abu Ihab Some people have a Mercedes and some people don't have a Mercedes.

Malek Some people shut up and some people should also shut up. (*To* **Mohammed**.) Who wants to know Malek Ahmad Mohammed Ibn Ahmad Malek Mohammed Ibn Mohammed Malek Ahmad Ibn Mohammed Mohammed Malek Ahmad Malek Malek?

Mohammed Walla. They gave me this machine (*a laptop*) and told me to visit these people (*a long list*) and to find out who is who. We have to know who everybody is.

Ashraf *brings the coffee.* **Abu Ihab** *brings the juice.*

Abu Ihab First the juice. (*To* **Mohammed**.) Tfadal. Drink.

Ashraf The coffee will get cold. (*To* **Mohammed** *with the coffee.*) Tfadal.

Malek Why do I have juice and coffee? Who ruined the order?

Abu Ihab So you don't know who is who?!

Mohammed Of course I know who is who. They told me to count the people so I count.

Ashraf It's good to count people.

Mohammed It's good to have something to drink. Bless your hands.

Ashraf I will count the people. One. Two. Three. Four. Tfadal.

Malek One hundred per cent. We're counted.

Mohammed I have to count one by one. So which one of you is Malek Ahmad Mohammed . . .

Abu Ihab They forgot who we are?! I remember everyone. There isn't one in the whole city I don't remember. Ask me.

Malek Abu Ismail, with the khishkhash? Do you remember him?

Abu Ihab Of course. Every year, in the third rain, not the second, in the third rain, we went to the orchard with the women and the truck. He had 500 trees. We spent two days. We put the sheep in the ground, cooked it, worked, and then we ate.

Ashraf Did you count Abu Ismail?

Mohammed I don't know which Abu Ismail you're talking about.

Abu Ihab Abu Ismail with the khishkhash? They forgot you, Abu Ismail, rest in peace, ya Abu Ismail.

Ashraf Rest in peace, my brother.

Malek Agh, Abu Ismail and the khishkhash . . .

Mohammed Rest in peace? But if he's dead, he's not counted.

Malek, Abu Ihab, Ashraf Astaghfirullah Al Adheem.

Malek Why??

Abu Ihab Of course he can be counted.

Ashraf That's a mistake.

Malek OUT!

Mohammed Let me explain. My job is to count the ones on top of the ground. The living.

Ashraf It's a job?

Mohammed Of course it's a job. So which one of you is (*very fast*) Malek Ahmad Mohammed Ibn Ahmad Malek Mohammed Ibn Mohammed Malek Ahmad Ibn Mohammed Mohammed Malek Ahmad Malek Malek?

Silence.

Malek Who feels like dancing? I feel like dancing. And where is the fruit Abu Mohammed? Prepare the fruit. Come and let us dance to the memory of Abu Ismail. (*To* **Mohammed**.) You count tiktik boom tik boom, tiktik boom tik boom . . . Boom boom ta tatataaaaa. Boom boomboom.

And they get set up into a line and begin to do a small dabkeh. Very small. Very old. They pull **Mohammed** *from his comfort and they dance. Somehow the paper list of* **Mohammed** *gets involved in the dance. It's a very very long list on a computer printout.*

Abu Ihab No one dances anymore.

Malek That's not true. I went to the wedding and I danced. Agh, my heart.

Ashraf No, ya Abu Ahmad, you didn't die then and you won't die today. We have company. And dancing. And baking bread, inshallah.

Malek Yaaaa Abu Ahmad, where is the breakfast?

Abu Ihab Yaaaa Abu Ahmad, I am Abu Ihab and you are Abu Ahmad. And we had breakfast.

Malek Alhamdulillah. AND THE FRUIT?

Scene Five

Abu Ihab I'll tell you who everyone is. Hmmm. Abu Ayyman. He lives in Shati Camp.

Ashraf He died in Shati.

Malek Abu Ayyman died? When is the aza? The funeral?

Ashraf Ya zalameh, he died a long time ago. We went to the aza, rest in peace.

Abu Ihab And Abu Mohammed who lives in Zeitoun and sold jackets and wedding suits in the Fras Market. Then Abu Ziad who lives in Sabra and who had three sons killed in a car accident and then was never the same and he never spoke after that. Ah, Abu Mahmoud, Abu Marwan, Abu Wael, brothers, they all live in Daraj and made couches and chairs and sets for the newly-weds. But they closed and now they don't even open the shop anymore. They sit on car seats by Tariq's garage who fixes the flat tires. Abu Mousa, Abu Tariq, Abu Midhat, Abu Taher, all of them live in Nassr and have grocery shops. They moved from Shati. And then to Sheikh Radwan. Yes. And then, let me think, next to them was Im Qais who made dresses and then her daughter . . .

Mohammed (*interrupting from Im Qais*) Malek Ahmad Mohammed Ibn Ahmad Malek Mohammed Ibn Mohammed Malek Ahmad Ibn Mohammed Mohammed Malek Ahmad Malek Malek . . . which one of you is Malek Ahmad Mohammed Ibn Ahmad Malek Mohammed Ibn Mohammed Malek Ahmad Ibn Mohammed Mohammed Malek Ahmad Malek Malek?

Malek Ya Sidi, it could be me. Say it again.

Mohammed Malek Ahmad Mohammed Ibn Ahmad Malek Mohammed Ibn Mohammed Malek Ahmad Ibn Mohammed Mohammed Malek Ahmad Malek Malek. Are you him?

Malek Who wants to know?

Mohammed Ya Sidi, they want to take care of everyone. They want to remember everyone. They want to make sure that everyone is fine. They want to make sure everyone has what he needs. They just want to know who is 'everyone'. That's all.

Malek Let's say for example that I am Malek Ahmad Mohammed Ibn Ahmad Malek Mohammed Ibn Mohammed Malek Ahmad Ibn Mohammed Mohammed Malek Ahmad Malek Malek.

Mohammed Then I will open this labtob and open your file and write down that you are alive, that you live here, and that I visited you today and that I counted you.

Malek Labtob? File? Yes. I am Malek Ahmad Mohammed Ibn Ahmad Malek Mohammed Ibn Mohammed Malek Ahmad Ibn Mohammed Mohammed Malek Ahmad Malek Malek. Open your contraption. I heard of those machines. What does it say about me?

Ashraf My grandson has this contraption.

Abu Ihab My son and my grandson have this contraption. This contraption is a jinn.

Malek Quiet. This contraption does everything. I'm buying one. Five hundred dollars American.

Mohammed I'll open it. Sit. Sit.

They make a kind of office around the laptop. This 'office' has to be really make-shift from the stuff you would find in the houses of these men. **Mohammed** *would sit on some sort of 'chair', but we can't hide his face with the screen.*

Scene Six

Mohammed (*opening the computer*) We put this here. If the battery is dead we use electricity. If there is no electricity, we use the battery. If we have both, we use electricity. If we have neither we wait for lunch. Ah. Electricity.

Malek Of course!

Mohammed We press this button. And . . . (*It takes a while.*) it . . . turns . . . on . . . usually. . . . God is great, it will go on.

Malek WAIT. Before we record who is who, yours truly wants to go skybing with my son Ahmad who lives in Neeeuw York. What do you say?

Abu Ihab I thought you want to see your file.

Malek I don't have a file.

Mohammed   Everyone has a file. (*To* **Ashraf**.) What's your name?

Ashraf   Ahmad Ahmad Mohammed Ibn Ahmad Ahmad Mohammed Ibn Mohammed Hussam Ahmad Ibn Mohammed Mohammed Mahmoud Mohammed Ahmad Mahmoud Ashraf Ahmad.

Mohammed   Ahmad Ahmad Mohammed Ibn Ahmad Ahmad Mohammed Ibn Mohammed Hussam Ahmad Ibn Mohammed Mohammed Mahmoud Mohammed Ahmad Mahmoud Ashraf Ahmad. Enter. And here you are. You see. You exist. And you live here. And your wife is gone. And your children, some have died and some have travelled, right.

Ashraf   Im Mohammed was clever. And the boys died fighting. And my brother Abu Imran ran to the West Bank, he has five boys. They all study. Does it say all this? Is this written? They are all lawyers and builders. All five. What else does it say?

Mohammed   Your ID.

Ashraf   What else? What about my work, my house, the names of Abu Imran's children, how smart they all are, what about my shop where I built furniture? And the men who worked with me? And when Mohammed got married and he fell off the roof the week before and he couldn't dance at his own wedding. But he danced because he was strong even though it hurt. God gave him strength.

Malek   That was a good wedding. He fell off the roof fixing the boiler. Curse all the boilers. Write: I am Malek Ahmad Mohammed Ibn Ahmad Malek Mohammed Ibn Mohammed Malek Ahmad Ibn Mohammed Mohammed Malek Ahmad Malek Malek. Enter. My son is Ahmad Malek . . . wait . . . (*He takes a tiny paper out of his pocket.*) His skybe name is Ahmad 40162.

Mohammed   Ahhhh. So you are Malek Ahmad Mohammed Ibn Ahmad Malek Mohammed Ibn Mohammed Malek Ahmad Ibn Mohammed Mohammed Malek Ahmad Malek Malek. I never would have guessed. Enter.

Abu Ihab   Yatik al afia.

Malek   What does it say about me?

Mohammed   That you live here.

Malek   And?

Mohammed   That's it. And your ID of course.

Malek   That's it? That's it? Write. I am Malek Ahmad Mohammed Ibn Ahmad Malek Mohammed Ibn Mohammed Malek Ahmad Ibn Mohammed Mohammed Malek Ahmad Malek Malek. I have twelve sons. A dozen. And daughters somewhere. All beautiful. All married. I have forty grandchildren. Boys and girls mixed. I don't remember their names but every one of them has to be counted. You hear me. Write. Press Enter. I worked for forty years. And then another forty. I built a house. And I built another one when the first one exploded. Write. I fought in 1936, 1948, and again . . .

Abu Ihab (*interrupting*) I drove the taxi for forty years. And I'm waiting forty years to drive again. My wife, may she rest in peace, made eleven children, God keep them, and they made children. And then the four boys went to Norway. They don't live here anymore. But they made children. They all made two. That's how they do things there. But they have eight children in Norway making children. Write. Eleven and eight and everyone who comes after them. You understand. But count them. Write eleven children. Eleven children who are making children in Norway but they are only in Norway for a year or two. Enter. (*Pause.*) They will come back one day, inshallah. Count.

Ashraf People stopped buying couches and furniture when the money stopped coming in. So we began to make chairs and beds. And soon that stopped because we couldn't get the materials in. I started to make tables, big and then small. But who needs tables big and small when no couches are coming. What happened to that carpentry shop, ya Abu Ahmad, you're the oldest, what happened to my carpentry shop? I made ten children and three daughters. There are two twins, boys, Mohammed and Mahmoud. They are thirty-four years old next winter.

Malek Ahmad 40162. In Neeuw Yooork.

Mohammed Abu Ahmad, you don't know how to work the contraption.

Malek I know. You don't think I know. Ahmad 40162. There are 40,162 Ahmad's that you have to find ya Abu Counter and they all have news for you.

Abu Ihab I drove a bus. I am Abu Ihab the Bus Driver.

Malek I fought in four wars, maybe five, or six. We fought all the countries one by one. Why aren't you writing?

Mohammed I don't write. I only count. (*To* **Abu Ihab**.) What's your name?

Abu Ihab You don't write? You only count? Nice. Then. He is One. He is Two. I am Three.

Mohammed You don't want to tell me your name?

Abu Ihab No.

Mohammed Then you won't be counted.

Abu Ihab I don't want to be counted.

Mohammed But then you won't get what everyone else gets. No one will know that you live here. No one will know how to find you.

Malek Eh. . . . Everyone knows how to find him. He's Abu Ahmad the Bus Driver.

Abu Ihab Ya, Abu Ahmad . . . I am Abu IHAB the Bus Driver.

Malek That's what I'm saying and everyone knows where to find us. Even Abu Counter.

Abu Ihab Khalas, I don't want to know and I don't want to be counted.

Mohammed   Astaghfirullah Al Adheem.

Abu Ihab   I know who I am.

Mohammed   I have to count you. What's your name?

Abu Ihab (*No answer.*)

Silence.

Scene Seven

Abu Ihab   I drove a bus for a long time. But then they changed all the drivers and remade all the streets and no one knew where anything was anymore. That was then, but now I can only drive from Beit Hanoun to Rafah. Not like before when we drove the merchants and the visitors from Ras Al Naqura to Eilat, from Al Quds to Cairo. (*Not loud and proud.*) I am Abu Ihab the Bus Driver. (*Pause, sigh.*) I drive a bus.

Malek   Tell me, ya Abu Counter of People, did you count yourself?

Mohammed   Me? I was counted a long time ago. Look. (*He types his name.*) You see. Mohammed Mamdouh Mohammed Ahmad Hussam Othman Mohammed Ali Othman Ahmad. And where I live. And my ID. (*Pause.*) That's me. (*Pause.*) That's all of me!

Malek   That's all of you?

Abu Ihab   How many children do you have, God keep them all. Abu who are you?

Ashraf   What was your work? What did you make?

Malek   Who is your mother and father? The most important people.

Malek *looks at the audience.*

Malek   Who are you all?

Ashraf   Look at all these children.

Abu Ihab   Mashallah. Mashallah. We stand like fools and they watch us.

Malek   We have to know who they are. What will happen if we stop knowing who is coming and going? (*Speech.*) What will happen if we stop knowing our neighbours and the sons of our neighbours. What will happen to us if, God protect us . . . Yalla . . .

Malek, Ashraf, Abu Ihab, *and all the drama assistants on the side go into the audience and ask the kids their names, the names of their mothers and fathers, where they live, where they are from, what they like to play, etc. This will break everything up. We need to give it three–four minutes max.* **Mohammed** *is at the computer furiously typing. When* **Malek, Ashraf**, *and* **Abu Ihab** *come back on the stage, happy knowing the whole audience, they stand behind* **Mohammed** *reading out loud what he has typed about himself.*

Malek (*reading for* **Mohammed**) I am Abu Ahmad. (*To the others.*) Like me. (*Reading.*) I have three boys, Ahmad, Ali, and Mohammed and four girls. Ahmad is married and has six boys called Mohammed, Sami, Ibrahim, Amer, Hussam, and Kamal. His wife Ward is waiting for the girl and they will name her Maryam when she comes. Inshallah. The second boy died when he was two days old, rest in peace yabba, habibi . . .

Abu Ihab (*continuing reading*) . . . but the third is strong and he's handsome and a fighter and he makes me proud. He is also married and has four boys and four girls . . . a match . . .

Malek (*to* **Abu Ihab**) Abu Ahmad, let's make lunch while Abu Ahmad writes in his contraption.

Abu Ihab I am Abu Ihab and you and Abu Counter are Abu Ahmad. What's wrong with you today? (*To* **Ashraf**.) Come Abu Mohammed, let's prepare lunch. Abu Ahmad the Counter will be writing for many hours.

Malek And then, there was Abu Mahmoud with the horses. Did you know him? He taught his horses to dance. Yalla ya shebab, let us dance again. I feel like dancing. TikTik Boom, tiktik boom, tiktik boom . . .

Malek, **Abu Ihab**, *and* **Ashraf** *do a small little dance.*

Ashraf (*Coughing to get attention.*)

Malek What? Talk.

Ashraf (*embarrassed*) Shoo yanni skybe?

Abu Ihab No laughing! It's good to ask. You're smart to ask, ya Abu Mohammed.

Malek Skybe, yanni, is when a telephone marries a television. They do it on the combuter. So you can call and see the person you're calling and it happens over the internet. The internet is a big thing that is connecting the whole world and they call it the world wide web yanni, www because it's one big spider web. But don't be afraid because there's no spider. Just a web.

Mohammed Here. Watch. Here he is. Ahmad 40162 in NeeuwYourk. Call. It's ringing. I love skybe.

Malek AHMAD??? AHMAD!!! I AM YOUR FATHER. I SEE YOU. DO YOU SEE ME. HERE I AM HABIBI. WE ARE COUNTING YOU. HOW ARE YOU, MY HEART? DO YOU SEE ME? I AM OLD, HUH? HABIBI, HOW ARE YOU? GOOD INSHALLAH. HABIBI. I SEE YOU. WE ARE COUNTING YOU. MY HEART. HERE IS ABU AHMAD WHO CAME TODAY TO COUNT US. DON'T WORRY. YOU ARE COUNTED, HABIBI, MY HEART, YA MY SON. HOW ARE YOU?

Music. End

Play #2: The Mothers

Characters

Im Ahmad, *the oldest, maybe sixty, married to Abu Ahmad.*
Maryam, *the youngest; very, very, very pregnant; married to Saed.*
Ward, *married to Ihab who is the son of Abu Ihab the taxi driver; in the text she is called Ward but at some point she is called Im Ahmad which means there are two Im Ahmads so we call Ward as Im Ahmad 2.*
Im Ramiz, *forty, married to Khalil.*

The relationships here have some relevance to other characters in this collection.

We are in the courtyard of **Im Ahmad**, *where there is an oven, where cooking often takes places, especially in summer. There are pots all over. These are pots of descending sizes for cooking a sheep to boiling an egg. Also, they have large and small utensils to accommodate the pots. The mothers are just cooking together and each mother has a different number of people to feed. Because we can't use real food, we have to have a clever story of pretend food around and about. There are also burlap bags of food, e.g. fifty kilos of rice, sugar, etc. It's a normal regular day, so to say. The women are dressed in every colour in the world. One big assortment of all colours and kinds of women's clothing and tastes.*

Im Ahmad (*alone*)   Good morning on this glorious day and my thanks to God. Inshallah, INSHALLAH Abu Ahmad will stay with his friends all day in their diwan. Let them play together all day, inshallah. Married for fifty years, God keep and protect him, but inshallah let him play with friends. Today he asked for spinach. He read on the internet that spinach keeps you young. So he wants fifty years worth of spinach to make up for his lost youth. He says I made him old because I didn't make him enough spinach. You can die from such a man, learning the internet at his age, may God keep and protect his soul. (*Shouting.*) Ya Ward, where are you. It's almost evening.

Ward (*shouting from inside*)   Don't exaggerate. You always exaggerate. We haven't had the afternoon prayer. Calm. Stop pulling the feathers from the chicken before it's been slaughtered. (*She enters.*) I'm here.

Im Ahmad   So you want me to dance for you?

Ward *comes in with more cooking things. She is dressed for cooking. She settles in. They are preparing the food.*

Ward   What is that?

Im Ahmad   Spinach.

Ward   It's not good.

Im Ahmad   Shoo yanni, it's not good. Are you the genius of spinach?

Ward   You're getting old Im Ahmad. You bought it from Saman's shop, I can tell, and not from Sleiman. I told you to shop only from Sleiman if you want spinach. You go to Saman for bamia or green board beans. You want me to bring these back to Saman and get you new from Sleiman? I have to go to Sirhan for the honey and he is next to Saman and Sleiman. It's no problem. And never buy honey from Saman or Sleiman. It's bitter. Be careful . . .

Im Ahmad   Enough. Stop. Saman Sleiman Sirhan. You buy a different thing in a different shop. You think you're the smartest one to spend money? It's spinach. You cook it, you eat it, and INSHALLAH you get younger. Sit. Chop. And you go easy with the meat. It's expensive and it makes you die. That's what Abu Ahmad says and I swear to God if he says it, he's right. That's what he says! And you don't want to kill Abu Ihab God save him and protect him and keep him.

Ward   Abu Ihab will live to 120 INSHALLAH. But I don't think his mind will live that long. He confuses me with Im Ihab on some days and yehhhh – he wants me to make a wedding for Ihab and Ihab's been married for a long time. Rest in peace Im Ihab. Ahhh, God protect my father-in-law . . . and all the men. Walla, Im Ahmad, God give you strength and bless your hands. How are you?

Im Ahmad How am I??? I'm worried. I have eight daughters in all the countries. Name me a country, I have a daughter in it. I miss them. I want to see them. I want to visit them? I want them to come home every once in a while and eat my food. But there is no coming home these days. Alhamdulillah, Mazen is still here in eighth grade.

Ward You can always sky-ib-hun (Skype them).

Im Ahmad I can't feed them skybing. Abu Ahmad is skybing. He's yelling the whole night at all of Brooklyn, Neeuw Yourk.

Ward I skybe my sister every Friday. I haven't seen her in years except through the computer . . . it's six years already – I say your spinach is no good – and my brother, I haven't seen him in two years. And, Yousef ya,Yousef, it's been sixteen years . . . Aghhh my heart, agh my spirit, aghh my brothers, my sisters, God will care and bless and bring goodness to you. Inshallah. Why did we end up like this?

Im Ahmad They closed the country.

Ward Shoo yanni, the country is a shop? . . . They can close it and open it whenever they want? What a thing!

And they continue. A little cleaning up here and there. Maybe we have a baby in a box on the side. This would be **Ward***'s baby. Baby sound effects.*

Ward I have to visit the schools.

Im Ahmad Khair inshallah?

Ward Khair. But each one is in another school. They spread them like seeds in a field. One here and one there, one here and one there. I have to visit five schools to hear that the children are smart. They are all smart. From the biggest to the smallest. Twenty points from twenty, nineteen from twenty. That's what they bring. All smart. (*Pause.*) It's the fault of the other kids. This one pushes and this one pulls. The girls all have long braids. It takes me an hour every morning to get them ready. All day long girls pulling braids of other girls . . . from under the mandeel even. And the ironing, it takes me another hour . . . every shirt ironed . . . they look like doctors, God keep them. (*Pause.*) My day is over before it starts. It's not the afternoon prayer yet and I've done a day of work. Enough, I'll throw myself from the roof and we'll see if they miss me.

Im Ahmad Calm down, girl.

Ward (*crying*) Shoo yanni calm down. Everyone is yelling at me. A husband, a father-in-law, and ten children, and even this baby in my stomach . . . MAY GOD KEEP AND PROTECT EACH AND EVERY ONE OF THEM. I don't sleep from worry. I don't eat from worry. I have a head-ache from worry and from worry I'm going to get (high) blood pressure . . . and then an attack (heart). I know it. I feel it. They don't like me. And I don't want any more children. Ten is enough, God keep them all.

Im Ahmad No, no, no, no, ya habibti, they love you. We all love you. Khalas, come. Come. Come to me. Do you want me to fix your braids? I haven't fixed braids in two years.

Ward *lays in the arms of* **Im Ahmad**. **Im Ramiz** *enters. She is older than* **Ward** *and younger than* **Im Ahmad**. *She is carrying heavy things: bags of rice, or boxes of soap, it's a big load. She is physically strong as an ox, but she is not happy.*

Im Ramiz Ya'tikum el afieh. (*Seeing* **Im Ahmad** *and* **Ward**.) Who's sick? Who was killed? Who is getting divorced? Which rocket fell on whose house? Why are we crying on this day? (*She sits and starts to gently weep.*) So much pain, so many troubles, so many heart-aches. (*More weeping. Melodrama.*) I can't take any more bad news. How much can a person take? How much more? True, we are women! We are strong, and healthy . . .

Ward And beautiful . . .

Im Ramiz But how much can our hearts carry? How much can my arms carry? They are falling off. Someone help me.

Im Ahmad Yalla ya Ward, go help her with the packages. Enough sadness. We'll cry later. I haven't cried since last week. It's time. Later, after the evening prayer, we'll sit and cry until the night prayer. (*To* **Im Ramiz**.) Did you bring me the tray? Tell me you forgot the tray?!

Im Ramiz Don't give me your forgetting problems. I have your tray. (*Think.*) I borrow a tray and you count the days until I return it. Am I a thief?

Im Ahmad Shame on you, Im Ramiz.

Im Ramiz One time I broke your clay pot and I'm hearing it forever. I have your tray, God keep the trays and bless them.

Ward Are we crying now or later? Why are you in a bad mood, ya Im Ramiz?

Im Ramiz (*she starts weeping a little*) I'm not crying.

Im Ahmad It's Khalil?

Im Ramiz He said he was going for a week. He called me every day. Then he said he was staying longer. He called me every week. It's been three months. He calls me every month but what happens when he starts calling me every year. How many years? Where did he go? Why can't he get back? I don't know where he is. I don't know if he has money. He could be dead. Yeeeeeh! The children are asking for him every day and every night. My mother is worried. My father is worried. And I'm alone. We are all alone. Why did I marry him?! I curse the day I married him. I curse all the men. I curse the occupation. That's what I say.

Ward Enough . . . there's an explanation for everything. Maybe he lost his phone. (*Building it up . . .*) Maybe he was robbed. (*Building it up . . .*) Maybe he's in jail. (*Building it up . . .*) Maybe he's dead . . .

Im Ramiz *starts crying and* **Im Ahmad** *is beating* **Ward** *for being so stupid.*

Im Ahmad   Walla, he's not dead and he's not in jail. And not all the men are the same. Men are good. They shop. They fix the things that are broken. They eat the food we cook. They wear the clothes we clean. What would we do without them? God save you, Abu Ahmad. Bring the potatoes. I hope you bought enough.

Ward   Where did you buy them from? Sleiman, inshallah. He has the good potatoes.

Im Ahmad   Enough. (*They work. To* **Im Ramiz**.) You should go to an organization.

Im Ramiz   God help me from organizations.

Ward   I don't need organizations. I have schools. More than I can visit.

Im Ramiz   What kind of organization? My cousin works in an organization. She likes it very much. They play with children, some of the orphans, God save the orphans and bless them, God is big. Every week she goes to Khan Yunis and they take care of the orphans. (*Thought.*) And now my children are orphans . . . their father, lost in the world. I'll kill him when he comes back. Where does a man go? He leaves a wife and six children?

Im Ahmad   There are organizations who can help you find him.

Ward   There aren't enough eggplants. Listen, call Maryam and tell her to bring a bucket of eggplants. Tell her stop by Sirhan.

Im Ahmad   Maryam can't bring herself! Where is she anyway? I said I would get her in a taxi and she says 'no no the walking is good for me'. I say you need a taxi, she says she's walking. She'll have that baby on the street. Give me the phone. (*She takes her mobile and calls* **Maryam**.) WHERE ARE YOU, habibti? We are all worried that you'll have the baby on the street, God forbid. (*Listening.*) Outside the door?! So come in.

Ward (*taking the phone*)   Wait. We need more eggplants. (*Listening.*) From Sleiman or Salman? (*Listening.*) Good. You're smart. Not like Im Ahmad, she doesn't know how to shop. (**Maryam** *comes in on the phone*.) Come in. (*Listening.*) You're in? Where? (*She sees her.*)

They all laugh. **Maryam** *is very, very, very pregnant. She can hardly walk. She is young. This is her first baby. The three women surround her and touch her belly.*

Im Ramiz   It's a girl. Your stomach is wide.

Im Ahmad   It's a boy. See how your belly sticks out in front.

Ward   Sit, my sister. (*She takes out a coin on a string and hangs it over the belly until the coin starts to swing.*) Look. It's a boy. What could be clearer. I'll go to Abu Ala and get the wool. Light blue and dark blue. When the baby comes out, we'll put the hat on his head. He'll be like the moon.

Maryam   I need to sit, habibti, I need to sit. I swear to God, I don't know how you all do this so often. It's so heavy. I left my house – when – it took me an hour. The streets are full. A thousand kids going to school. Alhamdulillah. But they shouldn't step on my feet, pushing me here and here and there and there. I couldn't walk. And try to find a car. And where is that husband? After the morning prayer he left the house. Where? Where! He says he's going to prepare for the baby. How does a man prepare for the baby? Here are the eggplants. Look, my hands are so swollen I won't be able to do anything. Look at me. I'm useless. I'm ugly. I'm so tired. (*She starts to cry.*)

Ward (*pouring tea*)   Drink, habibti, drink. It's camomile. It will make you happy and calm. I was ugly when I was pregnant. We are all ugly when we have this big stomach. It will go when the baby comes. And we'll be beautiful again. We have to be beautiful.

Im Ramiz   I was beautiful . . . so why did he leave and WHERE IS HE?

Im Ahmad   Enough, ya Im Ramiz. You should go to an organization and they will find him. I will go with you. Everything always end up well. And if not, that's what God wants. Enough tears. Did you bring the nuts?

Im Ramiz   I bought all kinds. I was so upset I bought every kind there was. There must be five kilos of nuts. All the kinds. And I'm going to sit and eat them all. And be fat and ugly.

Ward   And how much did you pay? More than you should. You also don't know how to shop. The wrong shop and the wrong price. I know it. Show me the packet.

Im Ahmad   Quiet! You don't know a nut from a banana, an orange from a lemon, a king from a sultan.

Ward   Meeeeee??? Be careful, Im Ahmad. I'm the smartest one in the neighbourhood about shopping.

Im Ramiz   I went to Ez-Zawyeh, I counted the shops, eight shops and it's the ninth on the right.

Ward   That's if you went in from Fahmi Beek Street. Tell me you went in from the side of the mosque. Then you know where you end up. At the shoe fixer, on the dirty end of the souk. You go in from the end where the people go in. Not from where the carriages and donkeys unload the grass.

Im Ahmad   Queen of the market, stop yelling.

Ward   If it wasn't for me, Im Ahmad, you would starve to death because you, ya sheikha, you don't go out. And why? Ask her why. Because she's afraid something will fall on her. Look up! What is there that will fall on you? Look, is anything falling? Nothing is falling. Nothing is coming and no one is coming. This is how it is and that's the end of the story.

Im Ramiz   Then how will Khalil ever come back? (*And she weeps.*)

Maryam   He won't fall from the sky, my sister. You have to stop crying, it's no good for me and the baby in my stomach.

Im Ahmad   Let her cry. It's good to cry. The baby will get used to crying. He'll come out crying. We're all crying. The whole country is crying. Give me that pot. Not that one. The other one.

Maryam Why don't you go out, Im Ahmad? Go out. See the world.

Im Ahmad So something can fall on me? I saw the world. I don't want to see it anymore. I went to Turkey. I went to Egypt. I went to Jordan. I went to Greece. Big deal. It's all the same. Here, you go outside, and something will fall on you and kill you. And then you're dead. I go out for weddings and for funerals. That's enough. And I will come to you when the baby comes and I'll take a taxi. Special. (*Special taxi means not a collective taxi but an actual taxi.*)

And they continue. The phone of **Maryam** *rings.*

Maryam (*seeing the number*) It's Saed. (*Answering.*) What Saed, how are you? (*Listening.*) I told you, I'm with Im Ahmad and Im Ahmad. (*Listening.*) I told you. Im Ahmad says hello. And Im Ahmad the other says hello. And Im Ramiz says hello. What do you want? (*Listening.*) What are you doing in Shajaiyya? (Eastern neighbourhood.) You'll get shot. (*Answering.*) White. All white. (*Listening.*) Im Ahmad says it's a boy but I want it white just in case. (*Listening.*) Any colour you like, habibi, whatever you want. Ya tik al afia. I'll see you later. (*Closes the phone.*) He's a carpenter today. A Masters Degree in journalism and today he's a carpenter. Yesterday he was an electrician. Tomorrow he will be a plumber. Alhamdulillah, he keeps himself busy and the house is getting prepared.

Im Ramiz (*crying crying crying.*)

Im Ahmad (*to* **Maryam**) Look what you did now.

Maryam What did I do? Ya Im Ramiz, habibti, I'm sorry, habibti, Khalil will come back. One day soon, inshallah, Khalil will be back. Here, feel the baby. He's jumping around. He'll be born soon. (*Her phone rings and again it's Saed.*) Not now Saed. This is not a good time. (*Listening.*) No, it's not the baby. It's Im Ramiz.

Ward Enough sadness. It's a nice day. Everything smells good. The food. The flowers. The air. God is great and Alhamdulillah we are all healthy and what more can you ask. Who wants coffee? (*And she starts with the coffee: a thermos and cups.*)

As they are drinking coffee, all the phones start ringing. First **Ward***'s, then* **Im Ahmad***'s, then* **Maryam***'s, and* **Im Ramiz** *calls her house when she sees that phones are ringing everywhere. We hear parts of each conversation. There is no real hysteria. They have done this a thousand times. There is concern. But no panic. All the conversations happen more or less at the same time but it has to be orchestrated so we hear the main point of each woman.*

Ward What do you mean the teachers are on strike? (*Listening.*) Don't leave from the school. (*Listening.*) Where are they going? Don't stay alone, you hear me. Stay with your class, stay with the girls in the your class. I'm calling your brother. (*She calls another of her kids.*) Sharaf, do you have a strike in your school? (*Listening.*) Where are you? I want you to come home. Where is Ismail? (*Listening.*) Keep him by your side. Go to Ahmad, I'm calling a car. (*She calls another of her kids.*) Hadeel, Hadeel, why are you crying, stop crying, yamma, go to Ola's class. A car will come bring you home. There's nothing to cry about. Stop crying. Khalas yamma. (*She calls her husband.*) Ihab, what is this, the teachers are on strike? (*Listening.*) They aren't on strike? Why are the kids out of school? (*Listening.*) Which holiday? There is no holiday? Send three cars to go get them. Now. Ihab, bring them to me. You know I have blood pressure, you want me to have a heart attack? Bring them to me.

Im Ahmad   Who is this? (*Listening.*) Abu Ahmad? Where are you? (*Listening.*) What's falling? Abu Ahmad, what's falling? Stay where you are. I'll come get you. (*Listening.*) Ya Abu Ahmad, where are you? I'll come get you. Here I'm putting on my abaya. I made spinach. Yes Abu Ahmad, you'll be young again. You will fight again. (*Listening.*) Yes, I know this is your last chance to fight. Stay inside. I don't want anything falling on you, God save you. (*Listening.*) Who is that? (*Listening.*) What guest? (*Listening.*) Now? (*Listening.*) Yes. Is anything in the sky? (*Listening.*) What do you see? Which way is it flying? (*Listening.*) Is anything coming out of it? (*Listening.*) You have to bring him home? (*Listening.*) (*Listening.*) Are the men still all there? I'm coming to get you. (*Listening.*) You have a car? (*Listening.*) Yes, I'm making the spinach. Just stay where you are.

Maryam   What, ya Saed? (*Listening.*) Stuck? Who is with you? (*Listening.*) And there are no cars? (*Listening.*) The road is closed? Are you sure? I don't hear anything. It's calm here. Im Ahmad (Ward) is talking to her kids. I will stay here. You come to get me. (*Listening.*) I will call a car. (*She also calls the same company as* **Ward***'s husband.*) It's busy. Should I call you a car? Everyone is calling for cars. (*Listening.*) What happened? (*Listening.*) Turn on the television. Saed, what will you do? (*Listening.*) When? (*Listening.*) Come get me. I can't get home by myself. (*Listening.*) Listen, I will stay here until you find a car. But if it's dangerous, don't come this way. I will stay with Im Ahmad and Im Ahmad. It is quiet here. (*Listening.*) The baby won't come today. He knows it's a bad day to come. He'll wait until tomorrow or the day after, inshallah. (*Listening.*) We're cooking. Spinach. (*Listening.*) I know you like it. Be careful. Call me.

Im Ramiz   It's me. Did anyone call you? (*Listening.*) And you had the phone the whole time next to you? No one called? (*Listening.*) Who is that? What did they want? (*Listening.*) Yamma, I don't want to talk to them. They know where Khalil is and they won't tell me. I know. They talk to him. (*Listening.*) I don't believe them. (*Listening.*) OK. (*Waiting.*) Hello, wife of my uncle. How are you? Alhamdulillah. (*Listening.*) I understand, believe me, I understand, but then where is he? Why doesn't he want to talk to his children or his wife? (*Listening.*) They are all in the kindergarten, why what's happening? (*Listening.*) From where? (*Listening.*) Im Ahmad's kids said it was a holiday. (*Listening.*) You have all six of them? Bring them home. I'm coming. (*To the mothers.*) There is no holiday. Something is happening.

Im Ahmad   Something is happening.

Silence. Sound of bombs, low distant, nothing serious. Continues on. Grows slowly.

Ward   That's nothing. It's an Apache (helicopter) coming, it's hanging in the sky in the north.

Im Ahmad   Are the kids OK?

Ward   Abu Mohammed is picking up all the kids in buses and vans. He is sending all the taxi cars he has.

Im Ahmad   And Saed? Will he get back or do we have to arrange something?

Maryam   He's coming here. It will take him some time.

Im Ahmad   Stay, stay. Any which way the day is broken. And it started out so nice.

Ward   Im Ramiz, you want more coffee?

Im Ramiz   Pour. Pour.

Im Ahmad   Let's have breakfast.

Ward   Everyone is coming here.

Im Ahmad   Good. We'll be together. Do you remember when there weren't telephones? How did we live? I'll tell you. You told a neighbour who told the next neighbour who told the next one and by the end of the day everyone knew what had to happen.

Ward   Now we have a mobile. Now after an hour everyone knows what has to happen.

Im Ramiz   Pour the coffee. Pour the coffee.

Ward   It stopped. I don't hear anything.

Im Ahmad   Give me the tomatoes. And the onions. And the peppers. Wait. Look. Soon something will fall.

Maryam   This baby is jumping and jumping and jumping. Like a kid in school.

Ward   Soon. Just wait. Soon you'll be running to schools and running from schools. That's how it is.

Im Ramiz   Pour the coffee. (*She weeps.*)

Im Ahmad   Don't be sad.

Ward   We are all a little sad. That's how it is.

Maryam   But the baby is dancing.

And slowly they drink coffee, they talk but we don't hear it, music (low) covers their conversation, the conversation of women sharing secrets and calming down before yet another storm. Sound of the helicopter gets louder, and louder . . .

Play #3: The Brothers

Characters

The Gangs are teenagers, fourteen to seventeen-year-boys. Kids.

Gang One: This duo are the more intelligent and street smart of the two groups.
Boy One, **Mazen**, *the leader, aka King Mazen. He is the smartest of the group, he is soft, basically rational.*
Boy Two, **Sirhan**, *friend of Mazen, aka Arab the Arab. He knows how to follow the right people.*

Gang Two
Boy Three, **Ihab**, *the leader, aka Sultan. Although there is potential, he is a show-off, he thinks he knows things that he has no clue of. In fact, he is a follower who plays a leader. But he looks good and people like him for the first five minutes before they see his true colours.*
Boy Four, **Mohammed**, *friend of Ihab, aka Big Boy* **Titi**. *He is a nice boy, but he makes all the wrong choices. He goes where it's easiest and doesn't really care until someone gives him a reason to care . . . usually fighting or joining a collective cause against someone or something.*

Monster One
Monster Two

An UNRWA school yard, with their version of a swimming pool in the middle of the playing area. This pool is like a huge rubber/plastic water tank that is about waist-high and made for about six kids but in Gaza they get ten in. Behind it, a basketball court. Basketballs.

The courtyard is grey concrete. UNRWA schools, depending on how much money they have and where they are, are usually blue and white but can also be colourless. Gang One will be in blues and purples and Gang Two in reds and oranges. Needs choreography. Rhythm, exciting, a little suspense, upbeat, hip.

Ihab *enters. It's a stylish walk, confident, an I-own-the-street kind of walk. I'm cool. Then a jump. A spin. A trick. He has a stick and does a trick. He thinks maybe someone is following him. He 'takes care'. Practices with his stick. He whistles.* **Titi** *appears at the other end of the courtyard (stage, playing area, however wide we can make it, distance is needed). He whistles back.* **Ihab** *whistles the answer code.* **Titi** *whistles back. Finger whistles so they are loud. Answering the code.* **Titi** *finds a stick so he has one too. They meet centre stage. They do a stick thing, let's say a ceremonial hello after following a workshop in stick dancing.*

Ihab   Salam!

Titi   Salam!

Ihab   OK?

Titi   OK.

They 'pose'. They stand and let people watch how 'fabulous they are' and how dangerous they are . . . as if they are being watched by young boys.

Titi   Swimming pool!

Ihab   Swimming pool? (*Wait.*) Water.

Titi   Water.

They move around the swimming pool. Dance-like walking. They consider the possibilities this pool offers. Around one way. Around the other. Checking it out. Good pool. They take a few steps back. And with some kind of flying leap, jump into the pool. The splash should be interactive. And with music, they are goofing around in the pool. Laughing but a little rough and tough, a little drowning each other . . . on the edge of violence.

Titi   Great.

Ihab   You call that great?! You know nothing of great.

Titi   Yeah?

Ihab   Great is if we hang in this pool all day and no one throws us out.

Titi   Yeah, that's great.

Ihab   Yeah, that's great. Again?

They get out of the pool and again with some kind of flying leap, they jump again into the pool. And again they start goofing around and splashing and not noticing that **Mazen** *and* **Sirhan** *are approaching.*

Mazen *and* **Sirhan** *are coming from the opposite corners (where* **Ihab** *and* **Titi** *did not come from). They don't see the two in the pool from the start. Their approach to the playing area is similar to* **Ihab***'s and* **Titi***'s but at some point they notice that there are two boys in the pool. Sneaking, dance sneaking, likes cats approaching and then retreating, they arrive at the pool. Again, this is built on movement and dance.*

Capital letters can mean shouting or conviction or provocation. The tendency is that **Titi** *shouts,* **Mazen** *doesn't,* **Ihab** *and* **Sirhan** *both play with it.*

Sirhan WHAT ARE YOU DOING IN THE POOL?

Ihab WHO ARE YOU TALKING TO?

Mazen YOU.

Ihab ME?

Sirhan YES YOU.

Titi IS ANYBODY TALKING TO ME?

Sirhan OUT OF THE POOL.

Ihab ME???

Mazen YOU!!!

Titi WHY?

Sirhan BECAUSE WE WANT TO GO INTO THE POOL.

Titi OH YEAH!

Sirhan YEAH!

Titi YEAH!

Sirhan YEAH!

Ihab (*calm*) Wait, wait, wait, wait, wait, wait. Don't you see, boys, that I'm in the pool. And that I am going to stay in the pool . . . with my friend Big Boy Titi. ALL DAY.

Sirhan OH YEAH.

Titi AND ALL NIGHT.

Mazen (*calm*) OK. Stay in the pool. I think I'm going to hang around this pool . . . ALL DAY . . . because it's a NICE DAY, and with my friend Sirhan Arab the Arab.

Mazen *and* **Sirhan** *'walk' around the pool, provoking a little, maybe splashing, threatening a little, so* **Titi** *and* **Ihab** *can't get out of the pool. And all this is movement and acrobatics. Cool.*

Ihab I'm swimming. I ENJOY SWIMMING. Don't you see that I am enjoying swimming?! The sun is hot and the water is cool. Swimming is good for you. You don't get blue legs if you swim. That's what my mother said. Come my brother Big Boy Titi, swim with me.

Titi And I'm SWIMMING. I'M HAPPY. VERY HAPPY.

Ihab Notice the excellence – the genius – of our swimming and our breath . . .

Titi And no blue legs.

And of course as they swim, **Mazen** *and* **Sirhan** *are at the edge of the pool. They provoke. They poke. They splash. They touch heads and feet.* **Ihab** *and* **Titi** *start grabbing back from the pool. A fight starts. All four end up in the pool. Fighting and dancing. It's so great to be in the pool but ya still gotta fight to get the other ones out. Someone manages to throw someone out of the pool and they all end up out of the pool. Again, practised movement and dance. Otherwise it's just four guys getting out of a pool.*

During the next few replicas . . . the boys get towels of different sizes, all white. **Mazen** *and* **Ihab** *use the towels to make turbans and gowns for themselves and* **Titi** *and* **Sirhan** *use the towels to wrap them around their waists and heads. They should look like two gangs of pharaohs from different families.*

Mazen THIS ISN'T OVER.

Ihab DID I SAY IT WAS OVER?

Mazen You don't know when it's enough. You don't own the pool.

Ihab Is someone speaking to me? Titi, do you hear someone talking to me?

Titi Huuhhhh. . . . I have water in my ears . . . what did you say . . . it's dirty water.

Sirhan You're such a . . . (*the rest of the sentence would be 'idiot' or 'moron' or some other insult*).

Mazen (*interrupting him*) Don't say it! It's not the fault of Titi.

Titi I didn't do anything. I didn't say anything. You came. WE WERE IN THE POOL FIRST. YOU CAME AND THEN ALL THE REST.

Mazen Cool out, Big Boy Big Boy, TITI. Give it a rest.

Ihab When it suits you?! I don't want to give it a rest. (*Pause.*) I am a black belt in taekwondo. Big Boy Titi . . . take your stance!

Serious but funny! The kids perform Korean taekwondo moves that they learned at the workshop. You can also use the Korean names of these moves.

Titi Ready motion.

Ihab Front stance.

Titi Tiger stance.

Ihab   Back stance.

Titi   Block, down low back . . .

Ihab   Reverse punch . . .

Titi   Scissor block, middle punch . . .

Ihab   Twist block, reverse punch, strike . . .

Titi   Hammer twist, side punch . . .

Ihab   Hook punch . . .

Titi   Side kick . . .

Ihab   Tornado kick . . .

Titi   Axe kick . . .

Ihab   Spinning hook kick . . .

Titi   Roundhouse kick . . .

Ihab   I WIN.

Mazen (*to* **Sirhan**)   How about a little practicing . . . me and you . . . before our next class . . .?!

Sirhan   A practice session. I'm red. You're blue. And the bell rings. DINNNGGGGGGGGG!

They begin to wrestle and box.

Both   Watch your left, watch you right, upper jaw, pow, watch your feet, dance, pow, upper left cut, lower left cut. We are the A Team making the A show. No cheap shots, agreed. Agreed. Let's try a flair flip and flair flop. Jump. I'm gonna get gold. No I'm gonna get gold. He's a low blow. And no potatoes. And here is my signature move. And it's a two shot. No it's a three shot. It's a knock out. No. He's up. And a jab. And a hook. And a glass jaw. And he's on the rope. And he's down for the count. And a hook. And a liver punch. Peek-a-Boo, a straight right, is he saved by the bell, it's a technical draw, he throws in the towel. (*They throw in the towels.*) It's a technical knock-out.

Mazen (*to* **Ihab** *and* **Titi**)   HA!

Ihab   You call that fighting?

Mazen (*imitating*)   You call that fighting?

Sirhan (*imitating*)   You call that fighting?

Ihab   Why don't you get out of the yard. We were here first.

Titi   Yeah! We were definitely here FIRST . . . swimming and having a good old time and you came AND RUINED IT.

Sirhan WE RUINED IT??? We came into the courtyard planning on playing some nice basketball and we find the two of you taking a bath.

Ihab At least we take a BATH.

Mazen Shoo yanni? What exactly are you trying to say?

Sirhan (*to* **Mazen**) That you don't take a bath.

Mazen OH YEAH?!

Sirhan OH YEAH.

Mazen WHY ARE YOU YELLING AT ME?

Sirhan I'M NOT YELLING.

Titi What a bunch of goof-balls. I never saw such goof-balls like those. Did you ever see such goof-balls as those?

Ihab Someone stole our basketball. You two stole our basketball when we were swimming. That's why you were sneaking in. Give it back.

Mazen I swallowed it.

Sirhan Yeah we swallowed it. Both of us.

Titi GOOOOF-BAAAAALLLLLS.

Mazen Are you starting a war?

Ihab I didn't say nothing. He has his own mouth and he speaks from it.

Mazen Then say I'm not a goof-ball.

Ihab I'm not saying. I'm not his boss.

Sirhan Oh gimme a break . . . everyone knows he does exactly what you say. He follows you like a shadow.

Titi And YOU DO EXACTLY WHAT HE SAYS.

Sirhan That's because King Mazen is smart. And you, you're not smart and everyone knows it. We don't need ears to hear what everyone says about you.

Mazen We do need ears.

Sirhan Of course WE NEED EARS.

Titi What do they say? WHAT?

Sirhan If you don't hear it, I'm not telling it.

Ihab (*to* **Titi**) DON'T YOU HAVE EARS?

Titi Of course I have ears. But they're full of water. What did they say those bandits.

Ihab THEY don't say anything.

Mazen Yes THEY do.

Ihab THEY DON'T. AND THEY SAY THE SAME THING ABOUT YOU.

Ihab *jumps on* **Mazan**. **Sirhan** *jumps on them and then* **Titi** *on top and they end up in one piece, tangled together but able to move as one piece. And as such they move around the stage trying to get free from each other.*

All Go left. I'm going left. Me too. Everyone stop. We start over. Now try the right. One step right. My right foot isn't around. I think I have it here. Well move it. OK. We have to get untangled. Whose foot is this? (*He tickles it, and someone laughs.*) It's my foot. Stop. (*Laughing as they try to locate who has whose limb.*)

And they do this for a while, laughing from the tickling, and collapsing on the ground angry, all in one pile. And they lie there.

Ihab I hate this life.

Titi (*hesitating*) Me too.

Mazen Why?

Ihab Everyone is – yech – you know – like – broken or busted up or dead or dying. I'm leaving . . . the minute I get some money together.

Sirhan Yeah. I'm leaving too.

Titi Where are you going?

Sirhan Don't know. First the money, then the border, and then the rest is up to God. Where are you going?

Ihab He's not going anywhere. Where are we going? With what? I'm staying. This is where I live. Where am I going? Here.

Mazen I'm going to university. HERE. First I have to do the high school test and then . . . A LAWYER . . . so if you get into any trouble – here's 'my card'.

Ihab Excellent . . . because I'm always in trouble.

Titi He's always in trouble. He's starting his third school because he keeps getting thrown out of the other schools he went to.

Ihab SHUT UP.

Mazen Which school?

Ihab Nile School.

Mazen I'm in that school.

THE BIG NOISE OF THE MONSTERS belching and coughing and groaning and growling. If you read how they speak at the end, you see that they are not such genius monsters. So it's a lot of scary noise, but stupid monsters!

Enter the **Monsters**. *They are strong and tough and mean and scary. They come in from yet a different side of the courtyard.* **Monster** *boys with bats. These characters can be padded and stuffed and made high and big.*

They have amplified voices.

Monsters One *and* **Two** We are Shareef and Sharaf and we are coming to play in the courtyard. Everyone in the courtyard has to leave. OOUT, OOUT, OOUT . . . WE WANT TO PLAY.

The four boys are laying alert. Now we have the dance entrance of **Monster One** *and* **Monster Two** *and how the four boys best strategize to keep alive and in the courtyard.*

Monster One What should we play?

Monster Two Fighting.

Monster One Good, let's fight.

Monster Two Ready?

Monster One Ready.

Monster Two One.

Monster One Two.

Monster Two Three.

The **Monsters** *punch each other and KNOCK EACH OTHER OUT. The four boys slowly approach the two bodies laying knocked out in the middle of the courtyard so that now no one at all can play.*

Mazen We have to move them.

Ihab We can't wake them up.

Sirhan Yeah, they'll kill us.

Titi They sure are big.

Mazen Why are they like this? Why can't they be normal like us?

Ihab Yeah, why can't they be normal like us?

Sirhan He sure is heavy.

Titi He sure is ugly.

Mazen Let's tie them up.

Ihab Yeah. (*To* **Titi**.) Go get rope.

Mazen (*to* **Sirhan**) Go get tape.

The two go and get this stuff. Meanwhile . . .

Mazen We'll tie them to each other.

Ihab They'll never be able to undo it if they're stuck to each other.

Silence.

Mazen   Where'd you learn taekwondo?

Ihab   From a film on the television. We copied it.

Mazen   That's how we learned boxing.

Both (*not in sync*)   Show me again.

Together a little boxing, a little taekwondo, a little wrestling, a little dance. The two boys come back with the rope and tape. During all the above, the monsters have been quite still but growling and groaning like small earthquakes and tsunamis every once in a while. Like after-shocks after the first hits.

Mazen   Let's get to it before they break us in pieces.

By chance, **Ihab** *and* **Sirhan** *work on* **Monster One** *and the other two work on* **Monster Two**. *And after they are all tied up in some ridiculous manner . . .*

Mazen   Let's wake them up.

Ihab   Yeah, wake them up.

Sirhan   What if they bust through our defences?

Mazen   We're four against two.

Ihab   But they are like six.

Titi   Maybe we can talk to them.

Mazen   Them? They listen to no one. They own the street.

Sirhan   What's the solution?

Titi   We can't just stand here with two monsters tied up blocking the courtyard. How are we gonna play?

Mazen   They sure would make good wrestlers . . .

Ihab   And taekwondo players . . . wow . . .

Titi   And basketball. We could get in the Olympics with them on our team.

Sirhan   Let's wake them up.

Mazen   HELLO.

Ihab   WAKE UP.

Sirhan   We're going to the Olympics. Get up.

Groaning and growling. Scary. Noisy.

Mazen   Hey monster, are you gonna play fair and be on our basketball team and be on our side?

Ihab   Or do we have to drown you in the pool?

Mazen   It's your choice.

Titi We don't care either way. But you'd be great in basketball.

Monster One No one ever asked us to play with them and go to the Olympics.

Monster Two No one ever asked us nothing.

Sirhan But you can't eat us.

Titi Or step on us.

Mazen You have to play fair and control yourselves and go by the rules.

Ihab And stop making all that noise. I can't stand all that noise.

Monster One WHAT NOISE?

Monster Two WHAT RULES?

Ihab THE rules.

Monster Two There aren't rules.

Mazen There are some rules. Now, we gonna untie you and tell you all about it, OK?

Titi And no funny stuff.

Ihab And we are gonna teach you stuff and you're gonna do it just like we say. OK?

Monster One OK.

Monster Two OK. (*To* **Monster One**.) Do you have idea what they're talking about.

Monster One (*to* **Monster Two**) Just say OK or they'll kill us.

They form two groups: **Ihab**, **Sirhan**, **Monster One** *and* **Mazen**, **Titi**, **Monster Two**. *The start to practice wrestling and taekwondo.*

Bigger monsters are heard coming, wanting to play and go swimming (and this would be very loud noises and done over the sound system).

Play #4: The Sisters

Characters

These are the little girls, ages eight to eleven. The relationships mentioned are connected to the characters in the other plays in this collection.

Hiba *wants to be a magician, a singer, her grandfather is Malek. Her mother is Im Ahmad 1 and her brother is Mazen, she is small, loud, intense (energetic, committed), leads . . . she is the second oldest of the group.*
Dalia *is clueless (scared, immature even for her age), lacks attention, has no idea how the world works, her brother is Titi and her mother is Ward, she is third oldest.*
Olala, *she is the younger sister of Maryam and wants to be exactly like Maryam: a wife and a mother. She is very pretty but she is naïve and simple. Her brother is Sirhan. She loves her grandfather who is Ashraf, she is the youngest.*
Joojoo, *a sad girl, the oldest.*

Hiba, **Dalia** *and* **Olala** *are jumping rope and* **Joojoo** *is sitting on a cart with wheels (so that she can scoot around the yard as she pleases). The three girls are singing a regular jump rope song, low . . . we almost can't hear them. During the monologue of Joojoo they slowly start to hear what she is saying and gather around her with the jump rope, and their snacks, and the junk they have in their pockets. Capital letters can mean shouting or conviction or provocation. Play with them.*

Joojoo I'm sitting here all day and I'm dreaming of chocolate. But my mother says chocolate is no good in summer. 'No chocolate in summer. It melts and makes a mess.' Stupid rule. Now I'm dreaming of a lollipop. But then there's a rule about lollipops: that they ruin my dresses because I suck them with my mouth open. HOW ELSE ARE YOU SUPPOSED TO EAT THEM? And I don't even like this dress. I don't even care if it gets covered with chocolate or lollipops or lentil soup that also makes my dress dirty because I don't like lentil soup. Everyone likes it but me. SO WHAT. Huh? Do you shoot someone because she doesn't like A LENTIL? And another thing. I don't like math. It's all numbers. And numbers never end. It's too much. Really. THEY NEVER END. Oh. And the colour PINK because I have these pink shoes that always kill me when I wear them and I'm not a person who wears pink shoes. Really, do I look like a PINK SHOE PERSON? (*Breath.*) What else. I don't like boys because they are always telling us what to do and they aren't polite. (*Breath.*) People aren't kind in general. Mostly. And I don't like my desk because someone wrote bad words on it with a knife. So now I don't like knives. (*Breath.*) I don't like clocks . . . because everyone is always looking at them like there's a secret hidden inside. The secret of the clock. There's a jinn in the clock. A genie. Sometimes she runs and sometimes she sleeps. She's never regular. NEVER. And those toys that fall apart after four minutes. I hate all those things too because what's four days? That's when the clock jinn is running and our toys are ruined. I really don't like that it's always my fault that everything breaks after four minutes. That's what they say. And now it's summer. I DON'T LIKE SUMMER. (*Breath.*) Or winter. Or Sun. Or rain. Or clouds or stars or night or snow . . . I LIKE ICE. That was a mistake. I hate mistakes. I like ice but we don't have any because the border crossing is closed. AND I don't like cars. They all smell and they run over people flat and dead. (*Breath.*) I don't like when girls show off especially when I don't like what they are showing off about. AND I don't like it that absolutely everyone lies to me. And lies to everyone else. (*Breath.*) And I don't like being tired all the time. I simply don't like that at all. (*Seeing the girls.*) AND I REALLY DON'T LIKE IT WHEN A BUNCH OF GIRLS ARE LOOKING AT ME WHEN THEY SHOULD BE JUMPING ROPE.

Dalia Who are you talking to?

Joojoo Everyone. Absolutely everyone. But NO ONE listens.

Dalia Don't you want to jump rope with us? It's your turn.

Joojoo I don't like jumping rope.

Dalia Yes you do.

Hiba Are you in your stupid mood again?

Joojoo And I don't like it when people called HIBA call me stupid. I don't even like the name Hiba.

Hiba So you are in your stupid mood. What happened? Yalla. Talk.

Joojoo I don't like talking.

Hiba You're sitting here for half an hour talking I-don't-like-this-I-don't-like-this. What's your story? Yalla, I'm listening with all my ears.

Olala You only have two ears . . . that's what keeps your head straight. Otherwise your hair will be ridiculous. My grandfather told me that. He's very smart, my grandfather. He knew a man with one ear. And his hair was ridiculous. He fought the English.

Dalia Everyone fought the English. I don't know what's wrong with them that nobody likes them. I love the English and I speak English. (*In English.*) What is it that your name is called? You are of a true beauty. I am Dalia. I am of a true beauty. They are a true beauty. He is beautiful. Them is beautiful.

Hiba You call that English? Jump. (**Dalia** *jumps aimlessly, obeying nicely.*) The English . . . the English came after the Turks and the Turks invented falafel. It was on TV.

Dalia (*jumping*) When did we come?

Hiba We were always here.

Olala That's what my grandfather says and – like I said – he's very smart. But he has hairy ears. Why is that?

Joojoo I HAVE THIS REALLY ENORMOUS HEAD-ACHE.

Hiba Let's jump rope and I'll tell you my secret. Last night I thought up a secret and I'm going to tell you because you are my best best friends. Yalla, Dalia and Olala turn the rope. Joojoo jumps . . .

Joojoo I HATE JUMPING.

Hiba Yeeeee, you're really in a mood. FINE. I'll jump and you sit on your carriage like an old lady. And I'll tell you my secret.

Dalia Can I tell your secret to my sister?

Hiba (*thinking*) OK.

Olala Can I tell it to my grandfather?

Hiba No. I don't like hairy ears listening to my secrets. He'll tell his friend with one ear and ridiculous hair and then everything will be ruined.

They start with the jump rope.

Hiba Turn it good. Faster. NO! Slower. (*She jumps.*) I had a dream.

Olala I had a dream too. But when I woke up I forgot it. Dreams are like that. You always forget.

Hiba   Can I talk? Can I?

Dalia   I never dream. I'm always too tired to dream. And my mother says dreaming isn't real life. She says we should be sleeping and not playing games when we sleep. She says dreaming is a waste of time because you always wake up screaming and then she says . . . .

Joojoo   WHAT'S YOUR SECRET?

Joojoo's *shout scares them (slapstick-ish) and the rope gets all caught up. It has to be a big, good thick rope. After they sort themselves out with coughing and ahhhing and yallah, twisting this way and moving that way. And 'oh take this end' and 'oh take that end'. They end up slightly tied, very close to hear the coming secret.*

Hiba   I am going to make magic. (*The girls listen, attentive, curious, with growing concern.*) (*Hiba continues, slowly and detailed.*) I'm going to learn magic . . . in a magic school . . . There is one . . . somewhere . . . in France . . . in Norway . . . in America . . . in Japan . . . in Egypt . . . I heard there is a magic school. I will have a magic uniform. I wear a big black hat on my head, it looks like a box and a rabbit lives in it. (*Their interest/concern grows.*) It has food inside. I will wear a sparkling dress with frogs and worms and snakes painted on it. There are many secret pockets in it so I can hide birds and scarves. (*Confusion.*) And the best part is . . . the black cape . . . made of silk and with purple and blue stars all over . . . it looks like the night. Inside, the cape will be golden gold. That's the uniform! For the homework, I will make people float, or fly, or completely disappear. I will cut some people in half . . .

Dalia (*crying*)   I want to go home.

Joojoo   STOP CRYING. I WANT TO HEAR THE REST.

Dalia *stops crying.*

Olala (*thinking*)   My grandfather has rabbits in cages on the roof. And he kills them and we eat them. Yesterday we ate Fluffy with rice and green beans. There was nothing very magical about it.

Dalia   Fluffy must have thought it was very magical.

Joojoo   I don't like rabbits. Every time my mother cooks them, we have a fight. She says eat and I say no and it goes like that until she hits me. WHAT ABOUT THE MAGIC?

Hiba   That's it. OH. Also . . . and this is the best part . . . I'm going to sing when I cut people in half . . . because that's interesting . . . otherwise I'm regular. So when I make a veil disappear, I will sing. Don't you find that unusual? Is that the best secret you ever heard?!

Joojoo   IT'S NOT A SECRET ANYMORE. Tomorrow the whole world will know.

Dalia   Don't touch my veil. If I lose another one I'm going to get hit by six sisters all at once. Make someone else's veil disappear. And I think your father is not going to let you do your secret. You have to finish school and then university or else you have to get married. No one is a singing magician. Not in the whole world.

Joojoo   SAYS WHO?

Dalia   Name me one singing magician in the whole world.

Joojoo   YOU DON'T EVEN KNOW WHERE THE WHOLE WORLD IS.

Dalia   Yes I do. It's that. (*She waves her arms around.*)

Joojoo (*making fun of her*)   It's not THAT.

Dalia   Then what is it?

Joojoo   I'm not telling because it's too much for you to understand and you'll DIE of fright if I tell you.

Hiba   You're all ruining my secret. (*Performance.*) My name is HIBA'S MAGICAL SINGING WORLD OF DISAPPEARING THINGS AND HALF PEOPLE.

Olala   That's not a name. And anyway, no one will let you do it because it's not acceptable. It's forbidden to make things disappear. I think it's a bad secret. And I'm not telling my grandfather because he won't let me play with you and he'll tell me to find a new friend but I like you. So you have to have another secret. Like mine.

Joojoo   YOU HAVE A SECRET?

Hiba   Stop yelling. My head hurts from you.

Olala   I'm going to be a mother. (*SILENCE.*)

Hiba   Start from the beginning . . . you are such a pain in the neck.

Olala   First I am going to marry and I will have many choices for marriage because that's how it is when you are very beautiful and my mother says I am. And my grandfather. I will have a lot of gold all over me and on all my fingers. And you will all buy very big dresses in pink.

Joojoo   I am not wearing a big pink dress . . .

Olala   And I will have the BIGGEST DRESS of all . . . and we will go to my very big wedding in my very big wedding in a very big hall by a big sea. I will have the biggest white dress ever made and big stars in my hair and silver on my eyes . . .

Joojoo   AND YOUR EARS . . . And your grandfather's hairy ears . . . And then you will have kids with silver stars in their ears who all look like martians. And then you'll need a BLACK CAPE to hide under. WHERE'S THE MAGIC?

Olala   Very funny. You don't scare me with your scary ideas. You don't even have a secret. You just roll around in the cart because no one likes you and you like no one.

Hiba   Everyone likes her and she likes everyone. Quiet before I make you disappear.

Joojoo (*to* **Olala**)   YOU ARE THE UGLIEST GIRL IN THE WHOLE WORLD.

Dalia   I want to go home. I want to go home right now.

Olala NO. Because I'm not done. And you can't make me disappear because I am here all the time . . . AND THEN I WILL HAVE MANY CHILDREN WHO WILL ALL BE GIRLS. And then I will get a son. NO. FIRST ONE SON AND THEN THE GIRLS. THAT'S WHAT I'M GOING TO DO . . .

Joojoo WHO'S EVEN TALKING TO YOU? DID WE ASK YOU A QUESTION?

Olala I'M TELLING MY SECRET DREAM.

Joojoo I THOUGHT DREAMS ARE A WASTE OF TIME.

Dalia THAT'S WHAT MY MOTHER SAYS.

Olala WHY ARE YOU YELLING?

Joojoo WHY ARE YOU YELLING?

Hiba NO ONE IS YELLING.

Dalia Are we jumping rope or not? Let's jump. Come on. I don't want to tell secrets.

Olala I just get so excited when I think of all those little girls in all those little dresses. And the weddings. And being grown-up. Imagine us being grown-up. We'll have everything and . . .

Joojoo *stands and pretends to faint and falls down and plays dead. All excitement, except from* **Hiba** *who sits on* **Joojoo**.

Hiba Listen oh girls, imagine us . . . turning around from city to city and making things disappear.

Joojoo (*she can't shout because* **Hiba** *is on her, but she tries*) ALL BAD THINGS WILL DISAPPEAR?

Dalia I don't want to go to cities. I want to stay home. Let's make things appear. Like cakes and juice. Let's have a birthday party. Come on. Let's pretend it's my birthday.

Joojoo (*she can't shout because* **Hiba** *is on her, but she tries*) ALL BAD THINGS WILL DISAPPEAR?

Olala Which cities? The cities in the whole world? Like China? And America?

Hiba Exactly. The cities where the whole world is. Canada.

Dalia I heard my sister talk about Canada. And Jericho.

Joojoo (*sitting by this time*) All bad things will disappear?

Hiba (*answering*) If you all help me . . . because I'm only one person and there are a lot of things that simply must disappear.

Joojoo Did you hear her? There are a lot of bad things that simply must disappear.

Dalia I don't want to go to cities. Why can't we just jump rope and have a party and play with our stuff? A black cape? It's the evil eye. I want to go home. You're always confusing me with your ideas . . . that's you Hiba . . . my mother always says you say crazy things and she's right. And no one likes Joojoo except you . . .

Joojoo I'm gonna punch you in the face.

Olala My grandfather says you have to look at the good things in life . . . and then you can . . . .

Joojoo YOUR GRANDFATHER IS BURNING A HOLE IN MY HEAD.

And a small entanglement of **Joojoo** *getting up and sort of accidentally hurting/ hitting the others but not on purpose . . . just a bit out of control . . .*

Dalia I hate you.

Olala You are mean and bad. And no one will ever marry you. EVER.

Dalia Your mother dropped you on your head . . . everyone knows she's always crying.

Olala And you never ever had a nice dress . . .

Dalia And everyone knows your father left and ran away to Norway. And you're ugly.

Olala And you're never happy . . . or happy . . . or happy . . . Or even happy . . .

Joojoo (*during this barrage of insults . . .*)   HAPPY BIRTHDAY TO YOU. HAPPY BIRTHDAY TO YOU. HAPPY BIRTHDAY POOR DALIA AND OLALA WHO DON'T EVEN KNOW WHERE THE WORLD IS . . . HAPPY BIRTHDAY TO YOOOOOOOU!

Meanwhile . . . **Hiba** *has run off the stage, between the kids in the audience, and from some hidden place gets a huge bag. She pulls it to the stage area. The three girls are looking in surprise (***Olala***) and scared (***Dalia***) and curious (***Joojoo***) at the giant bag arriving. Hopefully the bag is bigger than the actress playing Hiba. It should be.*

Hiba *opens the bag with flair. She has a complete collection of self-made stuff she has put together out of everything one can find in Gaza. The clothing and props are combinations of things that would never go together BUT they have to be pretty/ funny/wearable/with a purpose. It's a designer's dream. Our dresses and hats were big, using hoops as the form. Each was decorated with either soda cans, coloured plastic bags, coloured kitchen towels, or packaging.*

Hiba LADIES . . . AND LADIES. WELCOME TO HIBA'S WORLD OF . . . wait . . . WELCOME TO THE MAGICAL FRIENDS . . . wait . . . WELCOME . . . TO THE MAGICAL WORLD . . . OF HIBA . . . AND HER FRIENDS. I am Hiba the Magnificent, this is Joojoo also the Magnificent from Depths of the Ocean who can speak in 1,000 languages in a loud voice. That one is Olala the Magnificent of the Red Mountain who can lift 3,000 kilos with one hand. And this one is Dalia the Magnificent of the Desert, our most excellent assistant who can walk for three years without drinking anything. Welcome one and all.

Dalia   I don't want to be magnificent. I'm going home. (*And she starts to leave. Slowly.*)

Hiba   And Dalia the MAGNIFICENT.

Olala   I am magnificent but I'm not from the Red Mountains.

Joojoo   IT'S YOUR MAGICIAN NAME. . . AM I FROM THE DEPTHS OF THE OCEAN???

Olala   God keep them far. God keep them far. My grandfather says never play with magicians.

Hiba   WRONG. Because MY grandfather says that it was magicians who brought happiness by singing and doing magic. And that's why we have to sing AND do magic.

Olala   And stealing. They stole everything.

Hiba   No. The occupation stole everything. Not the magicians. Joojoo, yell at them.

Joojoo   WHAT DO YOU WANT ME TO TELL THEM?

Hiba   TO PLAY MAGICIAN WITH ME. I HATE JUMPING ROPE!

Joojoo   EVERYONE HAS TO PLAY MAGICIAN NOW. PLAY.

Joojoo, **Hiba**, *and* **Olala** *start to throw stuff around, shouting disappear, disappear, disappear. Here, if we want, they can go into the audience and goof around with the kids. Sprinkle stuff on them.*

Hiba   And now the song . . .

Joojoo   I don't know any songs.

Hiba   Everyone sings what she knows. DALIA . . . come back . . . we need you. (*She hasn't gotten very far anyway.*)

Dalia   Can I sing 'Rosanna'?

Hiba   Ah. Ah. Perfect. Ready.

They silently think of a song.

Hiba   Ready?

They all start to sing a different song. Nicely. Real singing. From the heart. Four different songs. During the song, the fabrics, balls, squirters, masks made of paper, and other magical junk is juggled and tossed and caught, things can come from hidden pockets, hanging off the costumes. The four girls find this all very funny, they giggle and laugh following the orders of **Hiba** *and seeing how magnificently ridiculous they look . . . how much fun it is to be silly and laughing . . . And now the four girls are standing on the stage among the strange objects and costumes around them. They know they will have to put it all back together again and hide it all from whence it came. For a moment there is a sadness as they look at each other and the kids in the audience (who can also be a little decorated and sprinkled).*

Olala If anyone saw me, I'll never get married. Maybe . . . we can be magicians for a while and then I'll get married? I have tingles in me. Like inside I'm laughing.

Dalia It's not really scary at all. Can we sing in those cities that are in the whole world? I'm just asking, not that I'm going. I'll never get a permit. But maybe we can go to Cairo. And see those pyramids that everyone is talking about. Can you sing there?

Olala I think you can sing anywhere where your mouth is.

Hiba Did we accidentally make anyone disappear? I hope not. We need everyone here. I have to be more responsible. That's my problem. I have good ideas but look at this mess. My mother is going to be very mad. Did anyone disappear?

Joojoo Well I'm still here. So all the bad things don't disappear do they?

Olala You're not bad.

Dalia You're just sad.

Hiba Should we play this game again tomorrow?

Olala Yes. Can I bring my grandfather?

Dalia It's not so scary. Really it's not so scary.

Hiba Let's clean up and think about doing it again tomorrow. Exactly the same but different.

Joojoo (*to the audience . . .*)   SHOULD WE DO IT AGAIN TOMORROW?

End.

3: A Human Writes (2012)

About the characters

This collection of three plays comes from an unproduced five-play I wrote in 2006. Because of that, the characters of King Mazen and Wazir Walid are the same in all three plays. The King is a young man, he came to power when his old father died, mostly unprepared. He is educated, he wants to do what is right. A Wazir is an Arabian high ranking political figure, if you will, and our Wazir Walid is old fashioned and conservative. He can be nasty but he has no actual power as the king is the king.

About the sets/costumes

For the plays in this collection, feel free to play with anachronisms. Gold coins and Q-codes, horse-drawn Mercedes, scrolls and ipads, hoodies over the jalabias and such. Have fun.

Play #1: The Weavers

Characters

Girl One, *perhaps with orange hair; has carpets, wool, a loom, and pretty things. A colourful space. Some money.*
Girl Two, *perhaps with black scraggly hair; has a dark, sad, poor environment.*
King Mazen, *a cool young guy.*
Wazir Walid, *an uncool old guy.*

Two spaces next to each other, they are two 'houses'. Each with a tiny little garden.

For the **King** *and the* **Wazir***, a moving 'throne' of sorts, like a pair of car seats on wheels, a small couch on wheels, he's a hip king, maybe bikes?!*

There are two songs for this play. They have not been composed, but were said as text. If you have the composers, they can be turned into songs and used as theme music throughout the play.

The Weavers' Song

You weave your wool by day or by night – at day by sun, and then the candle.
The colours give us feelings: one for hope, one for love, one forgiveness.
Endless colours for endless feelings.
Begin. Row by row and line by line. In from here. Out from there.
Begin. Row by row and line by line. In from there. Out from there.
Back and forth and forth and back. Day turns to night and night turns to day.
And we start again and we start again and we start again.
Before the moon comes back, the strings are all in place.
What once were strings of colours have now become our carpets.
Carpets to warm our house and feet.
To decorate our floors and keep the evil out.

The Song of the Royal Carpet

Green and gold and gold and blue like fish and sea and sky
Edges fringed, and diamond shapes surround the centre eye
The eye sees words that you've not heard and still remain untold
The carpet was a task of love for men that we behold
Early on one day of rest, the final threads were tied
We brought our treasure to the King whose presence was denied
His loyal staff received us well and took the piece we made
His smile was quite broad and wide and we were quite well paid
We have not seen the carpet since we left it on the ground
We hope it pleased his majesty and our note be found.

Act One

Scene One

There is a non-working radio in the space of **Girl One** *and a light lit in the space of* **Girl Two**.

The girls are NOT on good terms.

Girl One Is it plugged in? The speech will begin?

Girl Two Why do you keep asking?

Girl One It's a simple question.

Girl Two Then find the answer for yourself.

Girl One You are mean from the day you were born.

Girl Two And you are spoiled from the day you arrived on this planet.

Girl One Shhhshshshsh. He's starting.

Girl Two Don't shshsh me. Sshshsh youself. He's starting.

Girl One Shshhshsh.

Girl Two Shshshshsh.

King Dear Citizens. The situation remains as it is and we will continue with our efforts towards the betterment for the people of this land. Athough we are hungry, we are not starving because we are generous. Athough we are alone in the world, we are together with each other. Athough we are not rich in money, we are rich in history and culture and this richness gives us unity. Show me another kingdom like ours. You can't. Because there isn't one. This is both a pain and a privilege. I promise you again that together we will work towards lessening the pain and enjoying the privileges. I have asked the Royal Mail Service to begin delivery to each family, quarter by quarter, house by house, a starting package. In it will be some Hope, some Love, some Forgiveness, some Anger, and a small box of Freedom. Use them carefully until the next deliveries. (*Pause. Nudge from the* **Wazir**.) And remember to pay your taxes. God bless you all for all your work and thank you all very much.

Girl One Ohhhh finally I will have some Anger. And you will get it. I am tired of smiling.

Girl Two Good because you're unplugged now. (*Pause.*) Go pay your taxes? (*Pause.*) Enjoy privileges?! What privileges? What will I do with some Anger? I've been angry since the day I was born.

Girl One A bit of everything is better than nothing at all.

Girl Two Why isn't there a little bit of Work in the package?

Girl One You are never happy with anything.

Girl Two And you are always happy with everything. Why are we talking? We don't talk to each other.

Girl One True. I do not speak to people with whom I am presently not speaking.

Girl Two Then why are you speaking? The King didn't include a Box of Words in the package.

Girl One May I remind you that, as unfortunate as it is, we are neighbours and this entire conversation is completely contrary to what the King spoke about. Alone in the world, together with each other.

Girl Two You see?! Always happy.

Girl One That's not happy. That's logical.

Girl Two Yes, well you should go pay your taxes before your head gets chopped off.

Girl One My taxes are all paid.

Girl Two I have no income so I pay no taxes. Hamdalillah.

Scene Two

Two boxes appear, one for each girl. On the box it says 'From the King'. Inside each box contains small boxes.

Girl One *opens her box, takes the boxes with are named Hope, Love, Forgiveness, Anger, Some Freedom. She sits at her loom, humming and creating a song about the carpet she is weaving.*

The Weavers' Song (*both girls know the song*)
  Green and gold and gold and blue like fish and sea and sky
  Edges fringed, and diamond shapes surround the centre eye
  The eye sees words that you've not heard and still remain untold
  The carpet was a task of love for men that we behold
  Early on one day of rest, the final threads were tied
  We brought our treasure to the King whose presence was denied
  His loyal staff received us well and took the piece we made
  His smile was quite broad and wide and we were quite well paid
  We have not seen the carpet since we left it on the ground
  We hope it pleased his majesty and our note he found.

Girl Two *opens her box and removes the box called 'Some Freedom.'*

Girl Two I will never leave the Weavers' Quarter. I will never leave the house of my mother and my father, may God keep them. I don't care that I have no work. I have this house. I have this garden. And I have this little box. I am free to dream about weaving again. One day I will weave again.

She notices something on the earth in the garden.

Girl Two MY WATER IS RED. AND GREEN. AND PURPLE.

Girl One (*falling off her seat from the noise*) Who is shouting? What has happened? Who is attacking?

Girl Two MY WATER IS RED. AND GREEN. AND PURPLE. Who has ruined my water?

Girl One You scare me to death over purple water? It's dye, for the wool, it's made from flowers. It won't hurt you.

Girl Two I don't care if it's made from gold. You are ruining my garden.

Girl One If you put your water tank on the roof like everyone else, it wouldn't be affected from the dyes.

Girl Two   I don't want the water tank on the roof. I want it where it is.

Girl One   Then drink red water. It won't hurt you. It's from flowers.

Girl Two   AND THE PURPLE AND GREEN.

Girl One   Spices. Your water is not properly stored.

Girl Two   Your water is not properly stored or it would not be in my garden. And my water is none of your business. Solve it or I will make a complaint to the King.

Girl One   I am registered and I am allowed to weave.

Girl Two   But are you allowed to dye wool?

Girl One   All weavers dye their wool. Or should we paint the sheep?

Girl Two   The complaint will be made.

Girl One   And I will make a complaint that your water tank is not on the roof like everyone else's.

Girl Two   There is no decree that says a water tank has to be on the roof.

Girl One   But there is a decree that says that each house is responsible to maintain a ten-day supply of clean drinking water in case of drought. And you don't have that. You drink straight from the rain supply.

Girl Two   Fine. The fight is on.

Girl One   And now I have used up my entire box of anger! (*And she smiles again, with difficulty.*)

Scene Three

Enter the **King** *and* **Wazir**.

Wazir   Ta Ta Ta Ta Taaaaa! His Royal Highness King Mazen has arrived. Please take numbers and wait in the line that starts here. Remember to bow, do not look directly into the eyes of your King, and never turn your back to him. (*Pause. To the King.*) Your Highness, we need to create more Hope and Love and Freedom. We still have plenty of Anger and Forgiveness but I don't know how long this will last. People are shouting . . . from all the quarters.

King   These are very precious things to get.

Wazir   Do you have any ideas?

King   I will reflect. Somewhere, inside me, there are plenty of ideas. (*Quiet.*) Write! Thoughts on the search for Hope.

Wazir *has a scroll of old paper and an iPad . . . attached. We hear the girls fighting.*

Act One: Scene Three   105

Wazir Who makes the sounds of cats being cut into quarters? Who stops the King from his thoughts on the search for Hope? Who wants their heads chopped off?

King No need to be so rude. You told me that people are shouting from all the quarters. We are not chopping off heads. (*Looking around.*) Where are we?

Wazir In the Weavers' Quarter.

King Odd. Usually there is singing in the Weavers' Quarter.

Girl One *and* **Girl Two** *race in, take numbers, stand in some imaginary line but don't wait.*

Girl Two I hereby issue this complaint against Girl One for poisoning my water. Look. My water is all different colours. (*She has three small bottles of water: red, purple, green.*)

Girl One And I hereby issue this complaint against Girl Two for not having a two-week supply of fresh drinking water in case of droughts.

Wazir You are all under arrest. You have the right to remain silent and should you choose this right we will assume you are hiding something. You have the right to speak and we will be recording to every word. You have the right to be presented to the King by persons other than yourselves and if you have no one we will represent you free of charge, however, a donation of one gold coin is suggested. Do you understand these rights?

King No one is under arrest. (*To* **Wazir**.) Why are you so . . . immovable??? Let us listen to the complaints and then decide according to the logic and to the facts. Girl Two, your water is very pretty.

Girl Two It's poison. It's from the dye of Girl One. All day long she is dying wool and weaving carpets and making money.

Girl One It is not poison. The red is from flowers and the green is from spices and the purple is from fruits.

Wazir Are you paying taxes on your income?

King Will you please be quiet until we know all the facts. Take a deep breath. (*Breath.*)

Silence. The **Wazir** *is breathing. In the silence, the* **King** *takes the three bottles and slowly takes a sip from each one. All are watching the* **King** *and* **Girl One**. **Girl One** *is not afraid. The* **Wazir** *has stopped breathing completely and is turning blue from fear.* **Girl Two** *is afraid and nervous (that the water is really dangerous).*

King Ahem. Ahem. Ahem. The red is quite tasty, the green is a little odd but might be better if heated like a kind of spice tea, but the purple is quite delicious. My dear Girl Two. According to the law, this weaver is allowed to dye her wool as long as the dye is not harmful to the environment and as long as the water system does not interfere with the property of anyone else. Girl One. Although you have obeyed the law, your water does interfere with the property of Girl Two, though it is not your fault. You have not, however, considered that your neighbour does not have work and therefore does not have the money needed for a roof-style water tank which will allow her a two-week water supply. What do you say?

Girl One   Your Highness, I was not aware of the financial burdens of my neighbour. This information was not shared with me because of the pride of Girl Two. I know nothing about her situation at home. The only thing we share is the electricity and the radio and that is only to listen to Your Majesty's speeches. If I would have known, I would not have used up my whole box of Anger. (*To* **Girl Two**.) I ask you to to accept my apology.

King   Girl Two, what do you say?

Girl Two   Lack of information is no excuse for rudeness. (*Pause.*) But Girl One is right. I do not speak to her as a friend because there is a history to this fight. The weaving workshop I inherited from my parents, may they rest in peace, was bankrupt. In a neighbourly way, I paid a visit to Girl One to get advice. She received me in a good fashion but she cheated me with her advice.

Wazir   CHEATING? Chop off her head.

King   Will you please calm down? Really, you watch much too much television.

Wazir   My excuses, Your Highness. But cheating is not acceptable.

King (*to* **Girl Two**)   How were you cheated?

Girl Two   Look at her carpets. See how much work she gets. Her parents taught her how to weave and how to dye wool before they died. My parents died when I was very young. They left with me with no skills. No sheep. No loom. Only this empty workshop. We come from a long line of weavers. We made carpets for the kings and the royal courts for hundreds of years and I am the last one from our family. (*From 'The Song of the Royal Carpet', singing/saying*)

> Green and gold and gold and blue like fish and sea and sky
> Edges fringed, and diamond shapes surround the centre eye

Girl One   That's not my fault.

Wazir   That's not her fault.

Girl One   Thank you.

Wazir   You're welcome. Who was your father . . .

Girl One   Abu Mohammed the Weaver . . .

Wazir   Oh Abu Mohammed the Weaver . . . he used to make beautiful carpets out of the designs from Andalusia and Constantinople . . .

King   Ah Andalusia and Constantinople . . . we should arrange a visit . . . But . . . (*Pause.*) This seems to be my fault!

Wazir   Arrest her. Arrest them all. YOUR fault?

King   Yes.

Wazir   Your Highness, nothing is your fault. Especially when it comes to weavers and carpets.

King   This is not about weavers and carpets. I have to create Hope. Here is a chance and I didn't see it. WRITE! Royal Decree Number . . . What are we up to?

Wazir   (*on iPad scroll*)   Number three-two-zero-one.

King   Royal Decree Number three-two-zero-one. Creation of Hope of Friendship and Finance.

Wazir   Your Highness, I think you are the one watching too much television. I am your Financial Advisor. What are you talking about?

King   Girl One will redirect her coloured water away from the house of Girl Two.

Girl One   But I am not a plumber, Your Majesty.

King   And Girl Two, who has built a very lovely garden with a working pump and lovely trees, will do the work teaching Girl One how it is done . . . for the future.

Girl Two   But Your Highness . . .

King   Wait . . . think of it for a moment. (*All think.*)

Wazir   Chop off their heads.

King   Turn off the television! In return for the plumbing work that Girl Two will do in the garden of Girl One, she will be taught the fine art of weaving by Girl One. Girl Two will practice on the small sample carpets and Girl One will teach her new stitches and other skills related to carpet weaving. There will no be fighting, no yelling, all parties will behave in a cordial and friendly manner during the works and I expect a carpet made jointly by Girls One and Two before the next feast. For this carpet I will pay one hundred pieces of gold.

Wazir   Way too much for a carpet. I say forty.

King   One hundred and fifty.

Wazir   Sixty.

King   Two hundred.

Wazir   SIR . . .

King   Fine, one hundred.

Wazir   Deal.

King   The Decree of Hope of Friendship and Finance is hereby settled. Go to your jobs. (*Leaving.*) Any trouble and heads will be chopped. Are you happy?

Wazir   Not really.

Act Two

Scene One

*The **Girls** are in the garden.*

Girl Two   This decree is worse than death.

Girl One   Death is boring. You are such a rascal.

Girl Two   Me working for you?!

Girl One   Me teaching you weaving?! You can't tell a carpet from a sock. So . . . fix the pipes. Redirect them.

Girl Two   I need a plan.

Girl One   YOU DON'T HAVE A PLAN? (*But she has used up her Anger so it's weak Anger.*)

Girl Two   Missing your Anger?

Girl One   Missing LOVE.

Girl Two   I don't need a plan. I fixed everything in this house and built everything in this garden. I just need some silence. If you are able to do that.

Girl One   Fine. (*She starts humming the weavers' song.*)

Girl Two   Let us separate these two pipes.

Girl One   They are full of water.

Girl Two   Yes, green water.

Girl One   The King said it would make good tea. I will go make some.

Girl Two   I'm not drinking green tea.

Girl One   And you can fix the pipes without a plan?

Girl Two   We don't need a plan. It's simple. Hold this pipe.

Girl One   But you are not a plumber.

Girl Two   ALL POOR PEOPLE ARE PLUMBERS.

Girl One   You are the most annoying neighbour I have ever met.

Girl Two   Don't let go of the pipe. I will attach another one here, and one here, and that will solve the problem. I will be done with your coloured water. . . . (**Girl One** *drops the pipe.*) YOU LET GO OF THE PIPE. MY HOUSE IS FLOODING.

Girl One   The King said cordial and friendly. Stop yelling.

Girl Two   FINE.

Girl One FINE.

Pause.

Girl Two Enough. Now it's my turn. Teach me to weave.

Girl One But the pipe isn't fixed.

Girl Two It's half fixed. You let go and now we have to wait for the water to dry. Give me half a weaving lesson.

Girl One Really, you are the most annoying neighbour.

Girl Two A decree is a decree. Start teaching. Here are my hands.

Girl One GO WASH THEM.

As **Girl Two** *washes her hands,* **Girl One** *takes out some wool and the loom and the things needed for weaving. She brings a small stool from the house of* **Girl Two** *and puts it next to her own in her house.*

The girls are now at the loom where the carpet of the Royal Professor is in progress.

Girl One (*while showing and teaching how to weave.*)

> You weave your wool by day or by night – at day by sun, and then the candle.
> The colours give us feelings: the sunny pinks, orange pomegranate, the nighttime purple, blues, and greens.
> Begin. Row by row and line by line. In from here. Out from there.
> Begin. Row by row and line by line. In from there. Out from there.
> Back and forth and forth and back. Day turns to night and night turns to day.
> And we start again and we start again and we start again.
> Before the moon comes back, the strings are all in place.
> What once were strings of colours have now become our carpets.
> Carpets to warm our house and feet.
> To decorate our floors and keep the evil out.

Girl One You continue. I will make the green tea.

Girl Two

> Begin. Row by row and line by line. In from here. Out from there.
> Begin. Row by row and line by line. In from there. Out from there.
> Pinks and purples and blues and greens.
> Back and forth and forth and back. Day turns to night and night turns to day.

She gets into a big mess. **Girl One** *comes back with the GREEN tea.*

Girl One You ruined this carpet. Look what you did to the carpet of the Royal Professor. It has to be finished in two weeks and YOU RUINED IT.

Girl Two WELL LOOK AT MY HOUSE. YOU CAN'T HOLD TWO PIPES TOGETHER AND NOW MY HOUSE IS FLOODED.

Scene Two

Wazir Who makes the sounds of cats being cut into quarters? Who stops the King from his Thoughts on the Search for Freedom? Who wants their heads chopped off?

King I must ask the Royal Writer to compose for you some new announcements. This is the twenty-first century. You cannot go chopping people's heads off.

Girl One (*with* **Girl Two**, *noisy*) It is with great sadness that I inform you that the Decree of Hope and Finance isn't working. She has ruined the carpet I was making for the Royal Professor and he wants it tomorrow. I want to make another complaint right now. She tied all my wool in knots and now the whole thing has to be redone.

Girl Two (*with* **Girl One**, *noisy*) It is with great sadness that I inform you that the Decree of Hope and Finance isn't working. She has ruined my beautiful garden, flooded my house, and now I have nothing. I am making another complaint. She ruined my pipes because she doesn't understand instructions. She thinks everything has to be tied in knots at the end.

King Quiet. (*Louder.*) Quiet. (*Louder.*) Quiet.

Wazir Everyone is under arrest. Everyone is having his head . . . (*considering*) shaved. You have the right to remain silent and should you choose this right we will assume you are hiding . . .

King I SAID QUIET. (*Pause.*) Why is one forced to shout?! I must think upon that. (*To* **Wazir**.) Write that down. Thoughts on the Need to Replace Shouting to get Things Done. (*Inspecting all the damage.*) Hmmm. Hmmmmm. Oh hmmmm here. And yes hmmmmmm. Hmm. Hmm. I understand. Girls One and Two. Your problem here is one of coordination and patience. Girl Two is correct. Girl One does plumbing like a weaver and Girl Two weaves like a plumber. This type of work will never result in a carpet or a water tank. You have good intentions but terrible methods. Your task will continue because the Decree of Hope and Finance is now being changed to the Decree of Hope, Finance, and Education. Girl One. You are to explain the art of weaving to Girl Two BEFORE you put her in front of the professor's carpet. Girl Two. You are to explain the art of plumbing to Girl One BEFORE you put a wrench in her hands.

Wazir Hope. Finance. Education . . . All that remains is Freedom.

King The hardest one of all, my friend.

Wazir Friend?

King Sir. Girls, I leave you to your work. Don't give up. You are doing quite well considering. And here, I have for each of you a lovely plum (*any fruit in season*) from the Royal Garden, which luckily has a water tank in the right place. All that is missing is the carpet.

Exit **King** *and* **Wazir**.

Here we need some music. And plenty of movement. **Girl Two** *begins in her garden showing how plumbing works. There can be pipes and wrenches, and other tools of* plumbers. *The Dance of the Plumbers with lots of hand gestures and swinging pipes. And such.* **Girl One** *will do the same with the yarns, the bobbins, the loom, etc.*

Girl Two   I understand.

Girl One   Yes, I think I understand as well.

They go to **Girl Two**'s *side to work on the pipes.*

Girl Two   OK?

Girl One   OK.

Girl Two   ONE. TWO. PULL.

They pull or push and **Girl Two** *falls back and knocks herself out.*

Girl One   OH MY GOD. Girl Two. Wake up. Oh dear. Where are you hurt? What happened. I pulled. Was I supposed to push? I did exactly what you said. OH NO. My poor head will be chopped off. I must fix this pipe. And I must fix this girl. No I must fix the girl first and then fix the pipe.

Scene Three

Enter, of course, the **King** *and* **Wazir**.

Wazir   Should I help them?

King   No. Only in an emergency.

Girl One *brings red water in a glass and sprinkles it on the head of* **Girl Two**. *Then she puts some purple water and then some green.*

Girl One   Habibti, my neighbour, wake up. These are flowers and fruits and spices from the garden. They will help you. Wake up my neighbour. Wake up my friend. Wake up my best friend. My best best, best friend.

Girl Two   Ughghghghgh. (*Groggy.*) You tried to kill me? Why would you try to kill me? We were becoming best friends.

Girl One   I didn't try to kill you. I pushed instead of pulled and made you fall.

Girl Two   No, I said push and should have said pulled. It's my fault.

Girl One   Do you think we are really becoming best friends?

Girl Two   That's what you said.

Girl One   YOU HEARD THAT???

Girl Two   YOU WERE SHOUTING WAKE UP MY BEST FRIEND.

Wazir   What is with women? Never happy with anything. Why can't they just weave and fix the pipes to prove that the decree works?

King This is their nature. Hamdalillah, they are complicated and full of love. WRITE. The decree is now called the Decree of Hope and Finance and Education and Love.

Wazir Still missing Freedom.

King I'm working on it. Believe me, I'm working on it.

Girl One Let's agree that it was a mutual accident. No one's fault.

Girl Two Good.

Girl One You have a bump on your head. Wait. (*She goes and brings a very odd hat made of a water bottle but covered with a woven cover.*) This is good for headaches.

Girl Two It looks quite ridiculous.

Girl One No one is here.

Girl Two What if the King comes back.

Girl One The next time the King comes back, it will be to get his carpet ...

Girl Two And to give us our one hundred gold pieces. I never had one hundred gold pieces.

Girl One I never made a royal carpet. It's like making a national anthem.

King It's starting to get interesting, don't you think?

Wazir You are a very clever King.

King I see you have got some new sentences from the Royal Writer. Be careful how you use them. Let's see how this project turns out.

Wazir Yes, Your Highness. Whatever you say, Your Highness. As you like, Your Highness.

King Oh dear! I need to hire a new Royal Writer. Go back to the old text or we'll have chaos around here.

Wazir Whatever you say, Sir. Shall I arrest them all?

King NO.

Wazir Yes, Sir.

Again, they begin work. First they fix the pipe. Again movement and no text.

Girl Two It's finished. Look. You fixed the tank. No more water here.

Girl One Come on, let's go make a royal carpet. WASH YOUR HANDS.

Again, they begin work weaving the new carpet. It should be royally simple. Red and Purple and Green and Gold.

Girl Two It's gorgeous. It's totally gorgeous. Did I really make that?

Girl One You had some help, but yes, you really made it.

Girl Two It's so . . . royal. The King will adore it.

Girl One Do you think so? It always makes me so nervous to deliver a carpet.

Girl Two Now all we have to do is wait for the King to come. (*Pause.*) You know, I was getting used to your coloured water. And the King was right. The purple is really delicious.

Girl One There are other colours. I have orange from the khishkhash fruit, and dark red from the beets, and the gold comes from the apple. I have no way to store them. Only one tank.

Girl Two We can make small tanks. That's easy. With the gold pieces, we can buy some small tanks and then have all the water ready for dying and for drinking. And we can use my garden for it.

Girl One YOU WANT TO UNDO YOUR TANK.

Girl Two Why not? But can we?

Girl One I don't know. We will ruin the decree. The King will not be happy. He really might chop off our heads.

Girl Two Not if we prove that it helps. That it's better than his decree. What about this? (*She shows her box of Freedom.*) It's a very small box but this seems to be a very small issue. What do you think?

Girl One We can add mine to it. Then we have twice as much. You will keep all the coloured water in your garden.

Girl Two We can make the garden bigger and do all the weaving in your house.

Girl One This is a very good idea.

Scene Four

King Now look at that.

Wazir What, Sir.

King They are smarter than I am. They have solved it.

Wazir What would that be, Sir?

In the garden of **Girl Two**.

Girl Two Do you remember how we fixed it? All you have to do is unfix. Ready. One, two, push.

The pipes are undone.

Girl Two Lovely red water, delicious purple water, green for hot tea.

Girl One We have one more task. The note to the King.

King Let us listen.

Wazir I am all ears.

Girl One The Royal Carpet is made. Edges fringed, diamond shapes.

Girl Two In the centre is the eye that sees all.

Girl One The good and the bad and the wise and the wrong.

Girl Two The eye sees words that you've not heard and still remain untold.

Girl One The carpet was a task of hope for people to behold.

Girl Two And learning and sharing for friends everywhere.

Girl One The final threads are tied together to last forever.

Girl Two We are ready to bring our treasure to the King.

Girl One And we hope it pleases His Majesty for eternity.

King THAT'S IT. THAT'S IT.

Wazir I don't understand. What's it? What happened?

Girl One What are you doing here, Your Majesty. We just this second finished the carpet.

Girl Two Please, we didn't mean to change your plan. We just made some small adjustments.

King PERFECT. It's all Perfect. It can be a perfect work.

Wazir No, Sir, I don't think it can be a perfect work. Much too many imperfections.

King CHANGE THE DECREE.

Wazir AGAIN???

King Of course again. We can change things if we want. I am the King. WRITE!

Wazir I am writing, Sir. SPEAK.

King It is finally called the Decree of Hope and Finance and Education and Love AND FREEDOM.

Wazir You have solved it.

King These girls have solved it. My dears, here are your one hundred gold pieces. You are good girls. You have my blessings and the blessings of the whole kingdom. Tonight is a party at the castle. You are both invited. The carriage will pick you up in the evening. (*To* **Wazir**.) To the castle to start preparations.

Wazir Freedom? How did you do it?

King I didn't. They did.

Wazir Well, Sir, maybe we could discuss the credits later because credits, you know, they are part of our history and legacy and in such matters we should be careful to include those who designed and helped you, writing, driving, editing decrees . . . those people who, might, . . . (*Fade out his blabbering.*)

End.

Play #2: The Electricians

Characters

King Mazen
Wazir Walid
Man with the Event
Poor Man One
Poor Man Two
Shopkeeper with Extra Candy
Brother One
Brother Two

Scene One

King *at his desktop. Typing and busy with all kinds of kingly stuff. He's a nice young hip king.*

King (*happy, active, typing, going through his emails, deciding which ones he wants to answer*)   Dear Man with the Event, in response to your generous invitation, I am sorry to inform you that I will not be able to attend your event as I am giving a speech to the citizens on this day. Did you not get the notice of my event? 'The Tuesday Royal Speech of Useful Information.' May I suggest that you reschedule your event so you can come to my event and then I can come to your event. What is your event exactly? Thank you for thinking of us. Yours truly, etc. etc. CC events@king.com (*Choosing another email.*) Next. Hmmm. This one. Dear Shopkeeper. Thank you for your offer of a donation of sweets to our children but we are trying to have the children cut down on sweets because their teeth have to stay healthy and we don't want them getting diabetes. They have enough sweets from their parents. Should you like to export your sweets, we will be happy to process your order. The world needs sweetness. Please contact exporting@port.com. Yours truly, etc. etc. (*On to another email.*) Next. Hmmmm. No. Hmmm. This one. Dear Lady in the Garden, thank you for writing to me. Regarding your complaint, please accept my apology that the Royal Elephant has inconveniently squashed your garden of courgettes and eggplants. Rest assured that you will be reimbursed for the damage done and as further help, we will send you a pot of cooked and stuffed courgettes and eggplants and vine-leaves. Enjoy and to your health. Yours truly, etc. etc. CC cook@kitchen.com. Next. (*Next email.*) Hmmm. Hmmmm. Yes. Dear Twin Brothers, I would be very pleased to give you both a position at the electricity plant as your diplomas are very convincing. Unfortunately, at this time, we are not hiring electricians. As you know, the turbines are shut down since they were attacked by the enemy of the kingdom and we cannot get the spare parts we need to fix them. As soon as this most inconvenient problem is solved, we will contact you for work. Yours truly, etc. etc. CC manager@powerstation.com. And now I will send them all and then I can go have lunch. One little push of this little button, God is great, when they invented this machine with this little mouse. I love this little mouse. Send. (*Pause.*) SEND. (*Pause.*) I said SEND, SEND, SEND. WAZIR WALID. . . YA WAZIR WALID. GET IN HERE. HELP ME WITH THIS STUPID THING. THE MOUSE REFUSES TO OBEY ME.

Wazir *rushes in.*

Wazir   THE MOUSE IS HEREBY UNDER ARREST.

King   What are you doing, you fool? You can't arrest my computer. FIND OUT WHAT IS WRONG WITH IT. I WROTE IMPORTANT EMAILS AND PRESSED SEND AND NOTHING HAPPENED.

Wazir   The electricity is off, Your Highness.

King   NOW???? After I composed three royal emails? Where is my back-up? Where is my UPS?

Wazir   Your UPS should be working. Let me check. (*He does.*) The battery is dead, Your Highness. It didn't charge.

120   Play #2: The Electricians

King   You'll be dead soon if you don't find those emails. Where is the back-up? Curse this machine and all the machines in the land. It gives you every opportunity to interact with everyone in the world and then you need electricity to make it work. Why doesn't it come with a battery?

Wazir   It does, but that only lasts for a short time. It is called the laptop and it is only this big.

King   I don't like those little ones. My fingers get stuck, look at these big fingers, there is no room for me in there. I want a big laptop. With plenty of electricity. Can you get me that? I MUST FIX THAT POWER STATION.

Wazir   Your Highness, a HUGE laptop would be called a desk-top and that is what you have. These – inconveniently, and as you know – do not receive enough electricity from the kingdom and you, like the rest of the citizens, will have to wait for it to come back so we can HOPEFULLY INSHALLAH find your royal emails. Would you like to recite them to me so we can send them by horse and carriage. The horses are ready. Better yet. You can recite them directly to the receivers yourself and, at the same time, have a ride in the fresh air and be amongst the people.

King   EXCELLENT IDEA. Call the royal horseman. You can always count on a horse and a horseman.

Wazir   YES, SIR, WE HAVE EXCELLENT HAY. HAMDALILLAH.

Moving in a befitting carriage . . .

Wazir   Where to your Highness?

King   To the Man with the Event.

Wazir   ATTENTION ALL. THE KING IS MOVING IN THE DIRECTION OF THE HOUSE OF THE MAN WITH THE EVENT. STEP ASIDE, YOU MAY WAVE BUT WATCH YOUR SHOES.

King   Maybe we should take the Mercedes? Security, you know?

Wazir   We're out of fuel, Your Highness. I sent you an email about it last week.

King   I didn't get it.

Wazir   Maybe it's in the junk.

King   Yes. The Mercedes is in the junk. God is great. I love the royal horses. Hamdalillah.

Wazir   And you are safe here among the people. No enemies in the sky today. Hamdalillah.

Scene Two

They arrive. Set has changed from the office of the King to Garbage Quarter.

Wazir   MAN WITH THE EVENT. ARE YOU HOME?

Man with the Event Yes, ya Wazir Walid, I am home. What brings you to the Garbage Quarter at this time of day. (*Seeing the* **King**.) Your Highness, you honour me with your presence. Whatever are you doing in the Garbage Quarter??? Take care, Sir. You never know what can jump out of the garbage and bite you?

Wazir Jump up and bite. This sounds like a security issue. We might need back-up.

King Thank you, thank you, thank you. Kind citizen, my computer is down and I'm here to answer your email.

Man with the Event YOU? But it's Garbage Quarter.

King No need to bow. As to my email: (*clears his throat*) the royal email stated that I cannot attend your event because I am giving an event to the citizens on that day and I would like to know why you are holding an event on the day of an event of the king?

Wazir (*to the* **Man with the Event**) What is your event? Why isn't it on my calendar? We all have calendars for events. Do you NOT have a calendar? Do you want a calendar? Do you want to be arrested?

King Calm yourselves. Let us listen. Speak.

Man with the Event Regarding your own event of last month in which you spoke of the need for people to help keep the kingdom clean and not randomly throw the garbage all about, I arranged an event to introduce the concept of all the different kinds of garbage that exist. I was going to do a demonstration for the people. But now I will move it to the following day. And I hope you can attend that.

King Excellent idea. I will attend. A man who listens, thinks, plans, and then acts.

Wazir And here is a gold coin for listening, thinking, planning, and acting.

Man with the Event God be upon you. Your Highness, would you like a demonstration?

King EXCELLENT IDEA. Listening, thinking, planning, acting and ENTERTAINMENT.

Man with the Event I need a volunteer.

King (*to* **Wazir**) Go.

Man with the Event All material woven from cotton, wool, silk, or brocade is kept separately. Jewels, real or imitation, should be removed from the material if applicable. Material woven from hemp or straw is considered paper. Paper is considered paper. They belong together. Material woven from threads that are not true cotton are considered plastic. Plastic is considered plastic and they all belong together. Sir Wazir Walid, pull out some of these items from the pile and put them here. (*He does.*) Very good. (*He finds a small mistake of a plastic bag and puts it in the right pile.*) Next. Metals of all kinds, be they tin, steel, zingo, copper, foil, cans, or any other material that goes 'klink' or 'klong' are in another pile. Sir Wazir Walid, find some of these. Batteries of all kinds, including the UPS, are separate from anything else on the planet and are a special case all together. Medicine is the same.

Never throw medicine down the drain or in the garbage. Never throw batteries down the drain. Never throw anything down the drain for that matter. (*Meantime,* **Wazir** *is all in a knot of junk.*) All food is separate. And is NOT garbage.

King   And what would this be? (*About his crown, which must be gold even if he is wearing jeans.*)

Man with the Event   Ahhhmmmm. The jewels would have to come out and go in the glass pile. Glass and jewels have similar properties, might I say. And the rest, Your Highness, is . . . is . . . metal. It goes with the tin cans.

King   Hmph.

Man with the Event   OR we could melt it – if need be – and make something else out of it. Your crown, Your Highness, is completely recyclable.

King   RIGHT! Excellent answer.

Man with the Event   For a most excellent King.

Wazir (*they are leaving*)   Was he trying to insult you with that tin can story?

King   No. No. Truth is sometimes painful. But his ability to improvise is excellent. I like him. And now off to the Sweets Quarter in the market. I want to see which of those shopkeepers has extra candy that he wants to give it away to the children.

Wazir   ATTENTION ALL. THE KING IS MOVING IN THE DIRECTION OF THE MARKET TO THE SHOPKEEPER WITH THE EXTRA CANDY. STEP ASIDE, YOU MAY WAVE BUT WATCH YOUR SHOES.

Again, the scene changes from the Garbage Quarter to the Sweets Quarter. Or it can all be one big market.

King   I smell something so sweet? Oh Shopkeeper, where are you, oh Shopkeeper with Extra Candy?

Wazir   Follow that smell. (*And they do.*) I smell cotton-candy. Yummmmmm.

King   I love it, but my teeth hate it. I smell chocolate and marshmallows.

Wazir   Delicious yummy chocolate. Nothing is better than a biscuit with a chocolate and marshmallows inside and when you bite it, it makes you dizzy . . .

King   Stop. I too am getting dizzy. (*Sniffing.*) What's that? I smell those chewy things. I love those chewy things. Let's buy half a kilo. No let's buy a kilo. All those shapes and colours, tastes and flavours. WHERE IS THE SHOPKEEPER WITH THE EXTRA CANDIES. I WANT A KILO OF CANDY. Blue snakes, white and yellow eggs, cola bottles. Sour fish. All the kinds. Two kilos. How many people live in the castle? Three kilos. WHERE ARE YOU OH SHOPKEEPER WITH EXTRA CANDY???

Shopkeeper with Extra Candy   That would be I, Your Highness. You would like three kilos of candy? How would you like it packed? Small bags, two hundred and fifty grams, half kilo bags, how do you like your candy?

King   YOU SIR, SHOULD BE ARRESTED FOR TEMPTING THE KING.

Wazir   ARREST THE SHOPKEEPER WITH THE EXTRA CANDY FOR TEMPTING THE KING.

Shopkeeper with Extra Candy   You have asked for three kilos. I am here to sell them to you. Why arrest me?

Wazir   Candy is bad!

King   CANDY, my little shopkeeper, makes you fat. It gives you spots on your face. It ruins and clogs up your heart no matter how old you are. It gets in your blood and makes it weak. And the more you eat it, the more you want it. Candy is expensive. CANDY, OH SHOPKEEPER, IS BAD.

Wazir   CANDY IS BAD.

Shopkeeper with Extra Candy   CANDY IS NOT BAD.

Wazir   WHO IS SHOUTING AT THE KING?

King   IS SOMEONE SHOUTING AT THE KING?

Shopkeeper with Extra Candy   No one is shouting at the king. We are all just excited about candy. Because candy IS exciting. It is not bad. Not if you eat it slowly. Carefully. Three kilos should last you three months. Not three hours.

Wazir   Do you want me to arrest him?

Shopkeeper with Extra Candy   WAIT.

King   SPEAK. Why did you email me offering to give candy away?

Shopkeeper with Extra Candy   Your Highness, I have extra merchandise. I ordered too much. I made a mistake. I thought to donate it to the children. Sir, candy is a present from God. Man has taken sugar and turned it into many things and candy is one of them. It makes you happy, it makes you laugh, it puts a smile on your face. It's pretty. You can share it with friends. Bring it to your children when they are good and excellent. It adds joy to a joyous occasion. Life is not only bitter. Life is sweet. And candy makes is sweeter.

King   Hmmmmmmmmmmmm. Hmmmmmmmmmmmm. And hmmmmmmmmmmm. (*To* **Wazir**.) What do you think?

Wazir (*nervous, very nervous*)   Hmmm. Hmmmm. Hmm.

King   ANSWER.

Wazir   Candy is . . .

King   . . . Good . . . if eaten in small amounts. We'll make a decree that says that three kilos of candy for the castle is the healthy amount, and one kilo per household of . . . ummmm . . . eight persons is the healthy amount, so neither people nor king will lose their teeth, or get fat, or get ugly. This will be the first email we send when the electricity comes back. Let us buy our three kilos and continue.

And they do.

Shopkeeper with Extra Candy   Enjoy your candy, Royal Sirs, and Families. I would give you a little extra but that would be against the law. Peace be upon you.

Scene Three

Wazir   Where to, Your Highness?

King   To the Twin Brothers Electric

Wazir   ATTENTION ALL. THE KING IS MOVING IN THE DIRECTION OF THE HOUSE OF THE BROTHERS ELECTRIC. STEP ASIDE, YOU MAY WAVE BUT WATCH YOUR SHOES. Sir, we are coming to the Electricians' Quarter. Here on your left, is the Weavers' Quarter. The Gold Quarter is further down. And the Internet Quarter is not far should you want to see a laptop. (*Pause.*) And way over there are the wonderful orchids of the kingdom. Hamdalillah.

King   Have a candy?

Wazir   Thank you. Who are these brothers electric?

King   I don't know. They want work and they have very good documents and diplomas. Let's have one more. Sit.

As they are resting . . .

Poor Man Two   The King arrested the Man with the Event. I think they are going to chop off his head. I hear he is headed this way with the Wazir by horse and carriage.

Poor Man One   What do you think they want around here? Maybe they are going to the Gold Quarter to buy gold.

Poor Man Two   And then they went racing their horses through the market and found the Shopkeeper with the Extra Candy. And they arrested him too.

Poor Man One   Maybe they are going to the Weavers' Quarter to buy a fine new carpet. I wonder what the carpet of a king looks like.

Poor Man Two   They're going to chop off his head as well. And they took all his candy.

Poor Man One   Maybe they are going to the Internet Quarter to look at the new iThings.

Poor Man Two   What if they are coming to the Electricians' Quarter?

Poor Man One   Then we're in trouble. There still isn't electricity.

Poor Man Two   We will all be arrested. And we will all have our heads chopped off.

Poor Man One   The king isn't the head-chopping type.

Poor Man Two   I hope you're right. Otherwise we have to watch three executions and then participate in our own.

Poor Man One   Maybe he's just going to the orchards to pick some fruit.

Poor Man Two   I don't think I could watch my own head being chopped off.

Poor Man One   Did you hear about garbage sorting?

Poor Man Two   That's gossip.

Poor Man One   And that the crown is made of tin?

Poor Man Two   Let's run.

King   We have a lovely kingdom.

Wazir   With a lot of problems.

King   Yes. Don't remind me. How do you see it all ending?

Wazir   With us all together. In one kingdom . . . that lacks nothing.

King   And how do we get there?

Wazir   That, Your Highness, is the job of a king.

King   Pass the candy.

Wazir   Try the green one. Like a sour apple.

Scene Four

Wazir   WILL THE BROTHERS ELECTRIC PLEASE STEP FORWARD.

Brother One *and* **Brother Two** *appear.* **Brother One** *is holding potatoes that are connected together. A lot of potatoes connected by wire.* **Brother Two** *has a garden hose snaked around him and holds a large full watering can. They also have cables attached from ear to ear, of each other and themselves. One has a battery taped to his hand. It looks both electric and explosive.*

Brothers One *and* **Two**   Oh Your Highness, welcome, welcome, what brings you to the Electricians' Quarter? We sent you an email but this is sooooo unexpected . . . Oh excuse us, Your Highness . . . (*They try to bow but it proves very difficult and they don't want to lose their stuff.*)

Wazir   What on earth are you doing??? (*To* **King**.) You said their documents looked good? But look at them. This is a definite security issue. TURN THE HORSES AROUND. I knew it was a mistake to go out. ABOUT FACE! WE NEED BACK-UP. HELLO. WAZIR TO KING'S GUARDS. ALL UNITS TO THE ELECTRICIANS' QUARTER. ARREST THE TWIN BROTHERS ELECTRIC. (*Stops to catch his breath and to see what is actually happening.*)

The Brothers Electric *in the meantime, have tried to undo some of what they are wearing and have ended up on the floor, legs spread, arms spread, complete surrender. And the* **Wazir** *has thrown himself on top of the* **King** *to protect him and they too are on the ground.*

King Are you done?

Wazir Thank God you're alive. (*To the* **Brothers**.) DON'T MOVE.

King Are you done?

Wazir We'll wait for the back-up.

King Would you mind getting off of me so I can stand up.

Wazir I don't think that would be a good idea.

King Why not?

Wazir Security.

King GET OFF ME THIS MINUTE OR YOU WON'T SEE CANDY FOR THREE YEARS. LOOK, THEY ARE LYING ON THE GROUND LIKE FRIGHTENED BABIES. LOOK WHAT YOU DID TO THEM. WE ARE HERE TO DELIVER AN EMAIL.

King (*to* **Brothers**) Are you gentlemen alright?

Brother One (*hesitating*) Yes, Your Highness.

Brother Two I think we will live, Sir.

King Well get up then, and . . . have a candy.

They do.

King WHY, WHY are you wearing potatoes and wires and hoses and batteries? You are an insult to Man with the Event. If he saw you, he would take you apart in five minutes. Start explaining. I am all ears.

Brother One If I may begin, Your Majesty, as you are well aware, we are short of electricity.

King As I am well aware. What else is new?

Brother Two We are trying to find other ways to generate power to ease some of the pressure in the kingdom.

King That is all very fine, but the contents of my email to you was to tell you that we cannot hire people because the power plants are missing turbines and we only have one left and it only takes a few people to run it.

Brother One We understand, Sir, and this is why we are thinking of OTHER ways to make electricity.

Brother Two Simple things that people can do at home.

Wazir We have four thousand unemployed electricians and you want more?

Brother One No, Sir, of course not.

King I still don't hear an explanation.

Brother Two Potatoes.

King Potatoes?

Wazir Potatoes.

King I think we should arrest the Brothers Electric.

Wazir BY THE POWERS GIVEN TO ME BY THE KING YOU ARE HEREBY UNDER ARREST AND YOU HAVE THE RIGHT TO REMAIN . . .

Brother Two WAIT. Let me finish the sentence.

King Fine. Start with the word 'potatoes'.

Brother Two Yes, Sir. Potatoes are an electric conductor. Look. If you put a steel nail in here, and a piece of copper in here, and you do that with all these potatoes, and then you take this wire here and attach it here and this one here to here and this here to here and once you have them all connected you take the two ends and, God is great, the bulb lights. (*It works.*)

Brother One And you can do the same thing with green lemons. And in the orchards, there are more lemons than potatoes. But that's completely up to you.

Brother Two And another possibility is this.

*The **King** and **Wazir** have calmed down, are sitting, eating candy, and watching the presentation.*

Brother One Water. Water also makes things work and look, we have a whole sea full of it, hamdalillah. The only problem is that it is flat. We need to raise the sea so that it falls this way. Watch.

*He pours the watering can of water down the hose that **Brother Two** has wrapped around him. And the water goes into a bowl that moves a rubber duck that is in the bowl.*

Brother One You see, the duck, like a boat, moved. We just need to raise the sea. Not raise it, make two levels out of it.

King You want to make the great White Sea two levels? You don't think that if GOD WANTED IT TWO LEVELS HE WOULD HAVE MADE IT TWO LEVELS?

Brother Two Of course. And given that, He also gave us the brains to think of changing and not destroying the great work He has done in our kingdom and on this planet Earth.

Brother One We heard the Man with the Event is sorting garbage. Marvellous!

King YOU WANT ME TO RAISE THE SEA?

Brother One No, Sir. We want to continue with our experiments, until we find work in the power plant, to see if we can raise small amounts of water that will create small amounts of electricity.

Brother Two And to be able to continue experimenting with the fruits in the orchard to see which ones are good electric conductors.

Wazir   We cannot be using FRUIT for electricity? Your Highness, please let me arrest them.

King   'The people who are crazy enough to think they can change the world are usually the ones who change it.'

Wazir   What, Sir?

King   This is the saying of the man who made my computer. (*To the* **Brothers**.) Are you saying that with potatoes and water and what-not, you can make electricity.

Brother One   Small amounts, Your Majesty, small amounts. Lights. The radio. The computer.

Brother Two   Your Majesty, we cannot drive a car with a potato, or heat or cool a refrigerator with green lemons.

King   We have four thousand unemployed electricians. These two men came up with several ideas that might help. That bulb is still lit. What would happen if we took these four thousand electricians and . . .

Wazir   . . . Turn the Electricians' Quarter into a . . .

King   . . . a research centre for . . .

Wazir   . . . Alternative means . . .

King   . . . OF ELECTRICITY. I LOVE IT. A BRILLIANT IDEA. WE WILL JOIN THE WORLD IN SEARCH OF A SOLUTION. WE MIGHT EVEN FIND IT. AND ONE DAY YOU WILL BE ABLE TO SEE OUR TINY KINGDOM SHINING LIKE A STAR FROM THE MOON. WE WILL JOIN ALL THE OTHER KINGDOMS ON THE PLANET AND SEARCH FOR WAYS TO MAKE BETTER PEOPLE ON A BETTER PLANET. THAT WILL BE MY LEGACY.

Brother One (*very hesitant*)   Sir, it's a great idea, but we are still only at the beginning. It's a huge race.

King   We will join the race.

Wazir   We have every right to be in the race. We are a kingdom like all others.

King   Well not exactly like all others. We do have some specific problems that are somewhat different from the others . . . BUT WHY NOT. WHY NOT. (*Pause.*) I want potatoes. And then we are going back to the castle. (*To* **Wazir**.) And you will make my mouse move and (*To the* **Brothers**.) you can expect a new email from me by the end of today.

The **King** *and the* **Wazir** *leave. Excited. Full of hope. Full with potatoes.*

Brother One   Are you thinking what I'm thinking?

Brother Two   He's going back to the castle and he's going to connect a hundred potatoes to his computer.

Brother One   It will work, if he does it right.

Brother Two It's not very convenient. Is it?

Brother One No. Not at all.

Brother Two It would be easier to raise the sea. That's just a question of levees and dams.

Brother One He's a good king in a very difficult situation. Only one turbine working.

Brother Two And a kingdom full of people.

Brother One God is generous.

Brother Two God is great.

Brother One ATTENTION ALL UNEMPLOYED ELECTRICIANS. ON ORDERS OF THE KING, WE HEREBY INVITE YOU TO OUR WORKSHOP TO BEGIN SEARCHING FOR NEW AND DIFFERENT SOUCES OF POWER.

Brother Two We begin tonight after the evening prayers. All unemployed – or employed – technicians are welcome. ON ORDERS OF THE KING WE ARE GOING TO TRY TO MAKE A BETTER WORLD.

King *and* **Wazir** *back at castle and computer. The computer is covered with potatoes and wires and lemons and hoses.*

King The mouse is not moving.

Wazir (*who is attaching and re-attaching everything*)   Let me try this one.

King Nothing.

Wazir Now?

King Nothing.

This goes on for a while, they get very frustrated.

King When the Brothers Electric did it, it looked very easy. What's wrong with you?

Wazir I am a Wazir, Sir, not an electrician. I think it was magic.

King There is no such thing as magic. Everything has an explanation. Even the things that don't have explanations. Try again.

Wazir Now?

King All we can do is to keep on trying.

Wazir Yes, Your Highness, all we can do is keep on trying.

End.

Play #3: The Cooks

Characters

King Mazen
Wazir Walid
Cook One
Cook Two
Guard
Royal Mother
Ahmad
An Old Man

Scene One: Prologue

Everyone is on stage: the **King**, **Wazir**, **Cook One**, **Cook Two**, *the* **Guard**, *the* **Royal Mother** *and* **Ahmad**. *They are in a central diwan of a dilapidated castle. Each character has carved out a small spot for him/herself so there are some 'rooms' but things over-lap into other 'rooms' as if each character or group of characters has to find his/her own small space on earth. Given this, we need a throne or chair or seat for the* **King**, *a table of some kind for both eating and the desk of the* **Wazir**, *a cooking block with lots of large pots and all things for the kitchen. (Let's say a throne-room marries a kitchen.) Pots ranging from tiny to enormous. Many long sticks for ovens, big spoons for wood for big pots. A big knife that does everything from cutting an onion to cutting a cow.*

There is a lot of noise as several conversations are going on at the same time. Nothing can be heard clearly. The text for this 'noise' will be conversations. **Cooks One** *and* **Two** *discussing the dinner, the* **King** *and* **Ahmad** *talking about the next iPhone,* **Wazir** *and* **Royal Mother** *talking about the* **King**, *the* **Guard** *talking to his walkie-talkie. People and conversations change. As all this is happening in the same central space, all characters make an effort not to see what is happening in 'rooms' they are not supposed to be in.*

Scene Two: The Play Begins

Wazir (*to himself*)   Aghghghgh. Another day of work. When will I retire. Where is the law that says I can stop working when my bones are creaking and my back is hurting and I can no longer follow the language of the king. (*Getting dressed in royal clothing.*) He talks like, like, one of those musicians, those silly poets. NOT THAT THE KING IS SILLY. ABSOLUTELY NOT A SILLY KING. It's just that he's . . . young. He's a young king. Not really an adult and thus not really wise. God rest the soul of his brother and his father. Why did this Mazen come out so . . . so . . . soft? Where are his . . . his . . . KINGLY QUALITIES. I fear I am losing ground. He seems to listen to me and then goes and does what he wants. And of course every decision he makes is wrong. Every one. He refuses to wear royal garments. He would rather take a horse and carriage than his Mercedes. And he likes to garden. WHICH KINGS GARDEN? Not in the history of royalty has a king shovelled in a garden. It makes me nervous. Every time he is out there, I am forced to invent an emergency. Last week, I sent him a letter as if from the Minister of Transportation saying there were too many horses and carriages on the streets and not enough cars. So what does he do? He asks to widen the streets for carriage and cars and add trees for shade and beauty and he creates 4,000 jobs. This is no way to run a kingdom. We need the people dependent on us so they won't rebel. Not that there is any reason to rebel. Just to keep everyone calm and in place. That's how it's always been. Right. I could retire but the Royal Mother will never let me. She also wants to retire and move to the countryside but not until her son the King is married, with children, and not until he GROWS UP AND STARTS ACTING LIKE A KING. AND NOW . . . I must go to greet my King and begin this very long day. I am running out of money so today I have to teach him about a deficit.

Play #3: The Cooks

Guard By order of the Great Wazir Walid of our King Mazen I hereby issue Royal Decree Number one-five-zero-seven-one-nine-five-two-two-six-xero-two-one-nine-five-two. The decree herein states that as of today our kingdom is in a state of deficit. (*Pause.*) In simple language, we are running out of gold.

Guard (*listening into his walkie-talkie*) Yes. Yes. Yes. Really? Immediately. (*Announcing.*) Ya Security Guards of the Royal Court, set up the scanning devices and disguise them as horses. (*Announcing.*) Ya Cooks of the Royal Kitchen! This evening the King and our Great Wazir will be having a meal together.

Cook One *starts to cook. He is the head chef. Silent. Serious. Not likely to smile or laugh. An excellent chef.* **Cook Two** *has become assistant chef. The opposite of* **Cook One**. *Always talking, moving, doesn't seem to have a real job other than to be the assistant to* **Cook One** *when needed.*

Cook Two (*reading the newspaper*) Did you hear about the deficit?

Cook One I heard. Believe me, I heard.

Cook Two (*reading*) The prices are going up. Three gold pieces for anything with wings, four gold pieces for meat, four-and-a-half gold pieces for fish and anything that swims and doesn't have a back-bone or a brain.

Cook One (*cooking*) The King and the Wazir are dining together. I wonder what that is about. I need a lamb or two. (*He goes out.*)

Cook Two (*continuing reading*) And the fruits. No. No. Yeeee. Two gold pieces for anything from a tree. Half a gold piece from anything from the ground. Those who climb the ladders get paid more than those who bend down to collect.
Not fair.

Cook One (*coming in from out*) There are no more animals in the yard. Just Lulu, that skinny rooster who wakes us up. What will I slaughter?

Cook Two (*reading*) Even the spices: one gold piece for the whole set. It used to be half a gold piece for two sets. How are we supposed to enjoy the good taste of food without spices?

Cook One (*serious in thought*) I have nothing to slaughter but Lulu. Hmmm. Maybe we should have falafel and humous. The King loves it. And we'll show him we're trying to save money. (*Short breath.*) But the Wazir . . . he will not like it! He will be INSULTED. Oh Lulu. Listen Lulu, the Wazir is a powerful man. And he is not on the side of the King. This is between me and you, ya Lulu, so we have to show him we respect him.

Cook Two I was thinking we could open a restaurant but now the banks can't lend any money. This story is serious. I hope we get paid this month.

Cook One Lulu, I will make you taste just like a sheep. Your death will be more valuable than your life.

Cook Two If you slaughter Lulu, who will wake us up?

Cook One The iPhone. (*He breaks the neck of the chicken, we hear the sound of the chicken alive and then dead.*) Ahh Lulu, I will cover you with spices and you will be like the lamb at a wedding.

Cook Two Here's an article about the Dead Sea. It's drying up. It's all turning to salt. Salt is getting cheaper.

Cook One Lulu doesn't need salt. He needs fresh yogurt and three kilos of bones.

Cook One *is very busy with the rooster and his pots and all kinds of things from all kinds of bags, big and small. It looks like he's making magic in the large pot.*

Cook Two (*reading*) It says that the seas are drying in a phenomenon called 'the warming of the globe' ya'ni, it's too hot, the ice is melting and making floods and we, here in the desert, don't have ice, so here the sea is drying up instead of the ice and we are left with the salt.

Cook One Like the beginning of time. In the beginning there was only salt.

Guard (*to walkie-talkie*) Yes. Understood. (*Announcing.*) The Wazir has arrived.

Cook One And the food is ready. Are they in their places?

Cook Two Ready as always.

Guard (*announcing*) The Royal Dinner is served to the guests of the King, may God keep you all.

Cook One Enjoy.

Guard Tasting the royal dinner!

King Do we really have to do this every time?! We have the same two cooks for my whole life and I'm still alive.

Guard (*officially*) Your Highness, the food must be tasted! Suppose the back door was left open . . . and someone snuck in . . . and dropped something into the pot . . . The food must be tasted.

Guard *tastes the food.*

King And?

Guard The food is not poisoned!

Wazir What is the meal?

Guard Lulu in sauces and spice.

Scene Three

The **Cooks** *serve the meal. (One bowl of something and a spoon.)*

Wazir (*ceremonially*)   Good evening, Your Majesty, I hope everything is well with you and may God keep you forever in good health and good spirit so you can rule the kingdom as all those who preceded you.

King (*cunning*)   Good evening, ya Wazir. I hope all is well with you.

Wazir   It is.

King   Let us eat first and talk business later.

Wazir   An excellent suggestion, Sir. (*Eating.*) What is this meat?

Guard (*announcing*)   What is the meat?

Cook One   Sheep, Sir.

Guard   Sheep, Sir.

Wazir   It doesn't taste like sheep.

Guard (*announcing*)   It doesn't taste like sheep.

Cook One   It's sheep.

Guard (*announcing*)   It's sheep!

King   It's sheep. I think it's good. Eat. Eat.

They eat silently, tension, curiosity. **Cooks One** *and* **Two** *are watching closely . . . trying not to watch of course.*

King (*suddenly*)   WHAT DO YOU MEAN WE HAVE A DEFICIT?

Wazir (*completely off guard*)   Whaaaa . . . Wee . . . ummm . . . we . . . it happened . . . it was when . . . (*Pause. Thoughts.*) Your Highness. (*Pause.*) You spent all the money. (*Pause.*) The gold bags are empty. (*Pause.*) It happens. (*Pause.*) You see, in economics the theory states . . .

King   ME???? BRING ME THE ACCOUNTS.

Guard (*in walkie-talkie he mumbles some incomprehensible code words. He leaves the stage and comes back with a box spilling over with receipts. Announcing.*)   THE ROYAL RECEIPTS.

King   Give me one. (*Looking at it.*) I didn't order fifty sheep, twenty-five goats, and two hundred ducks.

Cook One   That would be the Wazir who placed an early order for next year's feast.

Guard   That would be the Wazir who did that for the feast next year.

King   Listen, my best guard, you are glued to me like a stamp. We are all in one room. I hear. Believe me, I hear. Calm down . . . until I need you. OK, my man?

Guard (*announcing*)   Yes, Sir.

King   Give me another receipt. (*He reads.*) Who ordered a Jacuzzi?

Wazir Your Highness, that is my gift to you on the anniversary of your eighth year as King. And now you ruined the surprise!

King And you bought it with the people's money?

Wazir The gift is from all the people.

King You asked all the people?

Wazir Your Highness, as Wazir, believe me I know what the people want.

King (*Oh right!*) Yes, I understand. (*Looking at another one, getting louder.*) And five thousand swords. Who bought these?

Guard That would be I, Your Highness. It's for your security detail. We bought some extras and spare parts as well. Leather handles.

King (*angry but under control, to* **Wazir**) So tell me, oh my Wazir, how much money do we actually need? I mean to keep the kingdom running.

Wazir After PERSONALLY going over the accounts myself, the deficit stands at one million two hundred thousand gold pieces and four hundred and fifty coins.

King How long do I have?

Wazir Some days.

King You mean to tell me that in 'some days' my kingdom will stop functioning.

Wazir I'm afraid so.

King Sir.

Wazir Yes, Your Highness.

King Give me your purse of gold. (*Given.*) And your chequebook. (*Given with difficulty.*) And your credit cards. (*Given with more difficulty.*)

Wazir Your Highness, how am I to run the kingdom?

King You are not. I am.

Wazir But Sir, you are just . . .

King Just what?

Wazir The King, Your Highness.

Silence.

King How much is this royal ring worth?

Wazir You cannot sell the royal ring.

King How much is this royal ring worth?

Cook Two According to the newspaper, and the rates on the gold exchange, I'd say it's worth twenty-five per cent of what is needed. A quarter of a million pieces of gold. That's about one hundred and twenty bags full.

Wazir Stop listening to Royal Conversations.

Cook Two Yes, Sir.

King I'm going to my office. No one bother me.

Wazir What about the coffee?

King Yes, right. Cook One, bring the Wazir his coffee and I will take mine at my desk.

Cook One Your Majesty. About the kitchen and food supplies. (*Quickly.*) We need an alarm clock.

Guard Your Majesty. About the kitchen and food . . .

King (*to* **Guard**) I heard. (*To* **Cook One**.) What about them?

Cook One There is not much left.

King (*to* **Cook One**) Be creative.

Cook One May God keep you.

Wazir I can't drink coffee myself!

King Why not?

Wazir You cannot sell the ring, Sir.

King Why not?

Wazir This is most rude.

King *leaves with the* **Guard** *close behind.*

Scene Four: The Next Day

Guard One and all and all and one! His Majesty King Mazen has asked you not to worry yourselves about Royal Decree Number one-five-zero-seven-one-nine-five-two-two-six-zero-two-one-nine-five-two. He is looking into the financial accounts of the kingdom and asks for your patience.

Wazir WHAT? Where did you hear that? Who told you to speak?

Guard The King himself. (*listening into his walkie-talkie*) No. No. No. Impossible? Immediately. (*Announcing.*) Ya Cooks of the Royal Kitchen, this evening the Royal Mother is coming for a meal

Cook One The Royal Mother?!?!?!

Cook Two (*reading the newspaper*) Someone is selling a ring for a quarter of a million gold pieces. I wonder who that could be??!?!?! Who can have such a ring? (*Reading further.*) Hmmm. Ooooo. Listen. It says that there is cow flu and bird flu and fish flu. Remember when you had the flu and I read the newspaper to you from cover to cover.

Cook One I will remember that day until the day I die. Each story was worse than the next. I became sicker before better. I couldn't cook for a week afterwards. The next time I get the flu, we will watch television and forget about the news.

Cook Two Last night on television I learned that one of the new kingdoms has stopped using gold and is using paper to make purchases. Paper instead of gold. (*He rips his newspaper in odd sizes and stuffs them into his pockets like a rich man.*) I'm going to buy some sheep . . . and a new rooster.

Cook One THE ROYAL MOTHER AND NO MEAT, NO BIRDS, NO FISH. (*Intense thinking.*) Hmmmmm. (*Intense thinking.*) Hmmmmm. (*Intense thinking.*) Hmmmmm. I will make (*Pause. Pause. Pause.*) a ROYAL SUPREME.

Cook Two Sir, I read the cookbooks from cover to cover and there is no such thing as Royal Supreme.

Cook One A Royal Supreme, my friend, is a new recipe. It is a creative dish of macaroni that looks and tastes like chicken in spicy sauce. And the Royal Mother loves chicken in spicy sauce.

Cook Two Very funny. I will send that to the newspaper for the daily cartoon. Here, take some paper (*newspaper money*) and GO OUT AND BUY A SHEEP!

Cook One STOP. There is no paper money. Stop reading the newspaper. It's the Wazir who is writing articles and making things up. I heard him talking to himself. (*Tiny pause.*) Go out to the royal orchards and bring me cucumbers, tomatoes, apricots, grapes, sage, basil, and most important bring ten beets. From the storage, bring me olives, pickled onions, pickled eggplants, and lemons. From the cupboard, bring me salt, red chillies, spice, and plenty of chilli, sweet and hot. And flour. I need a lot of flour. I shall add to it the juice of ten beets and have spiced macaroni casserole. And that is Royal Supreme. Go. Bring. Hurry.

The **Cooks** *are in the flurry of activity. Flour is flying. In the end we have a huge plate of red macaroni that is gorgeous. (We can make it from red candy and liquorice.)*

Guard (*to walkie-talkie*) Yes. Understood. Everyone stand ready! (*Announcing.*) The Royal Mother has arrived.

Royal Mother (*to* **King**) My son!!! My angel. My King. You look so hungry. You look undecided. You are the wrong colour. Your temperature is much too low. What are you wearing? That is not what a King wears. I sent you robes. Why don't you wear them? What are you wearing? You look like a peasant. Put on something red. You always looked wonderful in red. And your hair? Cut it. Comb it. Put on a crown. Do something. (*To* **Wazir**.) You! You aren't doing your job. This boy looks like a child. Not a king. Speak. Why does he look like he works in the market? It's been eight years. Why isn't he acting like a king yet?

Wazir (*whispering*) I have no idea, Ma'am. He is acting strangely since yesterday.

King Mother. My dearest mother. Catch your breath. Here, sit in my seat. Rule for a while. (*Pause.*) And calm yourself. Give some orders.

Royal Mother (*to herself*)   Just like his grandfather, that one. (*Pause.*) Fine. (*To* **Wazir**.) Make a royal decree that the King's hair must be combed twice a day. (*Pause as all wait.*) And make another one that he is to be dressed in robes EVERY DAY. With matching slippers and matching jewels. (*To* **King**.) If this is how you want to run your kingdom . . . Oh, your father, may God rest his soul, would be very unhappy with you. Where is the cook?

Wazir   Cooking, Your Majesty.

Royal Mother   At least someone is doing his job. Bring the cook.

Guard (*announcing*)   Bring the cook.

Cook One   Your Majesty.

Royal Mother   Show me your hands. (*He does.*) Turn them over. (*He does.*) Return to the kitchen. (*He does.*) I never liked that cook. Replace him. (*Seeing* **Cook Two**.) And him, too.

King   We aren't replacing the cooks. Can I have my chair back? Mother, we have some trouble.

Royal Mother   Not enough chairs?! (*To* **Wazir**.) This is all your fault.

King   Mother. (*Pause.*) Mother, my dear. (*Pause.*) How are you feeling, oh wife of my father?

Royal Mother   Thank God, I shouldn't complain. My Mercedes got a flat tire because the driver ran over a roof that fell off someone's house, what a pity, and we had to wait for my horse and carriage. That was a bother. You really should fix the roads . . . AND the roofs. (*Whispering to the* **Wazir**.) This is all your fault. Be careful or I'll replace you. (*Back to* **King**.) Otherwise, hamdalillah. I can't complain.

King (*whispering to* **Wazir**)   Didn't I ask that all the roofs be fixed? And the roads?

Royal Mother   What secrets are you whispering.

King   Nothing, my love, small talk between King and Wazir. (*Short pause.*) Mother, my dearest and most generous, I need to discuss something very important with you.

Royal Mother   YOU'RE GETTING MARRIED. But I haven't met her yet. I haven't tasted her coffee. Who is her father? How can you be so mean to me? What have I done that you ignore me? (*Whispering to* **Wazir**.) All your fault.

King   MOTHER I NEED TO DISCUSS YOUR GOLD.

Royal Mother   AHHHH. IT IS YOU WHO IS SELLING THE ROYAL RING. AND NOW YOU WANT MY GOLD. NEVER.

King   Mother. We need a million pieces of gold.

Royal Mother   Why? We have ten million gold pieces. Just yesterday I bought three hundred metres of brocade to recover the seats in the diwan. And ten new carpets. You must come see them. Oh those weavers are clever girls.

King Mother, we don't have ten million. We don't even have one million. It seems the money has been spent. Mother, my finest, my best, my beautiful, my flower, do you want me to have to close all the schools, all the hospitals and clinics, do you want to see all the shops empty again? People will blame me, and then my father, and THEN YOU!

Cook Two Your Majesty, do you know the cows and birds and fish all have the flu?

Royal Mother FISH DON'T CATCH THE FLU. WHO IS TEACHING THIS BOY? FIRE THAT COOK. (*Whispering to* **Wazir**.) Your fault. (*Exaggerated.*) Bring me my medicines.

Guard (*shouting*) Medicines for the Royal Mother. Make space. Everyone move away from her. (*He has powders and drops and flowers and such to sprinkle upon the Royal Mother.*)

King Enough. There is nothing wrong with her. Mother? Get up so we can talk. Me and you.

Royal Mother (*getting up*) Fine. (*Calling out.*) But first we should eat.

Guard (*announcing*) The Royal Dinner will be served to the King and the Royal Mother, may God keep you all.

Cook One Is everyone in place?

Guard Everyone is in place.

Cook One Enjoy.

Guard Tasting the royal dinner!

King (*repeating, as one would as a habit*) Do we really have to do this every time?! We have the same two cooks for my whole life and I'm still alive.

Guard (*officially*) Your Highness, the food must be tasted! Suppose the back door was left open . . . and someone snuck in . . . and dropped something into the pot . . . The food must be tasted.

Guard *tastes the food.*

King And?

Guard The food is not poisoned!

Wazir What is the meal?

Guard (*announcing*) What is the meal?

Cook One Royal Supreme.

Guard Royal Supreme.

King (*to* **Guard**) I asked you to stop doing that.

Guard Yes, Sir.

Royal Mother I have no meat.

Wazir Where is the meat?

Royal Mother The cooks forgot the meat! Replace them. Put their heads in the pot!

Guard (*announcing*) Chopping off the heads of the cooks.

King NO CHOPPING HEADS. MOTHER, BE QUIET. Bring in the cooks.

Guard (*announcing*) Bringing in the cooks.

King My mother wishes to know what is the Royal Supreme and where is the meat? Can you explain it to her, please?

Cook One (*flustered*) Oh Royal Mother of our Royal King. There is no meat in this dish because . . .

Cook Two We received a message that you did not want meat this evening. God save your Royal Highness and his Mother the Royal Mother. That you are an example to the people that we do not need meat every night.

King And tomorrow it will be in the newspaper. 'Royal Mother refrains from eating meat to help her son the King reduce the deficit.'

Royal Mother (*to herself*) Did I send a message? (*To the others.*) Well. It's about time they start writing about me again. My husband dies, and they forget their queen. Fine. But what is Royal Supreme?

Cook One Royal Supreme is an excellent new dish prepared carefully in my kitchen . . . with the best ingredients . . .

Cook Two It is Royal Macaroni, Maam.

Royal Mother MACARONI? My medicines. Immediately. (*She starts her fainting again.*)

King MOTHER! (*To* **Wazir**.) Why is she like this? Why is she so dramatic about everything?

Wazir She is an extraordinary mother, Your Highness.

King Mother, get up or I'm going to bed and no one will eat!

Royal Mother (*getting up, giving up her game*) Fine. Let us eat. (*They eat.*) Tell me, dear King, when will you marry and bring us the heir to our kingdom? I am bored and I need your children to raise. To prepare them for their futures.

King Mother, who is the king?

Royal Mother Why, you my dearest! I remind you every day. (*Whispering to* **Wazir**.) Your fault.

King Right. So tomorrow I am coming to your castle and we are going to discuss your gold.

Royal Mother *faints.*

Scene Five: The Next Day

Guard   Oh People of the Kingdom. The King has met with his advisors and regarding the Royal Decree ending with the numbers six-zero-two-one-nine-five-two, he asks you to kindly continue working and shopping and soon the shops and markets will be refilled. Inshallah.

Wazir   What advisors? Who is he talking to? Him and that impossible computer. I will throw it from the castle window and let the alligators eat it. ADVISORS?!?! GRRRRRR.

Guard (*listening into his walkie-talkie*)   Yes. No. Yes. Really? Immediately. (*Announcing.*) Ya Security Guards of the Royal Court, bring all the favourite toys of the King especially that laptop of his. (*Announcing.*) Ya Cooks of the Royal Kitchen! This evening the Royal Best Friend is coming for a meal.

Cook One (*unexpectedly excited . . .!*)   Ah, the Royal Best Friend Ahmad. He always makes a good guest. What do we cook for the boy?! What, what, what . . .?

Cook Two (*reading the newspaper*)   Here's an article on white bread and brown wheat. It says that we should avoid using white wheat and use brown wheat instead. Make something with brown wheat.

Cook One   STOP READING IMMEDIATELY and go bring me ten kilos of brown wheat from the storage, and three kilos of onions, ten oranges, fifteen large apples, bring me fifteen eggs, and a kilo of raisins, and butter, plenty of good fresh butter. And one-fourth kilo of cinnamon. And two kilos of sugar. No, make that one kilo.

Cook Two   And here's another article that says eggs and butter are bad. That they will destroy your heart like a bullet going through it.

Cook One   Not my eggs and not my butter. Run. We will make Ahmad a meal he will never forget. Run I say before I turn you into chopped meat.

Guard (*announcing*)   The Royal Best Friend Ahmad has arrived.

Ahmad   Bring out the music. Bring out the drums. Let's start the party. Your Highness, ya my brother, ya habibi, how are you, my friend, living alone in your castle?

King   Ya, my brother, hug me, kiss me, welcome, sit, yaaaaa. I am so happy you came.

They hug and look at each other with understanding of the general situation. Meanwhile, the **Cooks** *are cooking. The scene between the* **King** *and* **Ahmad** *is done for the ears of the* **Wazir**.

Ahmad   Now tell me about this deficit that you have? How could you run out of gold? Are you turning into your father??? YOU HAVE NO MONEY?

King (*whispering*)   I'm trying to keep it all calm but I can't find the gold. Either he spent it or hid it.

Ahmad (*whispering*)   We should try to find out. (*Pretending.*) NO MONEY. NO MONEY. What is your plan?

King Ahmad, my brother, you know I can't discuss royal business with you. Let's not talk about my problems now. Tell me about you. What of the family and the friends?! How is everyone? What is their news?

Ahmad Are you ready? Ashraf got married. And a kid is on the way. (*During the monologue of* **Ahmad**, *the* **King** *reacts to all the news accordingly. All for the sake of those watching.*) He married the daughter of his algebra teacher's youngest daughter. Beautiful. They have a tiny castle but they are very happy. Then, Khaled, he left the kingdom . . . yes . . . he got a scholarship to study cinema in England. He wants to return and make a film here. (*Louder.*) He wants to make a documentary about Wazir Walid because your Great Wazir worked under your grandfather King Mahmoud and your father King Mohammed and now you King Mazen. The rumour says he is a special Wazir!

King Oh he is special, that is sure. There is NO ONE like him.

Ahmad The day Khaled left for London he tried to visit you but your special Wazir wouldn't make the appointment. He said you, Your Highness, were too busy. He REALLY takes care of you. Here is big hug and good-bye from Khaled and he asks you to build a cinema for when he returns. Oh. The grandfather of Ayman died but he was one hundred and six so God keep his soul. And Aymam now has all the land because he has no sisters or brothers. And he says hello and if you need anything, just call him. He is planting the land with trees, beautiful trees with every fruit we have. He heard about your DEFICIT and he says in a year he will sell you fruits at a special price. And finally, my brother, me, your best friend in the whole kingdom, look at me and open your eyes, because I am getting married. What do you think. I found my princess. I gathered enough money from Weddings&Feasts.com and that's how I found her. Her sister was one of my customers.

King I am going to make you a prince. Right now and right here. (*He makes a kingly gesture.*) You are now Prince Ahmad.

Wazir (*bursting onto the scene, no longer able to keep silent*) THAT IS NOT HOW YOU MAKE A PRINCE. You must first make a son in order to make a prince. You cannot just go around making anyone a prince.

King Says who?

Wazir Every king who came before you.

King Is it written?

Wazir Yes.

King Where?

Wazir In the hearts of the royalty.

King All the more reason that Ahmad will be a prince. Bow to Prince Ahmad of the Great Dot Coms.

The **Wazir** *bows very rudely to* **Ahmad**. **Ahmad** *takes out his sword, the* **Wazir** *takes out his sword, and in half fun/half serious there is a small duel between the two. When*

Scene Five: The Next Day

Ahmad *sees that the* **Wazir** *cannot keep up with him, he drops his sword, as if he lost.*

Wazir (*tired from the duel*) I still have it in me!

Ahmad Difficult to win from, Sir Walid.

King A truly special Wazir.

Wazir (*tired from the duel*) After our meal, I will take a nice hot Jacuzzi.

Silence. **Ahmad** *and the* **King** *look at each other.*

Wazir (*getting nervous*) WHERE IS THE LUNCH FOR THE ROYAL BEST FRIEND?

Cook One THE ROYAL LUNCH IS SERVED. (*Seeing* **Ahmad**.) AHMAD, MY BOY, MY SON, ARE YOU REALLY GETTING MARRIED?

Ahmad HOW ARE YOU, FATHER? Yes. And you will love her like I do. And it's only for you that Weddings&Feasts.com exists. A wonderful idea, Father. If the King allows you to leave his kitchen, you will come work in mine.

Wazir (*still nervous. To* **Guard**) TASTE THE ROYAL DINNER.

Cook One And did I hear that His Majesty has made you a prince? Are my ears working correctly?

Wazir Why is the cook listening in on the conversations of the king?

King Ya Wazir, lighten up your heart.

Wazir Your Majesty, we can't have a cook in the diwan. It's better if Ahmad goes into the kitchen.

King Have a seat, ya Great Wazir. Where is the music? Where are the drums? We're having a party. (*To* **Cook One**.) Tell us, ya Royal Cook One, what have you made us tonight.

Cook One Bread cake!

Wazir BREAD CAKE????

Cook One An excellent and CREATIVE new recipe. BREAD CAKE. I shall go bring it. DINNER IS SERVED TO THE BEST GUEST OF THE KING. My son.

Wazir (*to* **Guard**) Taste the royal bread cake. (*Silence.*) You can never know, Sir.

Guard (*pause*) It's (*Pause.*) very (*Pause.*) unusual.

Wazir What does it taste like?

Guard (*pause*) Bread . . . and . . . apples . . . cinnamon . . . oranges . . . it's quite delicious.

King Seeing as our Cook has prepared this lovely bread cake for his only son and my best friend Prince Ahmad, let us give thanks and enjoy it.

Ahmad   I LOVE BREAD CAKE.

King   DELICIOUS.

Ahmad   My father can make anything taste good. Even a newspaper. (*They eat.*) So what about this DEFICIT of yours. Where is all the gold, my brother?

King   Yes. You heard. It seems I have made a terrible mistake in running this kingdom.

Ahmad   Maybe you need advisors.

King   I have advisors.

Ahmad   Maybe you need new advisors. Advisors who understand the new economy.

Wazir   Understand what new economy?

Ahmad   The new economy, ya Wazir. Surely you, of all people, have heard about the New Economy.

Cook Two   He's talking about the paper money.

Cook One   Be quiet. Those two boys are planning something.

King   I have been studying this new economy. And maybe I do need some additional advisors. Ya Ahmad, I could always count on you.

Ahmad   My brother, I am at your service whenever you need and I am your friend for eternity. Hey, did you hear about the paper money?

Cook Two   I TOLD YOU.

King   Let us have our coffee on the veranda in the fresh air.

Guard (*announcing*)   King and Royal Best Friend moving to the veranda.

King   Cook, Father of Prince Ahmad, please write up this new recipe for your son so he can give it to his princess.

Wazir   That Ahmad was always trouble. What IS a dot com? New advisors?!?!?!

Scene Six: The Next Day

*Early in the morning. Everyone is sleeping except for the **King**. He is looking out a window.*

King (*slow*)   A beautiful morning in a beautiful country. Trees as far as I can see. Every year they come and go. Ah the mother of nature. Mountains that reach heaven. And a sea full of God's creatures. And people, how great is God. Men and women coming from their homes, to work, to study, to create the life of a country. People with spirit. Good people. (*Pause.*) The sky tells me it will be a nice day today. Inshallah. Sun or rain. Both are good. (*Short pause.*) How do I get the gold back? What did he do with all the money?

Scene Six: The Next Day

An **Old Man** *appears at the window.*

Old Man   We peasants, we like the rain better.

They look at each other.

Old Man   In the desert, rain is good. Look east, Your Highness, and that is where your desert begins. Rain is good.

King   Grandfather?

Old Man   Good morning to you, Your Highness, and peace be to the prophet. You didn't sleep.

King   And good morning to you. And let us hope for rain.

Old Man   So what's with your deficit? Did your father spend it all? I left him plenty.

King   No. Not my father. The Wazir.

Old Man   The Wazir, your father, they were two halves of the same loaf. Have a peach. (*He gives him a fruit, depends on the season, we change the fruit. But it has to be a fruit tree that makes jam.*) It's from my tree.

King   Your tree? You had an orchard. You had twenty orchards and thousands of trees.

Old Man   Now I only have a peach tree. And it only gives me fruit in the season. Now I eat peaches. In winter, I eat peach jam. I have a small boy who works with me. He's an orphan. We get along fine. He can climb high into the tree. I can't get there anymore. We live in a small room under the tree. You should come and visit.

Cook One *awakes and begins quietly to prepare some tea and dry biscuits. He sees the* **King** *and the* **Old Man**. *He recognizes the* **Old Man**.

Cook One (*to* **King**)   Good morning, Your Majesty. (*To* **Old Man**.) Good morning, Ya Haj.

Old Man   Yes, it's been a few years since the Haj. Hamdalillah. You were a skinny little boy, always playing tricks on your father, hiding the fish knife, eating the last of the honey. How are you, my friend? Still in the kitchen?

Cook One   I'll never leave the kitchen. You know that. What do you think of your Grandson the King? He is a good boy, no?! Let us hope it rains.

King   Let us sit.

Old Man   Bring an old man some tea and biscuits.

Cook Two *brings tea and dry biscuits.*

Old Man   And here are some peaches. What better breakfast is there?

Cook One (*to* **Cook Two**)   Bring some honey.

Old Man   That's a professional cook. One who can always make a good thing better.

The **Wazir** *wakes up but doesn't see the scene.*

Wazir Good morning, Your Majesty. I will get the cook to make us something to eat. I hope he can find us something in the storage.

King Come good Wazir, see who is here.

Wazir (*to* **Old Man**) Your Majesty, what are you doing here?

Old Man Surprise, surprise. I heard my King was having some trouble. I thought maybe he needed some advice.

Cook Two (*to* **Wazir**) Have some tea and a biscuit.

Old Man And a peach from my tree.

Wazir It's a very tiring time, Your Majesties.

Old Man No more than any other time. There is no deficit. There is today and yesterday and before yesterday and tomorrow and after tomorrow and after that from the beginning of time to the end of time. (*Pause.*) Gold is like kings. One day they are on thrones and one day they are under peach trees. We go up, we go down. Like the trees, sometimes we are full and sometimes we are empty. But the fruits always come back. Unless the tree has a bug eating it. You must always spray for bugs. Isn't that correct, ya Great Wazir? (*To the* **King**.) What is important? We are here today. You, me, these two wonderful cooks. Prince Ahmad of the Great Dot Coms who will stand by you until death. And your mother. True royalty. She understands you and will help you like all mothers help their sons. She will not turn on you, Your Highness. She let you sell the ring and she returned the jewels of the crown. A few tears but she will work with you and the schools and hospitals will be open.

Guard (*announcing sleepily*) The kingdom is officially awake. Your Highness, where are you???

Old Man And this loyal guard, always at your side. (*Short pause.*) Do you know how strong the will of the people is? The will to live and populate this kingdom?! No king has ever been able to take that away. Look outside. People everywhere. Women are preparing their children for the day. Each one has a sandwich. Boys and girls walking to school. Fathers patiently waiting, knowing you will make the right choice. And the sea and the desert and the lands and all the animals will remain your friends if you are kind to them. This is what you have today. And tomorrow is coming. And today will pass. And that's how you fix a deficit.

Wazir You are as crazy as the day you quit! No king in our history every stepped down from the throne.

Old Man Then I am quite original.

King Wazir. Where is the gold of the kingdom?

Wazir You spent it, Your Highness.

King I did not spend it. You spent it. And WE would like it back.

Old Man A difficult request, boy.

Scene Six: The Next Day

Guard (*understanding*)   Your Highness, would you like me to spray for bugs???

King   No, no, no. Some bugs have to live. They make a balance.

Cook Two   Yes. A balance of nature.

Old Man   Lovely.

King   Great Wazir, your game is over. (**Wazir** *nervous.*) You will leave the castle today. (**Wazir** *frightened.*) You will take nothing with you. (**Wazir** *starts crying.*) Guard, you will accompany him to the house of my grandfather where he will become a gardener. The boy orphan will be in charge of him. He will live from the land. If he does not produce peaches then he will not eat. He will sleep on a bed of leaves outside the house until my grandfather fixes him. Should anything happen to my grandfather or to the orphan boy, you will put the Wazir in the dungeon. Is all this understood by everyone present?

Old Man   You are giving me work?

King   I am, Grandfather. Only you can fix this man. Enough work. I think that we should all have some peach pie and fresh milk. Can you arrange this for us, my best Cook One?

Guard (*announcing*)   Serve the Royal Breakfast to the Royal Household.

Cook Two   It's getting cloudy out there.

Old Man   It's going to rain. Hamdalillah.

Wazir   How am I to live outside, under a tree?

Old Man   We will soon find out. It's not difficult. Many people do it.

End.

4: Lost and Found (2013)

Play #1: The Room

Characters

Samar, *younger sister of Sara, age six to eight.*
Sarah, *older sister of Samar, age eight to ten.*
Mayar, *their cousin, age seven to nine.*

Late at night. Mayar's room. There is an area that isn't the room of Mayar. In the room, there are three single mattresses, one that clearly belongs there. Nice girl-room-things are scattered around making up a room that once was for one and now is for three. Pretty and crowded. There is also a carton or box on the stage.

Capital letters can mean shouting or conviction or provocation or simple emphasis.

Samar *and* **Sarah** *appear, dirty and dusty and scared. They don't go into Mayar's room until noted.*

Scene One: Samar

Samar (*at the entrance*)   I have a very nice room. We are six girls in this room. My share is small but hamdalillah we all fit. My part is nice. I have nice things in my part. When the baby was born, yes we have a new baby, Siba, the seventh girl, when she came we had to buy another mattress for Mahmoud. He's the first boy and the most important of us all. Because of how life goes, I got a new mattress. It isn't completely new because the new ones come wrapped in plastic and smell new but it was new for me. It went to Mahmoud. And his went to Samia and hers to Safa and Safa's to Sarah and Sarah's to Saja, and Saja's to me, and mine went to the poor, and Salwa's had to be thrown so she sleeps on the couch and Siba sleeps with my mother. When I got my new mattress, I put all my things on it. All of us put all our things on our new mattresses except for Salwa on the couch and Siba who doesn't have things yet. Everything worked out. It was a whole day of moving beds around the room and we laughed even though my father wasn't happy. Men are not happy. When he left, all the girls, we are six girls, seven, we are seven, I keep forgetting Siba because she's new. We arranged our things and some of us were fighting but mostly we were talking to our things and deciding where we would put them. I had a heart pillow that says 'Sweet Dreams' in English on it and that of course was in the centre of the bed. I also have a clock with a flower on top and three fish and two cats glued on it. It used to ring. A cat and fish playing on a clock!? But the ringer is broken. Mahmoud says it needs batteries but we don't have any. (*Breath.*) I have a very soft blanket and it smells of . . . it smells of me. That's funny. (*Pause.*) I like cats. I had a small white cat stuffed with cotton, on the bed, she had a red bow around her neck and I put a hat on her. I called her Mimi because Siba calls her Mmmmmm so I made it Mimi and thats a nice name for a cat. And I also put a bracelet on her, the cat, not my baby sister. A cat with a hat and a bracelet. (*Pause.*) Under the mattress was another story. I put my sweets there. And one time, oh God, I put biscuits there and it was very hot outside and very hot inside and all the ants from all the world found the biscuits and ate through the cellophane. I tried to wash the biscuits but they fell apart in my hands and my mother shouted 'No', so that was that. And the ants of the world were in my bed and on Mimi and I had to work all day to kill the ants and wash them away. And then it was fine. I slept even though I had no biscuits. (*Pause.*) And I had a feather. It was yellow, maybe from a big chicken, or maybe a pretend feather but it was very pretty and that was next to my pillow. Sometimes I put it in a book so it wouldn't get broken. We had a lot of feathers but we broke most of them. That happens a lot. (*Long pause.*) But now it's all gone. We came here waiting for a new room. Or a new house. I forgot what they said. All seven of us went to the cousins. Mahmoud stayed with my father in the broken house. And my mother and Siba run around visiting everyone everywhere. Today she's in the broken house.

Scene Two: Sarah

Sarah It's not broken. It's blown up. And the balcony flew away. I am one hundred per cent certain that someone found our balcony and sewed it onto their house. And our bedroom just fell off the house. Kablonggg. Lucky I wasn't in it or kablongggg on me and I wouldn't be here anymore. I would be with God and that's better than being here. I have nothing anymore. Nothing, nothing, nothing. I hate it here. Our house is scattered all over the city. Where are my clothes? Also scattered. Maybe I will see someone wearing my things and then what? Fight her in the street for finding flying clothing and socks. And where are my shoes? I have no shoes. Only my shib-shib. Like the Nakba. My grandmother said, 'We all left in our shib-shib because we were going to come back.' It's the naqba all over again. That's what grandmother said. I lost my boots. The ones with the fur. From Wahdeh Street. The good ones. (*Looking around.*) Where are we? Whose house is this?

Scene Three: Owls

Mayar *appears in her room and walks towards the two girls.*

Mayar You are in my house. I am your cousin Mayar. You are Samar and you are Sarah, right? Come in. (*No one moves.*) You can have my shoes. (*Looking at their feet.*) We have the same size. All three have the same size. It's good to all have the same size, no? Take any pair you want. Come in. The milk is on the stove. My mother is preparing things to eat. Come.

Sarah I don't want your shoes. I don't want anything ever again. I want to die. I don't have a cousin Mayar. Who are you?

Samar Don't say that now. Don't you want some milk first.

Silence.

Mayar Your room fell off your house? (*All considering this.*) You are all dirty and covered in dust and it's not regular dust. It's bomb dust. And your eyes are big like owls. And scared like owls. It must be the middle of the night. Let's drink milk and sleep. You are very tired. Come in.

Mayar *starts to pull them, first* **Samar**, *and then* **Sara**.

Sarah STOP PULLING US. What are you looking at? We aren't scared. You're scarred. You look like an owl. We are not owls.

Samar I would like milk. I'm so thirsty. I have dust inside me. I feel it. I can hear it.

Sarah   We aren't staying here.

Samar   Why? Why?????? I'm so tired. I'm so thirsty.

Mayar *runs to bring water and tissues.*

Mayar   Drink. And wipe your faces. (*Neither does.*) Come in. It's nice here. And we want to help. Because we are family. And you know we are cousins! We played together at the wedding of Im Basil. You can have whatever you need. That's what the family is for.

Sarah   WE DON'T WANT ANYTHING. (*To* **Samar**.) I want to go home. Father is there and Mahmoud and the baby and my mother. I'm not staying here. Where are my sisters? Why are we thrown out?

Samar   We were thrown out? I want to go home. (*Almost crying.*)

Mayar   You weren't thrown out. PLEASE come in. Come in. (**Samar** *and* **Sarah** *are tired. They take a step.*) Another step.

And very slowly, **Mayar** *leads the two girls into her room.*

Scene Four: Dust and Milk

The two girls are so tired that they just stand there as **Mayar** *is busy with tissues and cloths, washing their faces, taking off their coats, their shoes, etc. And talking the whole while.*

Mayar   Of course we played together at the wedding of Im Basil. We played at all the weddings. Maybe you have shock because your house broke. I would have a shock, too. I know what it feels like to have a shock. I had a shock, once. Lift your foot so I can take off your shoe. (*Possible that the girls start helping.*) And here is milk. (*Slowly silently,* **Samar** *and* **Sarah** *drink the milk. They are both relaxed.*)

Samar   Bless you, ya Mayar.

Sarah (*pause*)   What was your shock?

Mayar   What?

Sarah   What was your shock?

Mayar   I don't know but the doctor said I was in a shock. And also my mother. Do you really think your things are scattered all around Gaza?

Samar   One hundred per cent (*But* **Samar** *keeps falling asleep, not sound asleep but she is really very tired. And she wakes when something interests her.*)

Sarah   And the people found our clothing and they are wearing everything. If you found furry boots laying in the street – BRAND NEW – what would you do?

Mayar   I would ask around to see who they belong to.

Sarah   Well not everyone does that. Everyone takes them.

Samar   Do you think someone has Mimi?

Sarah   I think Mimi was blown to bits and is scattered all over the neighbourhood. Mimi has turned to dust. And everyone is breathing her in. Like our room and all the things that were in it.

Samar   No they aren't. You are a mean girl. I'm telling Mother. I want to go home.

Mayar   My cousin, tonight you have to stay here with me and your aunt and your uncle. Look at my nice room. Don't you want to stay here with me for a while. I'm all alone. No other children in the family. And no one is breathing in Mimi. Someone found her and will return her to you. And if not, we find someone else's cat or dog or giraffe or fish and you can take care of that one. That's what God would want you to do.

Samar   When do I see my mother?

Mayar   Tomorrow. Inshallah.

Sarah   And what about Samia, Safa, Saja, Salwa, and Siba?

Mayar   I don't know.

Sarah   We will visit them Friday.

Samar   WHERE ARE THEY?

Sarah   AT THE OTHER COUSINS. TWO IN A HOUSE. And Siba is with Mama.

Samar   And Mahmoud?

Sarah   With Baba. (*Pause.*)

Scene Five: Escape

Sarah (*realization of situation*)   WE HAVE TO LEAVE HERE. And go back home. Even if it's broken, we can fix it. We can help Baba build it. I can't stay here.

Mayar   IT'S THE MIDDLE OF THE NIGHT. And . . . and . . . you have school tomorrow and I didn't give you your clothes. There are a lot of clothes for you.

Sarah   Forget school. Forget clothes. We have to build our house.

Samar   We can't see the clothes. We have no clothes anymore. Look at us. Everything is ripped and dirty.

Sarah   We don't need things. We have to work. We have to find money. And we have to forget about everything else until we get our house back. You cannot be without a house. You cannot be without a house.

Samar   Baba will fix the house. Baba and Mahmoud and the uncles will help and fix the house.

Sarah   NO. We have to stop school and start to work. (*Pause.*) We have no house. We live in Block E house 37/268 and I won't leave it. That's what grandmother said. We have to work.

Samar   Work? What will I work?

Sarah   You will sell gum.

Samar   I WILL NOT SELL GUM. I AM GOING TO SCHOOL. I AM SOOOO TIRED. STOP SAYING THESE THINGS. I AM TIRED. I AM TIRED.

Samar *goes and lays down on one of the mattress and instantly falls sleeps.*

Sarah   I'm leaving. Give me clothes.

Mayar   Sarah, it's late at night. If you want to go I have to tell my father. Why don't you sit and take a rest. Sleep. Go tomorrow.

Sarah   You said you had clothes. Give me them.

Sarah *looks around the room finding dresses and eventually sees the box.*

Sarah   What's this?

Mayar   You can't have that?

Sarah   You said I could have everything. What are these?

Mayar   Boys' clothes.

Sarah   I can wear boys' clothes.

Mayar   NO YOU CANNOT WEAR BOYS' CLOTHES AND YOU CANNOT WEAR THESE.

Sarah   Don't bite me. You said, 'Oh you can have everything, oh I have things for you.' I want to get dressed and go out.

Mayar   I'm calling my father. YABA . . . (*But* **Sarah** *covers her mouth.*)

Sarah   OK. I'm tired. Let's go to sleep.

Sarah *and* **Mayar** *lay down on the mattresses.* **Mayar** *instantly falls asleep.* **Sarah**, *pops up, and silently escapes from the house.*

Mayar (*waking up, a minute later*)   Ya, Samar, your sister ran away.

Samar (*in that state of half sleep*)   Maybe she will find Mimi on the way.

Mayar   I have to tell my father. He will be angry at me. He'll blame me.

Samar (*in that state of half sleep*)   Maybe.

Scene Six: Sarah the Boy

Sarah *reappears at the entrance dressed as a boy.*

Mayar (*shouts with fear at first and then . . .*)   What have you done? Where is your hair? Where is your dress? What is on your head? Whose things are those?

Samar (*jumping with fear*) Do we have to run again?

Sarah I found them! I went outside and found the clothes of someone else's house. It was all neatly folded in the drawer that fell out of another exploded house. The cupboard was nowhere but this drawer was there on the street and the clothes were still folded.

Mayar But you look like a boy.

Sarah So be it. Maybe this boy has found my things and is wearing my dress.

Samar A boy in dresses is not right. The world is upside down. Listen to my heart beating. Everything is upside down. Boom boom boom boom. (*Short pause.*) You woke me up.

Mayar You look very strange. (*Pause.*) You came back.

Sarah No I didn't. I just wanted to show you how I look. I'm leaving. Right now. (*She doesn't.*)

Mayar You are a complicated cousin. It's the middle of the night. Come back into the room. Look at my things. Take anything you want. There are dresses and jeans and sweaters. And shoes. You can have it all. And let's go to sleep.

Samar I can't sleep because my heart is boom boom boom. (*To* **Sarah**.) You broke my heart. I'm telling mother tomorrow.

Sarah I will come in for five minutes but then I'm leaving. I don't want your things. There is plenty of everyone's things all out on the street. And I'm going to help my father fix our house and re-attach our room. And we will live with all of us in our house. I am not an orphan. I have a mother and a father and sisters and a brother and they need me to help.

Mayar But they brought you here.

Samar Yes. They brought us here to be safe. You have to stay. Come in. Sit down. And be quiet or my heart will have an attack like our grandmother. Or a shock.

Sarah *knows she has to stay.* **Samar**'s *words have touched her.*

Scene Seven: Mayar's Room

Mayar Let's sit. This is the best of the mattresses. And it's for Sarah. (*They all sit, maybe* **Samar** *close to* **Sarah**.) And these are my things. (*She takes a small tray filled with objects important to her.*) This is a doll from my uncle and she is called Daisy which is a kind of flower with a yellow middle. I would like you to have her, ya Samar, (*Breath.*) because when my brother Mahmoud was killed Daisy was my only friend. At night she whispers and says 'Sleep' and 'God is great' and 'I love you.' And if you hold her tight you sleep without any bad dreams and when you wake she says, 'Wake up because we have to start the day.' If you hug her, she whispers, 'Thank you.' And this, ya Sarah, is his kufiyah and you can wear it as a boy or a girl.

Scene Seven: Mayar's Room

Samar (*with a tin*)   What's that?

Mayar   Those are biscuits that my mother puts in this box in case I wake up hungry. Now they are for us. Let's see what kind of biscuits she put today and taste them. (*She opens them and shares them.*)

Sarah   And this?

Mayar   This is a photo of my uncle in Mecca. Look, Haj Ahmad has no hair and he is only wearing a sheet. I will make the Haj one day. My father promised me. After I finish school. The whole family will go.

Samar   Do you have a cat?

Sarah   Stop talking about the cat.

Samar   The cat is not dust. Someone found her and stole her from the drawer. And now someone is playing with her and maybe the hat fell off but Mimi isn't dust.

Sarah   Stop talking about Mimi.

Samar   Why is this happening to us?

Mayar   That's what I asked about Mahmoud. Why is this happening to me? It's from God.

Slight pause.

Sarah (*with a nice decorative box*)   What is this?

Mayar (*Pause.*)

Sarah   What?

Samar   What is it? (*Pause.*) Is it a secret in there?

Slight pause.

Sarah   If it's money, we won't steal it.

Samar   Is it money?

Mayar   It's not money.

Samar   What's in it?

Slight pause.

Mayar   It's a box that my grandmother gave me. It's old. My grandmother was also old. And she gave me this box. My grandmother was a good woman but she had many – she called them 'experiences'.

Sarah   Experiences? What kind of experiences? What are you talking about?

Samar   What's an experience?

Mayar   Something that happens. A lot of things happened to her. And she cried a lot.

Samar   Your grandmother cried???

Mayar   And that's why her mother gave her this box. And why she gave it to my mother and why my mother bought another one and gave it to me. It's an 'experience box'. I have one and my mother has one.

Sarah   You are crazy. I never heard of such a box.

Mayar   That's exactly it. This is a box full of stories.

Samar (*enchanted*)   A box full of stories. Let's read them.

Mayar   You can't read them. You can only tell them into the box. And only whispering.

Samar   I don't understand.

Mayar   You whisper your experiences into this box.

Sarah   So how do you remember them? What's in the box? Open it.

Mayar   I will. But you have to listen. You can't talk until it's your turn to talk. You have to be calm. No crying. No yelling. You just talk to it. And no laughing either. It's a game but it's not a game. Shall I open it?

Sarah   I'm not talking to a box.

Mayar   Then we don't open it.

Samar   I will play the game. I will whisper.

Mayar   So we open it. (*She opens the box.*) Hello Box of Experiences. I am Mayar. Today my cousins came because their house broke and their room flew away. At first they were very dusty and hungry but now not. Sarah is going to help her father build their house. And Samar will find a giraffe to take care of. I have invited them to my room to make them happy because their family is not together. I will now give you Samar who will tell you something.

Samar   Hello Box. I am Samar. I never spoke to a box. I lost my cat but I also lost my sisters who now live in the houses of my other aunts and I don't know when I will see them. I miss my mother who is in the broken house. Sarah is with me and she yells sometimes but don't hurt her.

Sarah   Box? Do you REALLY hear me? I am Sarah. I'm a girl even though I dressed up like a boy. Listen box, tonight there was a really loud noise and we fell and when we opened our eyes our room was on the street. Everyone came to help us, and shouting hamdalillah because we all lived. I will help my father fix our house so we can all be together. We lost all our pretty things but Mayar says she will give us her things. It was a really scary night, ya box. Really scary.

Mayar   And now we ask the box 'please remember my experience'.

Samar   Please remember my experience.

Sarah   Please remember my experience.

Mayar   Please remember my experience.

Scene Eight: Mahmoud

Mayar Shall we have biscuits and tea now?

Samar Yes, let's.

Sarah I like your box.

Mayar Me, too.

Sarah We can make one for when we go home.

Samar Mayar?

Mayar What, my cousin.

Samar You are a nice girl. I like you.

Sarah Mayar?

Mayar What, my cousin.

Sarah What's in the box over there?

Mayar Clothing.

Sarah So why can't I open it?

Mayer (*bringing the box. A solemn gesture.*) These are the clothes of my brother Mahmoud. We emptied his drawers and put his things in this box. My mother couldn't do it. Then one day her sister came and they did it together.

Sarah Rest in peace, ya Mahmoud. I didn't play with him a lot. He was older and a boy.

Mayar Oh he was very nice . . . and so clever. He could fix ANYTHING. The electricity, the water, the roof, and he even fixed my doll when her head fell off. And it never fell off again. This is the doll. He would throw me up in the air and then catch me, the way brothers do that. He did that all the time and he never dropped me. (*Pause.*) He called me 'little sister' because I am the youngest. And I loved when he did that. All these things are from him, because he worked.

Sarah Is that your shock? When he was killed?

Mayar Yes. I'm sure, yes. That's when it happened. (*Pause.*) You are my guests and we talk to each other and talk to the box and wear nice dresses. And this box of Mahmoud's clothes . . . we packed it tonight to give to your father to give to your brother Mahmoud. That's how they wanted it.

Sarah We should tell that to the experience box.

Samar And also that we can stay here until our room is attached to the fixed house.

Mayar And that we stayed up very late tonight.

Sarah And that I yelled and even ran away.

Samar   And that I lost my favourite cat Mimi who turned to dust and everyone is breathing her in. She is part of everyone now.

Sarah *and* **Mayar**   Stop talking about the cat! (*And laughter.*)

And continued whispering and laughing and eating until they end up in a huddle where their faces are no longer seen.

End.

Play # 2: The Shop

Characters

Salwa, *oldest sister, engaged, around seventeen to twenty.*
Marwa, *middle sister, aged twelve to fifteen.*
Maryam, *youngest sister, aged six to eight, she's a little girl.*

The scene is one of an exploded market. All merchandise been flung everywhere in every which direction. Whatever has landed on the ground is now in the hands of the stall owner of that space. There are boxes of all sizes and all items that are usually found in the market. It is chaos in every colour.

We will use a dirty white stage cloth. We will use a thick line of pink chalk around the stage cloth and to define spaces. The stage is filled with a combination of pieces of broken buildings that will later be used as market stands of different heights and sizes. Examples: a cement block can be used as a tiny sales counter, a broken table can be used as another for other wares, but we are going to build four or five various market stands by the end of the play.

The girls are wearing cleaning clothing. They know they are going to a dirty broken place so they wear whatever they can find at home that they don't care about. Maybe a brother's old shirt, or a rag skirt. Funny cleaning clothing. When they enter, these outfits are hidden by the regular long black abayas or black cloth coats.

Salwa *is carrying a video camera. And* **Marwa** *has a tripod and* **Maryam** *has a little microphone.*

Scene One: The Shop – Before

The girls arrive from the back. Or they are there, depending on if this is an outside show or in the theatre.

Marwa   WHAT A MESS!

Salwa   What were you expecting?

Marwa   A mess.

Maryam   Where are we?

Marwa   At the shop.

Maryam   This is our shop? Where did our shop go?

Marwa   Up. And then it all came down.

Maryam (*looking up and then down and around*)   And it went in all directions. (*Short pause.*) Maybe it crossed over the border. Maybe it's in Canada.

Marwa   What do you know about Canada.

Maryam   All the older girls in schools are talking about Canada. It's (*pointing far*) theeeeeeere. Far.

Salwa   Enough silly talk. Let's get started. Marwa, put the camera stand here.

Marwa *sets up the tripod. They are not one hundred per cent sure but they figure it out because they are clever.*

Maryam   I hope it stands.

Salwa   Let me attach the camera.

Maryam   Whose is that? Where did you get that?

Salwa   From Yussef. He lent it to me. (*Stops for a sad sigh.*) Give me the microphone.

Maryam   Which is that?

Marwa   Ya Salwa, don't worry. There will be a wedding.

Maryam   What's a microphone?

Salwa   With Babba wounded and mother running from hospitals and houses to visit the wounded and the sad. How? When?

Maryam   What's a microphone?

Marwa   God will solve it.

Maryam   WHAT'S A MICROPHONE? (*It's a working mic.*) Oh, so that's a microphone.

Marwa   Turn on the camera.

Salwa   Stand in the middle. One, two, three. OK, it's on.

All three start talking at the same time, shouting hellos and yelling that the shop is gone.

Salwa   LET ME SPEAK. (*Short stop.*) Hello Father. We saw how tired you were so we decided to leave the hospital but we will come back tonight. We hope you are feeling better.

Maryam   Because you were very sad this morning and we don't want you sad.

Salwa   We borrowed this camera from my groom so we can show you the shop. And we are going to see what the damages are and what we can do here.

Marwa   Hello Yabba. How are you? Feeling better? We are going to make you this video because we can't sit around doing nothing. We want to help you with our shop.

Maryam   Yabba, we put on cleaning clothes so we wouldn't ruin our school clothes. Look.

And here they open the abbayes and we see the funny cleaning clothes they are wearing.

Marwa (*to the camera*)   Yabba, this is the shop how it looks now.

Salwa   You see that all the merchandise from all the nearby shops got mixed up and a lot of it is ruined, broken, and some of it completely destroyed.

Maryam   And some of it went to Canada.

Salwa (*angry*)   Enough Canada.

Maryam (*to the camera*)   Yabba, Salwa is yelling at me. She is sad that she won't have the wedding. We will have the wedding, right, because Marwa said God would solve it. I love you, Babba, come home soon. (*To Salwa.*) Your turn.

Salwa (*to the camera*)   So here is the shop and we are going to fix it and you can watch.

Marwa   Like a film. Let's start.

And from here, they are more in the play than the video, but talking to the video.

Marwa   This is the shop. My grandfather made it and filled it with whatever the people needed. We sold all kinds of things. All three of us came to the shop to help. Even Maryam.

Maryam   I would count things and when I got to twenty-four I would put them aside and start another pile again from one. It's my system.

Salwa   And now it's completely destroyed and there is no explanation for it. Planes came and bombed the houses, the schools, the shops, and then they stopped. And they didn't tell us why they started or why they stopped.

Maryam   Another strange system. They ruined our shop. And now there is nothing to count.

Maryam   We sold eevveerryytthhiinngg . . . eevveerryytthhiinngg!

Scene Two: Introducing the Family

This can all be to the camera and audience. Or both.

Salwa   My father runs the shop. Everyone knows Abu Yahya.

Maryam   That's you, Yabba.

Marwa   His moustache goes like this.

Maryam   My mother is tall. No moustache.

Salwa   Quiet.

Maryam   Called Im Yahya.

Marwa   And we are three girls.

Maryam   Us.

Salwa   And six boys. Two killed in war.

All Three   Rest in peace.

Marwa   Yahya got married last summer.

Maryam   We have a new baby.

Salwa   They wanted to call him Marwan.

Maryam   After our brother.

Salwa   But it came out a girl.

Marwa   So she is called Marwa. Like me.

Maryam   I am called Maryam except my mother calls me Mimi and Yamma or Pain-in-the-neck.

Salwa   I am Salwa. And I am engaged to be married but we might have to postpone it.

Marwa   It will happen. It will happen.

Maryam   Welcome.

Scene Three: Cleaning

From here, they are busy with the shop. This scene of the cleaning is both playful and sad, with **Salwa** *realizing all that has been lost,* **Marwa** *trying to understand how to help, and* **Maryam** *curious and a bit scared.*

Salwa   We have to start to clean it or the rats will come.

Maryam   Which one is the rat?

Marwa   It's the giant mouse with the long tail and the long teeth and if it bites you then you die right there on the street.

Maryam   Yabba, you tell us if you see a rat coming. OK.

Salwa   We have no rats. They were bombed to death. (*Taking something.*) We can use this as a broom.

Marwa   Here is a rag.

Maryam   That was my blanket! What happened to it?

Salwa   It stopped being a blanket. Now it's time for cleaning.

Maryam   It's a very strange piece for cleaning.

Marwa   Look for something that can be a bucket.

Maryam   What's wrong with our bucket?

Salwa   It's broken. Use this tin can for a bucket.

Maryam   Everything is something different. It's like a game.

Marwa   It's not a game.

Maryam   It is. This is not a blanket and that's not a bucket.

Scene Three: Cleaning

Salwa Keep looking.

Maryam (*taking something that isn't a sponge*) So this is a sponge.

Marwa That's the idea. Now try to find something that actually sucks up water.

Maryam What a mess they made. Look. All these houses are the same. The shops are all like ours. The vegetables are mixed with the t-shirts. The t-shirt can be a sponge. Yabba, look, the t-shirt is a sponge.

Marwa And the yarn shop is mixed with the suitcase shop. Everything is mixed up with everything else. All the yarn is ruined. Whose yarn is this?

Salwa Abu Ali's. Or Abu Sleiman's. Or Abu Mohammed. They all sold yarn next to each other.

Maryam Yabba, it's a big mess. Why did they have to make such a mess?

Salwa The broom is working. It's moving the mess.

Marwa Don't touch anything that looks dangerous.

Maryam I found a lollipop.

Salwa *and* **Marwa** Don't eat it.

Salwa Yabba, we hope you are feeling better as you watch this. Did Yussef come visit you? He said he would come with the family. Some of them are wounded but hamdalillah they are fine. And they send their regards Yabba.

Marwa If you see my mother tell her not to come because it's no good for her. It's too dirty and she still has a cold.

Maryam She has a cold for a year.

Marwa What should we do with the boxes?

Salwa The garbage goes here, make a pile, and the boxes go here so we can open them and see what's inside.

Maryam I will count each box to twenty-four.

Salwa We don't know what's in them.

Marwa Let's find out.

Maryam What box is this? Where are our boxes?

Marwa Someone else is opening them.

Salwa MY WEDDING THINGS WERE IN THE SHOP. I PUT THEM THERE FOR SAFETY. (*To camera.*) I'm sorry for shouting Yabba. I just remembered that everything we bought for the wedding was in the shop. And now someone else is opening it.

Maryam I can go look for them. Yabba, can I go look for them?

Scene Four: The Boxes

As they have been cleaning and moving things, they are making some order in which there are places to put things; they make a pile of items that are possible to sell. At some point, they have collected the closed boxes and have put them near each other.

Salwa   And now to the boxes.

Maryam   NO.

Salwa   Why not. We have to open them and clean this up. We can't just throw them.

Maryam   It's a bomb or a rat. Yabba, I'm not opening them.

Marwa   She's not wrong. How do we know what's inside. That it's safe.

Salwa   WAIT. There's a way. Look. I know this box. It was delivered the morning we closed the shop. It's from Waleed and Brothers. I signed for it. We can open it.

Marwa   What do you think's inside of it.

Salwa   Plenty of stuff. When he made the order, Father had told him to put a little of everything in it, just in case. (*To camera.*) Remember Yabba. We did it together.

Maryam   I think someone is hiding inside . . . from the bombs.

Marwa   Quiet.

Salwa   No one is hiding in there.

Maryam   How do you know?

Salwa   I know. It's a box. I know.

Marwa   Wait. (*Pause.*) People are looking at us.

Salwa   So what.

Marwa   What will the people say if they see us like this?

Salwa   That we are cleaning up. Like everyone else. Cleaning up from this huge mess that came out of the sky and took whatever we had. I don't want to talk anymore.

Maryam (*shouting*)   WE ARE FIXING THE SHOP FOR MY FATHER. (*Pointing to the video.*) AND HERE HE IS. AND HE CAN SEE YOU.

Salwa   Now this is how we're going to do it. Everyone go find a stick or broom handle or a long piece of wood. Anything strong.

Each sister finds something.

Salwa   We go box by box. We start with this one that I know. And we bang on it. If anything is alive in there, we will know.

Maryam   How?

Salwa Either it will run out the bottom or scream.

Maryam I want to go home.

Marwa I want to hit the box. Yabba, it's a good idea right? (*And* **Marwa** *hits the first box and then they stand silently and wait for a second.*) Nothing came out and nothing screamed. Let's open it.

Salwa Yabba, this is the first box.

Maryam *goes and covers herself with another piece of fabric or puts something on her head for security or maybe finds an empty box and puts it on her head. She is a bit scared.*

They open the box and dump out the stuff.

The things in the box are dirty or broken. They come from a shop that is a stationary/school supply shop with small relevant toys, gifts, and such.

Maryam (*looking*) Everything is horrible. Look Yabba.

Marwa (*looking*) Is it all ruined?

Salwa (*looking*) I don't think so. Yabba, you can see that we have a mess here.

Maryam A doll.

Salwa Wait. Let me look and let me think. Yabba, we are going to open the next box and if nothing runs or screams we will open them all.

Marwa *immediately begins to knock on the boxes.* **Salwa** *joins her. Also knocking. As each box is emptied . . .*

Maryam (*close to boxes to show her father the video*) Nothing ran and nothing screamed!

Scene Five: Fixing the Shop

There is a big pile of different kinds of things on stage. Shirts, shib-shibs, plastic flowers, nightgowns, pots, kitchen things, towels, clothing of several kinds. Depends on how many boxes you use. Coffee pots, clocks, books. Whatever is CHEAP. Empty cleaning bottles that we can fill with water. Empty cookie boxes that we can fill with newspapers, we need a collection of things. Also some of the stuff is dirty and we will have bottles of water on stage to wash a few small dirty things.

Maryam Yabba, it's all terrible. Nothing is beautiful. I'm closing my nose and my eyes and even my ears.

Salwa And also your mouth. Maryam, there is nothing here to hurt you.

Marwa And if there is, we will rescue you. Come on, we have to fix the shop. Babba is watching and he won't love you if he sees you being afraid. (*Pause.*) OPEN YOUR EYES.

No reaction from **Maryam**.

Marwa (*swinging plastic leaves over her head*)   I am the souk genie and you are mine now.

Maryam (*opening her eyes*)   There is no souk genie. (*Looking at the pile.*) Hey, look, a doll. It's mine.

Salwa   Nothing is yours. It's all for the shop.

Maryam   Yabba. . . .

Marwa   Stop bothering him. Let's start sorting this stuff.

Phone rings.

Salwa (*on phone*)   Hello. (*To the sisters.*) It's Yussef. (*On phone.*) Yes, we set it up. And it seems to be working. (*Listening.*) The red light is on. (*Listening*) We found it a complete mess but we have started to clean. And we just opened boxes. (*Listening.*) NO. I mean no you don't have to come. We can do it. (*Listening.*) Really you shouldn't come. Go visit the hospital. We are fine. Bye. (*She closes the phone quickly.*) IMAGINE HE COMES AND SEES ME LIKE THIS?

Maryam   Yabba, Yusseff called Salwa and wanted to come but she said no.

Salwa   Start sorting this stuff. Everything that can be washed, wash using the water in the bottles. No other water.

Marwa   And everything that can be fixed, we fix. There is all kinds of stuff here that can be fixed.

Maryam   What do I do? There is twenty-four of nothing.

Salwa   Right now you are going to grow up. You hear me. You are going to do what we do. You are going to help us get this shop in order.

Marwa   Because you want Babba to be proud of you and you want to help with the shop and the money.

Maryam   Yabba, I'm going to save you. Watch. I'm growing up now.

As they work.

Salwa   Anything of glass be very careful. Wrap your hands if you can. If it's broken put it on the side. BE CAREFUL AND DON'T GET HURT. If it's in one piece put it here with all things that are in one piece. Keep things together.

Marwa   So this dress is OK. I put it here. This is the dress department.

Maryam   Here is the head of a doll. And two legs. And here is the whole doll. All here are the doll's parts. I can fix it. (*Even though they are not the same doll, she finds a way to make one complete doll out of the pieces she has.*)

Salwa   Yabba, I think this is the best way to do it. I can wash these socks and make three pairs together. We can sell them again because they really are new. Just bombed. (*And she washes them. And puts them somewhere to dry.*)

Marwa (*shaking a small box*)   Listen. I think these are pencils. They sound just like pencils. We can open them and sell them just as they are. And there are a lot. (*Searching.*) And here are pens. Yabba, look, we have some things to sell.

By now the situation is like this: the pieces of the shop and the broken furniture have become small market stands and surfaces where they can place all the stuff they are sorting. Slowly it begins to look like a funny little shop with piles of this and that. Not a ton of stuff, but enough to make it look like a little shop that sells a few of everything. From shoes, to bags, make-up, dolls, bedding, all of it. We don't need a whole lot of text all the time but as they make or fix things they can comment. 'I finished another one.' 'This is in one piece. I just need to clean it a little.' 'I made another doll but it's a very strange one.' 'This is in perfect condition.' 'Yabba, what is this? I have never seen this. I will put it on the side.' Regarding the song below, it would be nice if were a song. Composer?

> It's just a fine day in our neighbourhood
> All the good people are preparing for the feast.
> The women are sewing and washing and cooking
> The men are hunting and shopping and fishing
> And soon the feast will come and all will be pretty and all will be fine.

> It's just a fine day in our neighbourhood
> All the good people are visiting the elders
> The women bring fruits and good sweets and new clothing
> The men bring the gold that twinkles in the sun
> And soon the feast will come and all will be pretty and all will be fine.

> It's just a fine day in our neighbourhood
> All of the children are happy and are safe
> The boys are learning and trying and the football is flying
> The girls are singing and clapping while watching their mothers
> And soon the feast will come and all will be pretty and all will be fine.

Maryam (*with a box*)   I think this box has a music box in it with a lady dancing in a circle like this. (*Does what the ballerina does inside a music box.*) There are six of them in here. All working. (*So she does six ballerinas.*)

Salwa   If you fall, you get a hit.

Maryam   WHY???

Salwa   I don't want you getting hurt.

Maryam   But if I fall, I'm already hurt.

Salwa   Yabba, what do I do with her?

Marwa   This box is empty. I wonder what was in it? Well, at least we have a box. It's not a very good one but we can use it.

The shop is as ready as it can be.

Scene Six: The Shop – After

The girls look at the work they have done.

Salwa   This is all we have?

Maryam   The shop came back.

Salwa   I would hardly call it a shop.

Marwa   It's almost a shop.

Marwa   Yabba, look. We made almost a shop. When everyone is back from the hospital and the clinic, we will fix it better.

Maryam *has been walking about looking at all the things. At one moment she sees a big box or bag or package.*

Maryam   There's another box.

Marwa   I'll bring it. Don't touch it. (**Marwa** *brings it to the stage and starts to hit it with a stick.*)

Salwa (*seeing the box*)   STOP. STOP HITTING IT.

Maryam (*scared*)   YAAABBBBAAAA.

Salwa   QUIET.

Short silence.

Marwa   What's the matter, ya Salwa? What is it?

Salwa   Don't touch it. (*She goes to it.*) This is MY box. These are the things I bought for the wedding. I hope nothing is ruined.

Marwa   Let's open it.

Maryam   Yabba, are you seeing this?

Salwa *opens the box and it contains her wedding dress, veil, and all that is included.*

Marwa   I told you God would solve it.

Maryam   And He did. Are you happy?

Salwa (*totally mixed up*)   Happy? Look at this shop! I'm happy for me but what about Babba? There is still the problem of the shop. And of all the relatives in the hospital. And all who died. And the wedding! How can I be happy when the world is like this?

Marwa   That's true. But Babba and Mamma will choose the appropriate time for you to marry Yussef and there will be a wedding. AND there will be a shop.

Marwa   Don't worry. Life goes on. Right?

Maryam (*who is holding one of the fixed dolls*)   Look at this new doll. I made it. I'm going to call her WaWa because she has a wound and all of us get wawas. And I will give her to the new baby Marwa.

Salwa   Give her? We will sell her. She's beautiful.

Marwa   Look, customers are coming towards us.

Maryam   How do you know they are customers?

Salwa   Because that's what a customer looks like, right Yabba? They are coming to buy.

Marwa   Babba, we have to go now and serve the customers. We will keep the money in the empty box and bring it to you in the hospital tonight. Say hello to uncle Musa, and uncle Fathi, and aunt Sana, and my cousin Maysa, and my cousin Ahmad, and to my mother give her a big hug and tell her if she has time to come to the shop.

Maryam   Yabba, I fixed a doll. Did you see? I have to go serve the customers. But the money is with Salwa.

Salwa   We hope you agree with what we have done and shown you on this video, and we will see you tonight.

Marwa   And feel good, Babba. Get better fast.

Maryam   God keep you.

End with the song if you like.

End.

Play #3: The School

Characters

Ala, *youngest.*
Sleiman, *older.*
Jaber, *we don't know, but the oldest.*

A place where there used to be a school. Maybe a wall of the school itself. There are pieces of the broken school around: parts of a bench, desk, green board, cupboard, wall, door, wires, broken building stuff, books, papers, files. The needs of the boys are in the set, except for what they specifically bring. A dirty white stage cloth (so we can use chalk on it).

Scene One: Prologue (totally optional)

Actor playing Ala   Hello everyone. Welcome. Is everyone comfortable? Can everyone see? (*Maybe some rearranging?*)

Actor playing Sleiman   Has anyone here ever seen a play. Raise your hand if you saw a play before today. (*He counts them. There are a few, or none, or noise. Deal with it.*)

Actor playing Jaber   We are going to show a play today so those who never saw one will see what it is and those who already saw one will see another one. It's all good.

Actor playing Ala   How it works is like this. I'm going to play a little boy called Ala. My real name is (*says real first name*) but in the play I am little Ala.

Actor playing Sleiman   And my real name is (*says first name*) but I am playing a boy called Sleiman. He is a bit older than Sleiman.

Actor playing Jaber   And me, my real name is (*says first name*) and in the play I will be a boy called Jaber. Is anyone here called Jaber? Raise your hands. And what about Sleiman, anyone called Sleiman? And where are the ones called Ala?

Actor playing Ala   When we count to three, you shout your name so we hear who we have here. ONE.

Actor playing Sleiman   TWO.

Actor playing Jaber   THREE.

And then calm them down again.

Actor playing Sleiman   Everyone quiet because we have one more thing to tell you before we start.

Actor playing Ala   It's important.

Actor playing Jaber   Ala, and Sleiman, and Jaber don't see you. They don't know you are here. They think they are alone. So they aren't going to talk to you. And there's nothing we can do about it. It's a little bit like they are in a dream world.

Actor play Ala   We see you again later, at the end. And then we'll talk. (*Music.*) Listen.

Actor playing Sleiman   The play is starting.

Note: Music has to set the whole thing up to shut the kids up if needed.

Scene Two: Ala

Ala *has a song that he will use in the play. Sometimes humming, sometimes singing parts of it, sometimes singing it all. It should be a good popular song, familiar but not one that everyone knows. Not rap. A good song that he likes that he learned about from his father who also likes music. Director's choice.*

Ala (*walking on stage from the back and singing his song in a low voice. Reaching the school/stage*) MY MOTHER SAID, 'GO TO SCHOOL' but the news said, 'NO SCHOOL TODAY.' My brother said, 'GO SEE', and the neighbours asked, 'HEY, ALA, WHERE ARE YOU GOING?' and I answered, 'TO SCHOOL', and they laughed at me. Then the man sweeping the street said, 'HEY KID, WHERE DO YOU THINK YOU'RE GOING?' and I said, 'SCHOOL' and he also laughed and said, 'GO HOME.' But my mother said, 'GO TO SCHOOL' and my brother said, 'GO SEE.' So here I am at school and no one seems to be here. (*Annoyed.*) I'm not going back home because there is so much noise there I can't even think. Everyone is home and all the relatives are coming to visit the broken leg of my father. It's a big story that he broke his leg jumping from the window. He thought the rocket was coming. But it landed one house over. He was alone in the house or we all would have had broken legs. We had to buy a lot of sweets for those guests. My mother worried that we wouldn't have enough sweets. It's a lot of work. But hamdalillah my father's leg has visitors. (*Pause with humming his song.*) Hello school. What happened to you? You are broken in a few places. Like my father. (*Looking and not quite knowing what he should do.*) Not even the teacher came. The news said, 'NO SCHOOL TODAY' so that's what everyone did. But you never know. (*Sees a piece of the green board.*) I guess this is where the teacher used to stand. Here. Like this. And the teacher knows everything. EXCEPT WHEN THERE'S NO SCHOOL. Sometimes when I'm sitting in my seat – where is my seat – it must be around here. (*Indicates some place and sits.*) (*Pause. Smile. Starts his song . . .*) When I'm sitting here watching the teacher, I think, 'Ala, what do you want to be when you finish with all this school?' And every time I come up with the same answer. I want to be a singer. (*Takes place of teacher.*) One, two, one, two, three. (*And he starts to sing his song. Let him sing.*)

Scene Three: Sleiman

A second boy can be seen coming from afar and we can see reactions as he hears this singing. He is somewhat concerned.

Sleiman   HEY, what are you doing?

Ala   Singing!

Sleiman   WHY?

Ala   Because I like singing and the teacher isn't here and no other student is here. Except now you're here.

Sleiman   We're the only two who came?

Ala What did you hear on the news? School or No School? And I'm Ala. What's your name?

Sleiman Sleiman. I heard 'School.' And boy was I glad. I was getting so bored at home. And I need my lessons. I have to pass.

Ala We're the opposite of boring. My father broke his leg. So, do you like singing?

Sleiman Me? Singing. I don't know. I never did it. I like history.

Ala I don't like history. Everyone's always fighting. First by fist, then with biting dogs, then on the horse and the knight, AND THEN came the guns and the planes and soon the tanks and afterwards the F16s and now . . . now the ones with remote control so no one knows who's fighting who with what.

Sleiman History is not only wars. Though there are plenty. For me, history is the big story of what's going on. History is the whole story that explains everything that happened and how we got like we got.

Ala The whole story? I like stories. Sindebad. Alla Eddin. Ali Baba. Shatar Hassan. Spiderman. (*Stop.*) You know where else you find stories? IN SONGS. Listen. (*He sings a good part of his song where there is some fitting content.*) You hear. Another kind of story.

Sleiman I never thought of it that way.

Ala Well, I'm going to be a singer when I finish school.

Sleiman A singer!!! And you'll get famous?

Ala I'll sing all the songs that I like. I hear a lot of them. My father likes songs. He also sings. But now, with his broken leg, he's shouting. Sometimes shouting singing. (*Singing.*) Ya woman make tea, ya woman bring the lunch, ya woman do the coffee, ya woman who broke my heart and then broke my leg . . .!

Sleiman That's funny. (*Short stop.*) I'm going to be a doctor of history. That's an expert. On the university level. Inshallah. I will study Gaza. From the beginning of time. You know that Gaza is very very old. Among the first civilizations. The most occupied piece of land in the world. It's famous.

Ala Gaza is famous. Good. Because then a famous singer will come out of a famous place.

Sleiman And if my book is published, then both of us will be famous Gazans.

Ala *sings a little more of his song.*

Sleiman Nice . . . (*Pause. He interrupts the singing.*) You know that history is just the news . . . but from different times.

Ala Yeah, that story will make you famous!!! You'll get thrown out of school.

Sleiman Listen: every day you hear the news, right? Mankind always wants to know what's new so from the very beginning there's been news. It started with a guy running around listening to what was going on and then running again to tell everyone.

Ala   You know you're a crazy fellow, right?

Sleiman   And then he got another guy to help so now he was listening and telling the other guy who told everyone else. This way the whole village knew the news in one day because there were two guys running. And when the caravans started, they got another guy who went with them. And when the caravans came back, they started running again to share the news. And soon they built the boats so new guys boarded the boats and went to other places and during the trip they told the news to other guys on the boats and other guys who got on the boats told them their own news. When the boats came back there was so much to tell that more guys had to start running. And if a boat sank, we lost a lot of news and we had to start all over again going back on another boat to the same place. Then of course they invented the train and all of a sudden there were loads of these guys coming and going and telling everyone what was going on everywhere so that everyone knew. You can imagine what happened when the cars came and the airplanes came and we have thousands of guys all over the place, even up in satellites, telling all the other guys what's happening so everyone knows everything that's going on everywhere. And sometimes a guy lied and we had two versions of the news. And sometimes a guy forgot stuff.

Ala   What happened then?

Sleiman   We lost the news. Or we got two versions of the news. Sometimes three.

Ala   And this is history?

Sleiman   EXACTLY. Old news is history. Can you sing a song about that?

Ala (*thinking about it*)   Whether a guy lied, died, or didn't tell a guy???

Sleiman   Yes my friend, that's history and that's why I like it. To figure out who told who what when.

Ala   So the explosion that broke our school is history?

Sleiman   You got it.

Ala   And no one came today because a guy didn't tell a guy.

Sleiman   Or two guys told two different stories. And that's why I came. Too many stories. Too much history. It seems as if you and I and the only ones who missed a guy. (*Pause.*) It's happening very fast. There are too many guys running. And too many of them are liars. That's another reason I want to study history. To catch the liars.

Ala   Wow. You are one weird kid. Listen, man, I'm gonna be a singer. That's news. Go run.

Sleiman   It doesn't work like that. It has to be important. And now there's a club of guys who decide what's important. And your singing, it's not important for those guys. It goes very fast. You have to catch it the minute it happens or it doesn't become history.

Ala   You're smart.

Sleiman   I guess everyone knows the school got blown up but no one knows where we should go instead. Someone's not running.

Scene Four: Singing

Ala   I like your story. Do you want to sing with me?

Sleiman   I don't know how.

Ala   Everyone knows how to sing. You just open your mouth and go (*singing*) aaaahhhhhhhh and eeeeeeee and that's singing. Maybe one day, you'll be singing history.

Sleiman   I'll try. (*He does it but it's all off key and sounds like a cat.*)

Ala   Yup. That's singing.

Sleiman   It doesn't sound too good.

Ala   It doesn't matter. The idea is not to be afraid. Just to do (*singing*) ahhhhhh and eeeeeeh. Because it feels really good. And then one day you find out that you can do it and you know a song and you sing. Let's do it together. One, two, one, two, three.

They sing.

Ala   Nice.

Sleiman   Nice?

Ala   Nice!

Neither knows how to continue.

Ala   So history is old news?

Sleiman   We live in strange times.

Ala (*pause*)   A guy didn't tell a guy and school closes.

Sleiman   Yup.

Ala   And then it's history?

Sleiman   Yup.

Ala   Wow.

Scene Five: School Starts

Ala   What should we do now? I absolutely cannot go back home. Every minute is a new visitor to see my father's leg. Everyone talking at the same time. Bringing food.

My mother is making me run here and there for stuff for the guests. I can't sing. I can't listen to music. It's like a hospital in the house. His leg is hanging on a rope from the ceiling. I can't go home now.

Sleiman   Me either. And the news said it was a school day. I heard it with these two ears.

Ala (*pause*)   What else do you know?

Sleiman   I know how to build a wall. Do you know how to build a wall?

Ala   Yup. I learned when our kitchen blew up. That was news! All the guys were telling all the guys all day long. But now it's history.

Ala   Do you know how to fight?

Sleiman   What do you mean? Like beating a guy up?

Ala   Yup.

Sleiman   Yeah, I know how to beat a guy up.

Ala   How come? Who's bothering you?

Sleiman   The neighbours. I walk by and they punch me and I punch them and that's how my day starts. Every day. The minute I leave the door . . . they are waiting. Sometimes they win. Sometimes I win.

Ala   Teach me.

Sleiman   You're asking a doctor of history to teach you how to beat up a guy?

Ala   Yup.

Sleiman   OK. We have nothing better to do and every kid should know how to defend himself.

They get into position for a fighting lesson. And **Sleiman** *and* **Ala** *work together.*

Sleiman   First you start hopping with your feet, like this, so they don't know where you are. The faster you hop around the more you confuse them. (*They are hopping around.*) Stop. Now. These are your hands . . . and this is two fists. And you start swinging them. All over the place. (*Both swing fisted hands and arms. Funny.*) Now here comes the hard part. You do both together. Hop and swing and hop and swing and hop and swing. And then, when you see the whites of the eyes of your enemy you aim straight for it and POW. (*And they stay moving and hopping and swinging.*)

Ala   OK, now you're my enemy.

Sleiman   OK.

Ala   And here we go. (*And they hop around swinging for a while until* **Ala** *punches* **Sleiman** *who is quite surprised and he falls to the ground.*) I DID IT. (*Seeing* **Sleiman**.) Hey man, are you OK? Sleiman, get up. Come on man, it wasn't that hard.

Sleiman (*from the ground. Mildly wounded*)   You're a natural talent. But be careful because if they get you first, if they get you first you're gonna lose all your teeth.

Ala   My grandfather lost all his teeth. But he sure can eat. I don't know how he does it. And he hits also. Come on, get up.

Jaber *enters from afar.*

Scene Six: Jaber

Jaber (*from afar*)   I SAW THE WHOLE THING. STOP FIGHTING. NO FIGHTING. FIGHTING IS NOT ALLOWED. (*He gets closer.*) Stop fighting this minute. What are you fighting about? Where is the teacher? Where are the students? (*Short stop.*) Where is the school? They announced that school has started. I came running but everyone stopped me on the way. 'Where are you running?' they asked. 'School is open,' I answered but they just laughed at me. (*Stop.*) Explain now. Why are you two fighting? And I'm not taking sides. I don't know how it started and I don't know you and I don't know you. I'm just here to study and go home. So stop fighting. YOU HEAR ME.

Ala   YEAH WE HEAR YOU. THE WHOLE NEIGHBOURHOOD HEARD YOU.

Sleiman   We weren't fighting.

Jaber   I saw fighting. I saw what I saw. This is a school. Well, it was a school. You can't fight in the courtyard. This is the courtyard right? Or is this class? Where is the school? How can there be school today if there isn't a school? Is the teacher here? Answer.

Ala   Hey, take a breath. Say . . . (*Singing.*) Ahhhhhh.

Sleiman   No one came today.

Ala (*insisting*)   Ahhhhhhh. DO IT.

Sleiman   A guy didn't run right.

Ala   Ahhhhhhhhhhhhh.

Jaber   What guy? (*And then . . .*) Ahhhhhhhhhhhhhhhhhhhhhhhhhhh.

Sleiman   Ahhhhhhhhhhhhhh. (*Silent second.*) (*To* **Jaber**.) Why did you come to school today?

Jaber   The news said it was a school day.

Sleiman   But you're late.

Jaber   I'm usually never late. Never ever. But the news kept changing and by the time I heard that school was open it was late. By the time I was dressed, the news had changed. I decided that it was better to come and see for myself than to stay home.

Sleiman   Now two guys are running in opposite directions.

Ala   Or when two guys say opposite things. I'm starting to understand.

Jaber   I came to school and you came to school and you too so school is open. We will have our lessons. I can't miss a day. Everyone has to sit down. We will wait two minutes, here is the watch, and if no teacher comes, I will blow this whistle and school will start. And we will study. No one will talk and NO ONE WILL FIGHT. Anyone who makes trouble will go the headmaster. Tomorrow. But we can't miss a day of school when school is open.

Silence. Suddenly **Jaber** *takes his whistle from around his neck and blows it. More silence. Or deafness. In this silence waiting for 'school to start'* **Ala** *and* **Sleiman** *are plotting something in whispers as* **Jaber** *arranges his books on his lap and on the junk next to him in the set. When he is done,* **Jaber** *looks at his watch, sees it is two minutes, and again blows the whistle.* **Ala** *and* **Sleiman** *are ready now.* **Ala** *goes to the front of the class.*

Scene Seven: History Lesson

Ala   Students, turn to page thirty of your history lessons.

Jaber (*raising his hand*)   Teacher, I don't have my history book. Should I go home and get it, I can run, and be back in five minutes.

Ala   NO. You may share the book with Sleiman. Today we will study the History of Yesterday. You are all familiar with this historical time? (**Jaber** *raises his hand.*) No questions at this time. The student Sleiman will begin.

Sleiman   The History of Yesterday by the Student Sleiman. I woke up and wasn't sure if it was safe to go out. I asked a few people but no one knew so we went to the television. The television has been on since the year 2000. The whole family sat together eating breakfast and listening to 106 new news stations. We heard that we should stay inside. Then we had lunch. And then we all went to sleep for a while. I played football in the room until my father shouted that this is no time for football when the world is falling apart. Afterwards we watched the 106 stations again and still didn't learn anything new except that there was an earthquake in China and we said, 'Ya Haram' because 300,000 died. Then my mother started crying and crying because she was cutting onions for a big meal that we ate because we were all very hungry. Then we watched a series. Police caught spies and women fell in love. We drank tea and ate biscuits and watched two films. One made us laugh and one made us sleep. So we slept. All eight of us. And that is my History of Yesterday.

Ala   Very good. JABER. Your turn. Come to the front of the class.

Jaber   THE HISTORY OF YESTERDAY BY THE STUDENT JABER. I woke up at four and prayed. There wasn't any milk so I went to my uncle's house but the house was sleeping. So I went upstairs to my other uncle's house and he said, 'Yes we have milk but where is your father and why don't you have milk for the morning?' I stood there until he finished yelling at me and gave me enough milk to fill half a glass. Back in my house everyone was waking up and yelling that there was no milk and when my brother saw what I had, he took it from me and drank it. Then he gave me three shekels to go to the shop to buy milk, which I did. And when I got back everyone was dressed and waiting for me. They took the milk and heated it and some spilled over so my father called all of us 'donkeys'. We are fourteen people so I only had half a glass of milk but it was very good. Outside was a pile of garbage from all the broken things that my mother and sisters threw away after they got ruined from the hole in the house. So me and my brother Ahmad, we had to put it in piles and tie it in packages that we could carry and bring them to the place where they said we could throw our broken houses and all our broken things. It was on the other side of the fish market past the port. As we walked, we heard the news from inside the houses and they said that we should NOT be outside. We got scared, me and Ahmad, so we put down the packages in a pile and sat behind them next to a house where we could hear the news. And like my fellow student Sleiman, we also heard 106 news stations saying that we should not be out here. Ahmad started to cry. I went to a house where a lady looked kind and asked her if she could talk to my brother Ahmad and maybe let us sit near her. But she only said WHY ARE YOU OUTSIDE, WHERE IS YOUR MOTHER? GO HOME. I got angry but I had to hold Ahmad's hand or he would die. I love Ahmad so I held his hand. Then we got hungry. This was really a big problem. So I decided to use all of my brains and step by step we pushed our first bundle forward while we hid behind it. We pushed and then we hid. We made a barricade of the bundle and then went back to get the next bundle. We passed a bread-shop. I asked the man for a bread but he screamed, 'YOU ARE NOT FROM THIS NEIGHBOURHOOD. GO BACK TO WHERE YOU BELONG.' After five hours we were back home with the packages and my mother and father both said 'YOU ARE GONE HALF A DAY AND YOU COME BACK WITH THE SAME GARBAGE WE SENT YOU TO THROW. HOW STUPID ARE YOU BOTH? AND JABER IS MORE STUPID BECAUSE AHMAD IS IN GRADE ONE.' I tried to explain but neither would listen. I asked where the lunch was but since we are fourteen people, it was already gone. There was just one bread left and they gave it to Ahmad and he wouldn't share it with me because he said I was a bad brother and made him cry. I went back up to my uncle to see if they were still eating and they were but no one said, 'Come, eat' so I went to my other uncle upstairs and I just looked at his face and decided to leave before anyone said anything. I walked to the shops next to our house and asked Abu Ihab if I could move some of his boxes to the top floor in exchange for a sandwich. And here I was lucky because he said yes. I moved maybe fifteen boxes from the first floor to the twelfth floor and then he gave me a sandwich and he even gave me a juice, may God keep and save and protect him. But now it was getting dark and all the generators were on and I hadn't done any studying at all so I took my book, this book, here, and I read. But my eyes were going fuzzy and I thought, 'Oh I'm going blind.' And I got scared. I said, 'Yamma, I think I'm going blind,' but she didn't answer me because everyone was talking but no one was really listening. I washed my face but there was no towel so I used my shirt only there was dust on it from the boxes of Abu Ihad and then I couldn't see anything at all. I sat for a minute blind and covered in dust, until – it was so strange – tears came out of my eyes and washed them clean. I waited for them to dry by themselves and again started to read but again everything went fuzzy. So I said to myself that I will go to sleep and when I wake I will pray and go to school. I prayed and asked God that I'm not blind. I got on the mattress with my three brothers and all night they were pushing me off and pulling the blanket. I also pushed and pulled. But they are three and I am one. When the dawn came, I could see, and I thanked God. And that's the History of Yesterday by the Student Jaber. (*And he sits back down.*)

Scene Eight: Recess

In total silence. Stunned. Then.

Sleiman   It's recess time.

Ala   Yes. It's time for recess.

Jaber   Is it recess already? The time passed quite quickly. Who said it was recess?

Sleiman   Oh it's recess. We had two history lessons. It's definitely recess.

Ala   Right. Two lessons and recess. The time flies when you study hard. Hey, you never told us your name.

Jaber   I did. I am Jaber the Student.

Sleiman   Well nice to meet you Jaber the Student. I am Sleiman the Student. And this one here is Ala the Student.

Sleiman   I'm in the fifth year.

Ala   I'm in the third.

Jaber   I was in fourth but they put me back in the third because there wasn't room in the fourth but then I was too smart for third and since there is no three and half they put me back in third. I went by myself back to fourth where I sat on the floor. I can't make a single mistake in the fourth or I won't move to the fifth and then I have to make it to the sixth. My father said at the end of the sixth I have to stop school and start to work. So I can't miss a day of school or an hour or a lesson. You understand. I have to learn everything to grade six. And then I will work making bricks like my father.

Sleiman   How old are you, ya Jaber the Student. You sound very grown-up.

Jaber   I'm old. Maybe thirteen or fourteen.

Ala   You don't know how old you are?

Jaber   No. Is recess over?

Ala   I understand your rush to get back but recess just started. Let's take out all our lunches out of our bags and we can share them.

Sleiman   Good idea. I have an apple and a sandwich and juice, and a cucumber. Oh, and chips.

Ala   I have a banana, no I have two bananas, no three, my mother probably got confused putting three in one bag. And a sandwich, and a juice, and sweets left over from last night.

Jaber I have water and a half a tomato. I'm lucky for this half. The other half got squashed on my brother's head and he has no snack today. My half is a bit squashed but hamdalillah, it's good to have something to eat.

Sleiman No big deal. We'll share it all.

And they set up some 'tray' of collective food, poor but a feast for **Jaber**. *And they eat and* **Jaber** *is trying not to eat fast as they share the different things. After they eat,* **Jaber** *gets 'stoned' from the combination of food and exhaustion. Of course one banana each. If it's not banana season, one small fruit each, no pits.*

Jaber Recess is over. We have to study.

Jaber *goes back to his seat and starts reading.*

Sleiman (*to* **Ala**) This boy is in a troubled situation.

Ala What should we do?

Sleiman He hasn't eaten well or slept in a long time.

Ala I have an idea (*Announcing.*) SPORTS TIME. ALL STUDENTS TO THE COURTYARD.

Jaber Sports? I can't do sports. I have to read.

Ala Today is sports day. Don't you remember when we left the teacher said, 'The first day back is sports day.'

Sleiman They said it over the microphone. Don't you remember?

Jaber (*not remembering*) Right.

Sleiman First we do a few jumps. (*And they jump.*) And now we run. Twice around the yard. (*And they do.*)

Ala Great. Everyone on the ground! On your stomachs. Push-ups. One and two and three. (*They do them,* **Jaber** *trying desperately.*) Great. And now on your backs. TURN OVER! (*And they do.*)

Silence.

Jaber I'm so tired. (*Speaking very slowly.*) There is always something urgent to do. Every time I sit someone is calling me to save them. Jaber we need flour. Jaber we need the pot from your grandmother. Jaber you can't go out. Jaber you can't have friends. And Friday. I have to help clean the house. Recess must be over. I have to go back to school so I get into the fifth grade. I'm so tired. Don't let me fall asleep. Promise me. Don't let me sleep. I'm afraid of sleep. I'm afraid of sleeeeeeee. (*And he falls fast asleep.*)

Scene Nine: Humanity

Ala Wow! What kind of life is that? He gives me an ache. I hurt everywhere.

Sleiman Something is not right in his house. We should tell someone. But who? We have to let him sleep.

Ala I don't know anyone like him.

Sleiman There are others just like him. There are plenty like him.

Ala We'll let him sleep and when he wakes up – if he wakes up – we can take him to my house. There are a lot of guests there. No one will notice. And we will feed him. And give him a shower.

Sleiman Good idea.

Ala And you come to. This has been quite a day.

Sleiman How come only us three came? Are we stupid?

Ala I think we came because we're smart.

Sleiman I came because it's very boring to be all day in the house for so many days. My brain was starting to feel like sand. I would move my head and hear sand. The whole family was like that. Everyone is nervous and has sand in his brain from the news and the history. The women kept repeating, 'Oh My God' and the men kept smoking. Sand and smoke. Inside and outside. And the house is really small. And we are a lot of people home for a lot of days. And I was missing school. I had no place to sit and no place to study. All that history was passing me by. No one even knows I came to school. And they won't know when I come back.

Ala And the other kids? Why didn't they come?

Sleiman Either they didn't hear the right news or they are just lazy.

Ala Yeah.

Sleiman I think the news changed while we were walking to school.

Ala The guys stopped running.

Sleiman No, the guys got a new story.

Ala We should find out what it is.

Sleiman Yeah, especially since we don't know if it's safe out here.

Ala You think it's not safe?

Sleiman This day is already history. Let's wake him up, and get to your house. Let's try to take a bus.

They go over to where **Jaber** *is sound asleep.*

Sleiman Jaber . . . Hey Jaber . . . you have to wake up.

Jaber I'm awake. What do you need?

Ala We need you to put one arm around me and one arm around Sleiman. And come with us to my house to eat. We will let you sleep there. And then give you dinner. And you can visit my father's leg and if my father is in a good mood, he will sing. And I will sing.

Jaber (*in his sleep*)   That's paradise.

Sleiman   Come on buddy. Hold on.

Sleiman *and* **Ala** *get* **Jaber** *to hold on to him, they collect their books, and slowly begin their walk off the stage.*

Ala   That isn't a school anymore. It was. But now it's history.

Sleiman   And tomorrow I have to be the guy who runs with the story of Jaber.

Scene Ten: Epilogue (totally optional)

Before they get too far away, they turn and run back.

Actor playing Ala   This is the end of the play.

Actor playing Sleiman   Thank you all for watching it. You were a great audience.

Actor playing Jaber   Now, we want to hear what you think of it.

And the workshop starts.

End

Play #4: The Brother

Characters

Mohammed, *oldest – nine or ten – brother to Hassan.*
Ibrahim, *middle – seven or eight – a boy from the same refugee camp.*
Hassan, *youngest – five or six – brother to Mohammed.*

The play takes place in a courtyard in a refugee camp.

Mohammed *and* **Hassan** *are alone in the empty concrete courtyard. Mid-day.*

Hassan   How many ways can a person die? Shot. Blown up. (*Pause.*). Falling from the roof. Falling from the ladder. Falling from the tree. Falling. (*Pause.*) Bad fish. Talal the fisherman died of bad fish. That's what they said. He threw up and threw up and threw up and died. And everyone said it was bad fish. The teacher said it was bad water. Death by bad water. Drowning. Two boys in my school drowned. Death by water. (*Pause.*) Getting stuck by a nail or bit by a dog or by a snake or by a rat or by a sick horse. Or being squeezed to death by the snake before he bites you. Or being flattened by a tank or a bull-dozer or a building on top of you. Or if they hang you upside down for a week. (*Pause.*) Or being very, very, very, very sick. Any place. Stomach, head, leg, brain. You can die from all those things.

Mohammed   Stop talking about this subject.

Hassan   Why?

Mohammed   Because I need to think and you're bothering me.

Hassan   What are you thinking about?

Mohammed   Babba.

Hassan   Why?

Mohammed   Because of what he said to me.

Hassan   WHAT DID HE SAY TO YOU?

Mohammed   He said, 'Ya Mohammed, now you are the oldest.'

Hassan   That's important.

Ibrahim *enters following a football. He comes dashing in, wearing pants and a jacket but he's a mess, with shirt out, hair messy.*

Ibrahim   Goooooaaaalll. That's how you do it right. You hit from here and you run and you kick and you do it. Gooooaaaalllll. Again. From the side, avoid the one to the left, and the right, and the middle and the back. Avoid them all. Just keep your eye on the ball and run. Kick and run. And then gooooaaalllll. (*Breath. To the brothers.*) I am the captain of the team. You are the mid-field and you are the goalie. I tell you what moves to make and we win from the team in Zeitoun. And we win from Nassr and from Darraj. We get gold medals. Everyone comes to see us play. Gooooaaaallll. (*He is getting a bit nuts, too much.*) The people come. They say 'Mabrouk.' My father is proud, your father is proud. Gooooaaalllll. The Minister of Sports comes. He eats lunch with us and we leave in a taxi and go to the helicopter. We have matching bags and training suits. We go up and over the sea and land in Ramallah. And Gooooaaaaalllll. (*Completely out of breath.*) I'm thirsty.

Mohammed   HEY! CALM DOWN. THERE ARE OTHER PEOPLE HERE.

Ibrahim WHO ARE YOU TALKING TO? I'M HERE TO PLAY FOOTBALL. YOU WANNA PLAY. IF YES GOOAAALLLLL AND IF NO DON'T YELL AT ME.

Hassan We can't play. Our brother died . . . in war. . .

Ibrahim I DON'T WANT TO TALK ABOUT DEATH. Do you play basketball? You have to be three metres tall to play. I'm going to stretch my legs. Get tall. I'm going to jump three metres up and put that ball right in the basket and then baassskkeeettt. And the score is 370 to 50 and we are winning. Basskettt. Bassskettt. (*Breath.*) Let's play tag. You're it. RUN.

Ibrahim goes running but **Hassan** *and* **Mohammed** *only watch him.*

Mohammed HEY, WHAT KIND OF A BOY ARE YOU? COME OVER HERE. WHO IS YOUR FATHER? ARE YOU DEAF? OR STUPID? WE JUST SAID SOMETHING IMPORTANT.

Hassan Maybe he is crazy?

Ibrahim Who are you saying is crazy? You think I'm crazy? I'm not crazy. I'm a man. That's what my father said this morning. So as a man I'm playing. And this isn't your courtyard. It's shared by all the kids. And the men! (*Tags him.*) You. You're it. RUUUUNNNNN!

And he runs again but **Mohammed** *and* **Hassan** *stay. When* **Ibrahim** *sees that they are not chasing him, he runs past them.*

Ibrahim GOALLLLLLLLLL! And the score is 3-0.

But as he runs by, **Mohammed** *catches him, and sits on him.*

Mohammed What's with you?

Ibrahim I made another goal and you lose. Hey, I'm thirsty. Do you have anything to drink? I really need something to drink.

Hassan WE DON'T HAVE AN OLDER BROTHER ANYMORE.

Ibrahim Let me go. Let me go. HELLLLLPPPPP. MURDERERS IN THE COURTYARD. EVERYONE HIDE.

Hassan What's wrong with you? Did you fall on your head?

Ibrahim I need water. Let me get water. Listen, let me go and I'll be quiet.

Mohammed And you will stop making us crazy . . .?

Ibrahim So you admit YOU are the crazy ones. Gooooaaaalllll!

Mohammed *is very angry and brings* **Ibrahim** *over to the side of the courtyard and sticks his head into a bucket of water. Just a dunk.*

Mohammed How do feel about swimming????

Hassan Oh no! We're in big trouble now.

Ibrahim (*coughing and scared*)   Why did you do that? I didn't do anything to you!

Mohammed   We told you our brother died and you say goooooal. Who is your father?

Ibrahim   Abu Mohammed.

Mohammed   Where do you live?

Ibrahim   In Block B.

Hassan   We live in Block B. Yesterday was the last day of mourning. Maybe you passed by. Maybe you understand now.

Ibrahim   American football. That's another one. All those giant men stuffed in their arms and the shoulders and that helmet. You can drop ten bricks on your head and nothing will happen to you. I'll learn that football and then nothing can hurt me. Not even you. GOOOALLLLLLL. 4-0.

Again **Mohammed** *drags* **Ibrahim** *to the water and dunks his head.*

Hassan   Be careful, ya Mohammed, you can die by drowning.

Ibrahim   I'm gonna kill you. I'm gonna kill you. I hate you. I hate you both.

Hassan   You started it. You're crazy.

Ibrahim   You're crazy. Where do you live?

Hassan   We told you. Block B where the mourning tent ended yesterday.

Ibrahim   RIGHT AND I LIVE IN BLOCK B WHERE THE MOURNING STARTED TODAY.

Silence of course.

Mohammed   Peace on your head.

Hassan   Who died?

Ibrahim   I'm not telling.

Mohammed (*to* **Hassan**)   I'm going to find out.

Hassan   And leave me alone with him? He'll kill me.

Mohammed   You won't kill him right? Because you know I'm going to your house right? So play football together. I'll be back. And if anything happens to either one of you . . . DON'T LET ANYTHING HAPPEN AT ALL. YOU HEAR. YOU HEAR.

Ibrahim   The whole neighbourhood hears.

And **Mohammed** *runs off to find out.*

Ibrahim   You're it. RUUUNNNNNN.

And they start playing tag. And quite suddenly **Ibrahim** *stops. They are both out of breath.*

Hassan (*tags him*)   You're it. Run.

Ibrahim   My mother died sleeping.

Hassan (*silent*)   She died sleeping? How does that happen?

Ibrahim   You go to sleep and you don't wake up.

Hassan (*Total silence.*)

Ibrahim   God comes and takes you while you're asleep so you don't feel anything.

Hassan   You mean she was surprised that she didn't wake up?

Ibrahim   I guess so. (*Tags him.*) You're it. Run. (*But they only jump where they are.*)

Hassan   Does that happen much? I mean we know when we go out we could get blown up or shot or run over by a car or squashed by a truck or even turned into dust from a bomb. But to die when you are sleeping? (*Pause.*) Does that happen a lot?

Ibrahim   We don't know anything. Only God knows. (*Tags him hard.*) You're it. RUUUUUNNNNNN.

And they run to escape life, tagging and running. And **Mohammed** *comes back also running so they are all running after each other. They are tired and hot and go to the water bucket and each one puts his head in the water.*

Hassan (*to* **Mohammed**)   He told me. How can that be? How can you go to sleep and not wake up? I don't understand how you die from sleeping?

Mohammed   She didn't die from sleeping. She was sick.

Ibrahim   CAN'T WE TALK ABOUT SOMETHING ELSE.

Mohammed   Your father wants you at home.

Ibrahim   I'M NOT GOING HOME. COME ON, LET'S MAKE SOME GOOOALLLLLSSS.

And he goes running with the football.

Mohammed   HEY, HEY, IT'S YOUR FATHER.

Hassan   I don't understand? She wasn't sick before she went to sleep. How can you go to sleep and not wake up? My heart is going boom, boom, boom, again. Listen.

Mohammed   That's from running. (*Yelling.*) HEY IBRAHIM, COME ON, WE'LL TAKE YOU HOME.

Mohammed *and* **Hassan** *go chasing him.*

Ibrahim   I'm not going home. Not now.

Mohammed   But your father is asking for you.

Ibrahim   NO.

Mohammed   OK. OK. Let's stay here.

Ibrahim I watched cartoons this morning. That was nice.

Hassan We didn't. Do you want to hear how our brother died?

Ibrahim If he was killed, yes.

Mohammed Our brother Khaled was in the shop buying a belt because his belt broke and my father said he needed a new one. He was with his friends Iyad and Yousef. They were getting belts with big buckles on them. I wanted one too but my father said no. Those are for men. And Khaled is a man but his pants didn't fit right. Before he left he said to me, 'Ya Mohammed, if I find a good belt I'll bring it for you tonight because after we go to the shop, we are going to the beach.' That's exactly what he said. And then he said, 'And next Friday I will teach you how to swim. You and Hassan will learn to swim next Friday.' That's what Khaled said. And he smiled and he went like this (*taps his own head as his brother did*). And he left for the souk. And then they got him. Helicopter from there, it flew this way, and then the bottom opened and the rocket came out and hit the shop of the generators which is eight shops from the belts. And all those boys got caught in it and they all . . . died. Right there on the street between the generators and the hats and music and socks and the sheets and the belts. All those guys.

Ibrahim Where's the football?

Hassan Over there.

Ibrahim Whose turn? (*As in tagged.*)

Hassan I don't remember.

Mohammed All those guys died together and we don't have our brother.

Hassan Who will tell us what to do? He told us all the secrets about being brothers. Brothers are the most important.

Ibrahim MOTHERS are the most important. I don't have a mother. She died sleeping.

Hassan Can you stop saying that!

Ibrahim She died sleeping. She died sleeping.

Hassan Goooaaaalllllll.

Silence.

Ibrahim Today my father told me that from now on I have to grow up, that I can't be a kid anymore. He said he needs me to understand grown-up things because my mother died sleeping. My sisters and brothers are with my aunts and uncles. I can't go back to Block B. I am here in the courtyard with my friends and we are going to be sportsmen one day when everyone is done dying. Their brother died. His name was Khaled. He could swim. I can't swim. Everyone is going to mourn or coming from it. Everyone loses someone in this life. My father said I am a man. I think I'm very short for a man. Here is Mohammed and Hassan. Brothers. We played all day today. Sports. Whoever wants to join, come and we'll teach you everything we learned. All you boys can join our sports team. But I have to learn to swim. (*Pause.*) I only have one question. Who is going to feed me now that my mother died? Who will bring me tea and biscuits at night? Who will make my sandwich? Who will say ya habibi do your homework ya smart one and ya habibi sleep well and I'll see you in the morning? And who will wake me and say good morning habibi how did you sleep???? (*Pause.*) I heard that you can die from not eating. The men in prison are dying from not eating. I don't understand.

Hassan   I am never going to sleep again.

Mohammed   You have to sleep. You know what they say of all the strong and great sportsmen. They all sleep ten hours every night. So they can be strong and great.

Ibrahim   He will never be strong and great. We are small and not great. And no one is talking to us. No is saying why things are happening.

Hassan   Maybe we are too small to be strong and great.

Ibrahim   I have to start. My father said I'm a man.

Mohammed   Mine too.

Hassan   We can start. Now. Right now. Right now. Today. We are strong and great.

Ibrahim   Head in the bucket?

Hassan   How old was Khaled?

Mohammed   He was a man. Maybe eighteen.

Hassan   Wow. I guess he knew everything.

Mohammed   He knew a lot.

Ibrahim   All old people know a lot. We are just . . . what are we?

Hassan   Boys. God is so amazing he took Mahmoud to be with him.

Ibrahim   My mother will take care of him.

Mohammed   And he will take care of her.

Hassan   That's nice that they are together.

Ibrahim   You're it. RUUUUNNNNN.

[Optional] *And they run nowhere and everywhere. Here they can go into the audience and start talking to the boys and hearing stories about who is who in the family, if they are oldest or youngest, how many kids, and who has died this year.*

Hassan (*suddenly*)   Baaaassssskkkeetttt.

Ibrahim   It's a football, you idiot.

Hassan   It's a basketball. It's anything. It's everything.

Ibrahim   You're crazy.

Hassan   No I'm not.

Ibrahim   Head in the bucket?

Hassan   Head in the bucket.

Ibrahim   No. Goooaaaaallllll.

Hassan   No. Basskkkkkeeettt.

Hitting and fighting – choreographed to some degree. The three boys fighting together, practicing like cats, can have a frightening aspect.

And when they are tired, they just stop. No reason to start, no reason to stop. Just energy out of control.

Ibrahim   I have a bump here.

Mohammed   Let me see it. It's nothing bad. We can wrap it up.

Ibrahim   I'm wounded. I can tell people I got wounded.

Hassan   I'm also wounded. Look. I'm bleeding. You can also die from bleeding. I know that.

Mohammed   You won't die. It is not a serious wound.

Hassan   But it's a wound? Right. I mean it's a real wound? Great and strong.

Mohammed   It's a great and strong wound.

Sitting.

Mohammed   Hey. (*Big thought.*) Listen. (*Another thought.*) Now I am the older brother. (*To* **Hassan**.) I am your older brother. (*To* **Ibrahim**.) And I can be your older brother too.

Ibrahim   Good . . . because you can't be my mother.

Mohammed   Right. But I will teach you about being a brother. No bothering your father. Our fathers are busy with death. And we can't worry them. We have to be men now. I have to be a man now. The big brother.

Hassan   I don't know how to be a man. Especially if I stop sleeping.

Ibrahim   I don't want to be a man now. (*Pause.*) (*Be careful that the next part is said very matter-of-factly: no pathos, no tears.*) I want my mother but she died sleeping.

Hassan   Please stop saying that.

Mohammed   Ibrahim, I'm going to ask you to stop saying that. Your mother died because she was sick. Not because she was sleeping. One day we will find out why. The doctor will tell your father and he will tell you. We are just kids in a difficult world. And I'm just a bigger kid in the same world. People die. But look, people also get born. People have friends. We have friends. We have brothers and sisters. It's good to have brothers and sisters. (*Pause.*)

Ibrahim   And I never had a big brother because all the others are girls. My mother waited a long time for me.

Mohammed (*thoughts fill his head*)   Sit! The big brother is the one who teaches you everything you need to know in this life. Whenever he learns something new, he tells the younger brothers so they know how to live. Now, I have to teach you the things I know because I am the big brother.

Hassan   What do you know?

Ibrahim   You're not my brother.

Mohammed   OK. I can be your friend-brother. All those sisters aren't going to make you a man. Be careful, huh.

Hassan   So now you are like Khaled?

Mohammed   Yes. But also no.

Ibrahim   I WANT A MOTOR CYCLE. And ride it from here to everywhere. Vrooom! Vrooom! Vrooom! Like this. (*And he's off running. But he 'drives' back and stops short in front of them.*)

What did my father say to you? Exactly. Word by word.

Hassan   I don't want to hear.

And he closes his ears but also listens.

Mohammed   He said, 'Please tell him that Abu Ibrahim needs Ibrahim by his side as the oldest son. Tell him I am sad and I need to see his face because he is handsome as his mother was beautiful.'

Ibrahim   He said that?

Hassan   I feel water in my eyes. It's that bucket.

Mohammed   Ibrahim, your father and you are responsible now for all your sisters. He needs you to help him. He wants to teach you to become great and strong.

Silence.

Ibrahim *kicks the football in the direction of home, a new direction, and he walks after it.*

Hassan   Where are you going? Is it a goal?

Ibrahim   I'm going home. See you in Block B.

And he's gone in a flash.

Mohammed (*starting to walk*)   Let's go.

Hassan (*starting to walk*)   Do you know other things to teach me?

Mohammed   I guess so because I'm older.

Hassan   Start with the good things.

Mohammed   Let's see. An older brother secretly gives his younger brother pocket money.

Hassan   Really??? What else?

Mohammed   He defends you when you get in trouble, in school, on the street, at home.

Hassan   That's a good one.

Mohammed   And the younger brother has to do stuff too.

Hassan   WHAT?

Mohammed   Give the remote control to him.

Hassan   What else?

Mohammed   Ask questions. That's very important. Ask a lot of questions. Until you know what you need to know.

Hassan   Really?

Mohammed   Absolutely. Start asking?

Hassan   Can we go visit Ibrahim?

Mohammed   Oh yes. We will find him and visit him.

Hassan   That would be really nice.

And they walk off the stage talking about these things but no one can hear them anymore.

End.

Play #5: The Tree

Characters

Ali, *a boy, ageless.*
A **Father**, *Abu Mohammed, typical.*
A **Grandfather**, *Abu Hassan, old, very old, angry, but with a heart.*

A large tree. In a forest or orchard. The tree has grown in such a way as to have a convenient place for this play to happen. An invisible tree-house.

Scene One: No Hitting

Ali *is running away from home. He has a back-pack with him. He runs. Out of breath.*

Ali   Don't even try to stop me. I'm leaving this house. I've had it. Don't tell me 'come'. Don't tell me 'go'. I'm gone. Out. You have one less son. Sell my mattress if you want. And my clothes. I'm not coming back. Don't call me. Don't even come look for me. You hear. You all hear? What's this? A tree. A rope. (*He starts to climb up.*) Don't even think of looking for me. What's the use of being a kid in this life? Everything you try to do – nothing works out. I studied and passed but all they say is don't get so excited because soon you're going to work with your father fixing cars. Fathers are worse than teachers. Teachers, at least you get to leave school. But my father, pow from here, and smack from there. Like he has nothing to do with his hands but bang on me. No one is banging on me anymore.

He climbs up into the tree and hides, but we can still see him. But it's a whole scene how he gets up there and settles in.

Ali (*to himself*)   I can live here. I'm safe here. And I have . . . (*Opening his bag.*) a sandwich, a blanket, a notebook. Do I need a notebook? Yes. To write my thoughts. And draw. One juice. Not enough. A lighter. Gum. A ball. That's all I need. (*Anything else that comes up that he might need will be in the bag.*)

A **Father** *enters. He is worried and annoyed and aggravated.*

A **Father** (*annoyed and aggravated*)   Where are you, you pain in the neck? Don't think I won't find you. (*Stop.*) Who left the door open?! (*Stop.*) I will find you. (*Stop.*) Where are you, old man? (*To himself.*) Too many people in the house. Someone always leaving the door open. No one responsible. WHERE ARE YOU?

Ali   Who are you yelling at? (*Eureka.*) You're someone's father. I can tell from how you talk. I see your hand in a fist. You're going to smack him when you find him. That's why he ran away.

Father (*surprised*)   Who's that? Who are you? Shame on you for talking to me like that? Where are you?

Ali   It's me. Up here. Who are you yelling at?

Father   I'm looking for my father. Someone left the door open and he decided to take a walk and now we can't find him. And he sometimes gets confused. (*Stop.*) What are you doing up there?

Ali   I'm running away. How does someone lose a father? What, you forgot him in the market? In a taxi? At the hospital?

Father   Watch how you speak. I didn't forget him. He left on his own. Did you see an old man pass?

Ali   How old?

Father   Old. An old man. What are you . . . stupid? Get out of that tree.

Ali   No. Shame on you for losing your father. And you call me stupid?

Father   Well look around up there and see if you see an old man.

Ali   No old man is passing here.

Father   Look that way then!

Ali   What's he look like?

Father   An old man. An old man. They all look the same. OLD.

Ali   And you're his son. No wonder he ran away.

*A **Grandfather** enters from behind the tree or from another side of the courtyard.*

Ali (*seeing the old man, shouting*)   Hey old man, run, your son is right there. He's going to catch you. Smack you. Hit you. Bang on you and lock you up. RUN.

*The **Father** goes to the **Grandfather**.*

Grandfather   You want to catch me? Here I am. Catch. Where are we going?

Father   Who are you?

Grandfather   I'm Abu Hassan, you idiot.

Father   You're not my father. (*To **Ali**.*) He's not my father.

Ali   It doesn't seem to make a difference to you. He's old. He's lost. Take him.

Father   Ya old man, I am Abu Mohammed. I am not your son.

Grandfather   A curse upon all the sons! They are all useless and selfish. All the sons were raised wrong. It's the fault of the women. Both of you, out of my way. I'm going hunting. And no one is going to stop me.

Ali   I'll go hunting. But I'm not coming out of this tree. If you want to hunt, you have to come up.

Father   My father is lost! He's lost. I have to find my father. (*Loud.*) YABBA where are you? Come out. We'll go home. It's lunch time soon. COME OUT, OLD MAN, YOU HEAR ME. COME OUT THIS MINUTE.

Ali   That's the problem . . . you only scream at him and promise to lock him in the house and then you expect him to come dancing over to you. (*Calling.*) Hey old man. Stay where you are. He has a really big stick. Or RUN.

Grandfather   Who's that? I have a really big rifle. Show yourself.

Ali   Look up. I'm here. In the tree. Like an owl. What's your name? Who are your sons?

Grandfather   I am Abu Hassan. And have no sons anymore. I returned them gave them back to their mother. She ruined those boys and now she can fix them.

Scene Two: Lost Men

Grandfather Hey you, up in the tree? Who are you? Why are you acting like an owl? Where is your father?

Ali I'm living up here. My name is Ali.

Grandfather You're living in a tree? That's a good idea. You should be called Hassan. The Hassan I have is broken. (*Pause.*) I know every tree in this orchard and I know every hiding place. But where did all the trees go?

Father Burned.

Ali Burned to ash.

Grandfather Burned?

Father Where did I lose him? Which way?

Grandfather How can you find him? That's more important. Who are you? What did you lose?

Father I just told you. I'm Abu Mohammed. I'm not your son.

Grandfather Are you calling me a liar? Give me my rifle. You're all no good. Go back to your mother.

Ali Abu Hassan, he's not your son. He's another man's son. He wants to hit his father and lock him up.

Father I don't want to hit my father. I want to find my father. He left the house and he lost his way.

Grandfather That would be me. I left the house. But I didn't lose my way. I'm right here. I know every tree in this orchard. Who burned down the trees?

Father God save you, old man, but you are not the old man I'm looking for. I'm looking for my father.

Grandfather Maybe I am your father and your forgot! Who burned down the trees?

Father In the war. They burned our trees in the war.

Grandfather Those dirt-bags. Which idiot burns down trees? How shall we eat without trees? (*To* **Ali**.) Whose son are you?

Ali No one's son. I live in this tree.

Father Hussssshhhh. Every boy is someone's son and no one lives in a tree except a bird.

Grandfather Wrong. I'm no one's son anymore. The whole family is with God and the others, I gave them all back to their mother. I'm on my own now. And I'm going hunting. Yallah. Are we going hunting? I have a rifle. Let's get the dirt-bags who burned down our trees.

Ali   And I have a stick. Together we're an army.

Grandfather   To the hunt!

Father   WE'RE NOT GOING HUNTING. BOTH OF YOU CALM DOWN.

Grandfather   WHO'S NOT CALM? WE ARE GOING HUNTING. AND WHY NOT?

Ali   Stop yelling, ya Father of Your Son.

Father   You two have to go home. People are worried about you. (*To* **Ali**.) Your father is looking for you and . . . (*To* **Grandfather**.) Soon it will be lunch time and your family will be waiting for you.

Grandfather (*nasty*)   And whose son are you?

Ali   He's the son of the father who is missing.

Grandfather   Your father is missing? We have to go find him. I have a rifle. Soon it will be lunch. His family will be waiting. How can you lose your father? You're really an idiot.

Ali   And I have a stick.

Grandfather   And what a good stick it is. Who loses a father? Let's go hunt your father and . . . (*Lost and confused.*) Where is . . . Where is the orchard?

Scene Three: Remembering?

Father   Sit down, ya Haj. Sit here. (*To* **Ali**.) And you come down.

Ali   I'm not coming down and I'm not going home. I can't live there anymore. Everyone is only yelling there. Ali do this and Ali do that. And Ali come here and Ali go away. And Ali give and Ali get. It's enough.

Father   Maybe my father will pass this way. I shouldn't move around too much. I'll wait here.

Grandfather   This tree was very small when you were born. (*To* **Ali**.) It looked just like you. It was short and small and angry all the time and we fed it and raised it right and kept the animals away and soon (*to* **Father**) it looked like you. It was big and fat and full of good things. You have good things. I see them. (*Touching the tree.*) And now it's old. And the older it is, the smarter it is. From the generation of my father or his father. I know this tree. We are very smart. We remember everything. I would hide in this tree from my father, may he rest in peace. He would yell and I would hide. And also from the wife, too. Where is she, that woman? She should come pick these fruits.

Ali   They are askadinyas.

Grandfather   Oh yes. Askadinyas. Ya woman, come and pick these fruits so we can eat them. And if I find one worm inside, it's your fault. She discovered spraying.

Spraying is bad. I say, 'Let the tree grow. It's God's tree, it will grow as God wishes, hamdalillah.' She says, 'Spray.'

Father Who are you talking to?

Grandfather Your mother. She's spraying the trees and then she's making lunch. I don't know where she is. Fixing her sons, inshallah. Maybe they went fishing. She doesn't listen to me anymore. (*Again, lost and confused.*) (*To* **Father**.) Ya son, what season is this?

Father Ya, Abu Hassan, I am Abu Mohammed. I'm not your son. Your son is at home. And he's waiting for you to have lunch. Where is your home?

Grandfather Here. I ran away from home and now I live here. Under this tree, and he is my up neighbour. He will leave me alone, right, you, you up in the tree? You, up in the tree. What's up there? Anything to hunt? I have a rifle. For hunting. It's the gazelle season. We can hunt a gazelle.

Father Why are you running away?

Grandfather Everyone is always yelling at me: Sidi don't do that, Sidi don't go there, Sidi don't eat that, Sidi sit, Sidi stand. Shoo ya'ni? I'm ten years old. I AM A MAN.

Ali It's not the gazelle season.

Grandfather Shut up and don't talk to me like that.

Ali Sorry, ya Haj. It's the gazelle season, as you said.

Grandfather That's what I said.

Ali Because you remember everything. Right. Because you're very old, right.

Grandfather Right. I'm very old. (*Stop.*) Askadinya.

Scene Four: Shooting the Sandwich

Father I can't just stay here. I'm going to make another turn. It's my fault he wandered off. He forgets things and now I forgot to lock the gate. It will get dark and we won't be able to find him until the morning. This is no good. (*Shouting.*) YABBA. WHERE ARE YOU? MAKE A NOISE IF YOU HEAR ME. YAAAAABAAA. (*He leaves.*)

Ali (*a little concerned, to* **Father**) Maybe bring something to drink when you come back. I only have one juice. Don't forget where I am. If it gets dark, I mean, you can find me here in the tree. I have a sandwich. OK?

Father There is trouble all around. Everything is trouble. You wake up and trouble. You go to work and trouble. You go home and you lose your father. What does this mean? YOU TWO STAY OUT OF TROUBLE. DON'T MOVE FROM THIS TREE.

Father *leaves.*

Grandfather Why is he yelling? There's no reason to yell. Is there a reason to yell?

Ali All fathers are always yelling and always giving orders. Ya Abu Hassan, let me see your stick.

Grandfather IT'S A RIFLE. I'm going hunting. What are you hunting up there? I would like to hunt a turkey today. Your mother will make something with the feathers. It's a cold winter. I hear a turkey.

Ali Ya Haj, I am Ali. Your son is home. What's his name?

Grandfather (*thinking hard not knowing*) I call him 'ya boy' and he comes. Three of them come. All the same. Sidi, give me a shekel. Sidi, give me a shekel.

Ali Yeah, that's what my father calls me. HEY BOY! My name is Ali. You hear. My name is Ali.

Grandfather I hear, ya Ali the best Ali!

Then **Ali** *makes the sound of a turkey.*

Grandfather (*hearing the sound*) The turkey has come to us to be hunted. He's hiding in the trees. But the idiots burned the trees . . . So where is the turkey?

Ali Ya Abu Hassan, he escaped. He's running away. He's running from his father. There's a big turkey running after him.

Grandfather It's his father. It's his wife. Everyone is running. I'm getting very nervous. Where's my rifle? Where is . . . what's his name? The one who was here . . .

Ali He went to bring water from the well. But here. Have something to eat. (**Ali** *takes his sandwich out of his bag and gives the sandwich to* **Abu Hassan**, *lowering it by hand in the plastic wrap it's in.*)

Grandfather (*as the sandwich comes down* **Abu Hassan** *'shoots' it*) Shooooot. I got it. I got the turkey. (*And he begins to walk like a turkey and then dramatically acts out the shooting and dying of the turkey.*)

Ali Did you get him?

Grandfather Yes, I got him right between the eyes. And now I'm going to eat him. Come down. Come, hey boy, and help me clean this turkey. WHERE ARE YOU?

Ali Why are you yelling at me?

Grandfather I'M NOT YELLING. I CAN'T HEAR YOU. COME DOWN AND HELP ME UP.

Ali I'm not coming down.

Grandfather THEN STAY UP.

Ali Eat ya Haj. Eat the turkey. Eat.

Scene Five: Generation Talk

The **Father** *comes back. He has water and a bag of sandwiches and a thermos of coffee.*

Ali So?

Father He didn't go home. His brothers are looking for him by the sea. The uncles are looking in the souk. And I have to stay in the orchard because this was his favourite place. (*Towards the* **Grandfather** *who is still lying on the ground.*) What happened to him?

Grandfather We hunted. Turkeys. I got it. Right between the eyes. I was attacked.

Ali (*playing*) Who attacked you, ya Haj?

Grandfather (*thinking and finally . . .*) The idiots who burned down the trees. Who else attacks us?

Father Ya Abu Hassan, did you fight?

Grandfather Everyone fought. Every day. From the morning to the night. From moon to moon and from year to year. That's how it is. And then one day they tell you, enough, you have to rest. You can't go out. And then your teeth fall out. (*Pause.*) I had a rifle. I NEEDED A TANK.

Ali Ya Haj, you don't need a tank now. They do it by remote. Like the TV. Click. Click.

Grandfather You stay up in your tree, you owl. You can be my son. Keep watch. Tell me if anything is going to fall on my head.

Father (*to* **Ali**) Will you come out of that tree and help me find my father? All you kids . . . you only do what you want. You never take responsibility, you only yell at your mother and aggravate your father. The new generation, they don't know how to be men.

Ali We know exactly what we're doing. We are going to school and we are learning and we will learn how to fix the country and the remote control. And we will replant the trees . . . so everyone can hide in them again.

Father (*to* **Grandfather**) You hear how they talk. You hear, ya Haj?!

Grandfather Your generation didn't know how to be men either. Us? We were the men. Including your mother. (*Stop.*)

Father I'm not your son, ya Abu Hassan. Your son is cooking a goat for you to eat. Go home.

Grandfather I'm not going home. I live here, now, under this tree. And you are my son because you found me.

Father One could look at it like that. (*He calms down.*) Who is hungry? I brought some things.

Ali   I gave my sandwich to the Haj.

Grandfather   Let's have lunch. I'm so hungry I could eat a goat.

Father   Good because I brought sandwiches.

Grandfather   Men don't eat sandwiches. They eat trays of meat and rice.

Father (*giving out sandwiches*)   Well this is a tray of meat and rice. Eat well. And here is water from the well. Drink. It's cold.

Grandfather   Bless the hands who made this. (*Low and fast.*) Bismillah Al-Rahman Al-Raheem. . .

And they eat, with **Ali** *up in the tree and the* **Father** *and* **Grandfather** *down . . . as always until now.*

Scene Six: Up

Grandfather   Where is the coffee, ya woman? Prepare the coffee. We have guests.

Father (*could be playing the wife, subtle*)   Fine, Abu Hassan, the coffee is cooking.

Ali   Ya Abu Hassan, ya Abu Hassan, up here, look up.

Abu Hassan *looks up and rediscovers the boy.*

Grandfather   Who are you?

Ali   Ali, your neighbour. Come on up, Abu Hassan. We'll have coffee up here on the roof in the tree.

Father (*quick*)   No, ya Haj, the coffee is here.

Ali   I'm not coming down.

Grandfather   He's not coming down. We have to go up. He's my neighbour.

Father   How are you going to get up, you old man?

Grandfather   Who are you calling old? You're the old man. Afraid to climb a tree.

Ali   Right. Can't you climb a tree?

Father   You can't go up, old man. You'll get hurt.

Grandfather   I can and I will. Throw the rope. Take the rifle. Open the sails. And watch out for pirates.

Father   Fine. Everyone watch out for the pirates.

Grandfather   And robbers and thieves and the idiots who burned our trees.

Ali   Exactly. We do as we want. We are men of our own.

Grandfather   Free men.

Father Fine. The free men will have coffee in the tree. We're coming up. TO TELL THE TRUTH, I SHOULD HAVE RUN AWAY FROM HOME. All day long Ya Abu Mohammed get this, ya Abu Mohammed get that, ya Abu Mohammed we need money, ya Abu Mohammed we need clothes. (*Climbing.*) How are you doing, Haj, climbing up Musa Mountain? I feel like I'm in a Tarzan movie. Yaaaaaaaaaaaaa!

The **Father** *and the* **Grandfather** *make it to the top funny and appearing dangerous.*

Father It's nice up here. You can see the sea.

Grandfather Any pirates?

Father No. Just some small boats. They are too close to the shore for good fish.

Grandfather (*standing and shouting to the boats*) GO OUT. FURTHER. FURTHER OUT.

Ali They can't go further out.

Grandfather Why not? The sea is big. We can catch a whale and eat it all winter.

Father They'll get shot if they go too far out.

Grandfather By who?

Ali By the idiots who burned down the trees.

Grandfather WHAT'S GOING ON? WHY ARE WE UNDER ATTACK AGAIN? WHERE'S MY RIFLE?

Father Ya Haj, sit and have coffee. Sit. Relax. We're not under attack. The boats will go out. We'll catch a whale. YA SAILORS, WE WANT A WHALE.

Ali This is nice. (*Pause.*) I have a blanket. Here, ya Haj. And you Abu Mohammed. Here. Wrap.

Father This is nice.

Grandfather This is nice. The men together.

Scene Seven: Women Work

Father (*to* **Ali**) Why did you run away?

Grandfather You ran away? (*And he smacks him: it looks hard but isn't.*)

Ali No one respects me. No one asks about me. No one listens to me. I got eighteen from twenty on my exam and no one said Mabrouk. I cleaned the roof and no one said Ya'tik El-Afieh. My father is only complaining. And my mother is only yelling all day. I go to school and I come home and nothing has changed. Babies crying and the house upside down. My things are ripped and ruined. Even my school certificate was ripped and I had to tape it.

Grandfather I knew that girl would make a bad wife. I told my son, 'Find someone else, find someone fatter and stronger', and now look. She ruins the food and the babies are crying.

Ali Who?

Grandfather Your mother.

Father Ya Abu Hassan, ya Haj, this is not your son. This is a boy who ran away from home.

Grandfather Me too.

Father (*giving in*) Me too.

Grandfather This blanket is made from a wild goat. I killed this goat. And your mother made this blanket. My wife was better than your wife. (*To* **Ali**.) How is your wife?

Ali I'm not married yet.

Grandfather Soon inshallah. Soon. I'll talk to your mother.

Father Ya Abu Hassan, tell us about your wife.

Grandfather The wife. All the women ignore us. They do what they want. THEY WORK! THEY BRING MONEY. THEY LOCK ME IN THE ROOM. THEY CRY. AND THEY DON'T MAKE COFFEE ANYMORE.

Ali Calm, ya Haj, calm down or you'll fall out of the tree.

Father But he's right, ya Ali. The women of today aren't like the women of the past. All the women are busy today. Most of them are busier than the men.

Grandfather ALL THE WOMEN WERE BUSY IN THE PAST. HUNTING AND FIGHTING. THAT'S WHAT WE ALL DID. HUNTING AND FIGHTING. And then cooking and eating. And taking care of the children. All these children. Where did they all go?

Ali My mother is so busy that she doesn't ask me about school or about football. And my father says she is cooking from cans. And he yells and she yells. And it's always the same story. And in the end they say, 'Ya Ali, go watch television.' I don't understand why they yell or what they want.

Scene Eight: Men Can

Grandfather We should build a fire. The winter is coming.

Father There's still plenty of time for the winter. We should enjoy the summer and this tree.

Ali I found this tree.

Father This tree has been here since forever.

Grandfather You and you, what do you know about this tree? My father planted this tree. My grandfather planted this tree. All around were trees. No one burned trees then. No one was that stupid. Boy, who's your father?

Ali Abu Ahmad.

Grandfather HEY YOU, BOY, there are at least two thousand Abu Ahmads. The one with the sewing machine? The one with the falafel? The one on the street to the port? The long one? The one with the moustache like this or like this? The one who wears glasses? You don't know who your father is?

Ali My father is Abu Ahmad who works in the garage in the east. He can fix any car.

Grandfather Well then he's smart. And that makes you smart. So why are you in a tree hiding from him?

Ali He's trying to hunt me. And hit me with his stick.

Father It's getting late. I have to check my house again. How can I be so stupid as to lose my father??? It's so nice up here.

Grandfather (*to* **Father**) You lost your father!!! (*He hits* **Father** *with his stick.*)

Father WAIT. WAIT. I didn't lose him. He went for a walk.

Grandfather (*quietly, nicely*) Well he's allowed to do that. He's a man. He's allowed to go for a walk wherever he wants. He shouldn't be locked up.

Father Yes, Abu Hassan, he shouldn't be locked up.

Quiet. **Ali** *has curled up in the lap of the* **Father** *and is looking up at the sky.*

Grandfather He'll come home. We all go home in the end.

Father Of course, no gets lost here. Someone will bring him home.

Ali Ya Haj, do you think so? We all go home?

Grandfather You are both good sons. I see it. I feel it. I know it. Old people know things. Secrets of life. Believe me, aside from the idiots who burned our trees, we are good men. All of us. I like this blanket. It's time for a nap. Let us rest . . . and dream of the trees that used to be here.

And they do.

End.

5: Thirteen Ways of Looking at a Blackbird (2015)

Ramadan was early in the summer which meant we had less time to perform, which meant more than the usual four plays, and only three actors per play. This collection is made up of six plays, written within three months. Each play was made three times and performed twice a day. Only four of the six plays are included here.

In 'The Boys Who Can't Sit Still' we had a fourth actor playing all the relatives. You can also do this with four actors.

In 'The Boys in the Mirror' we had a technician do the short role of Mirror Image Two.

In 'The Snow Trip' the Mother and Father were voices. They can be actors. In 'One Thousand Questions' the girls' voices can be actors' voices but cannot be seen.

Play #1: One Thousand Questions

Characters

Father/Husband
Mother/Wife
Twin 1 – Ahmad
Twin Two – Ahmadino
Two Girls' voices, if possible

Scene One

Husband *and* **Wife**   This is my husband. This is my wife. We are married and will soon start having our children, God willing. This is where they will sleep. This is where they will sit and study and eat and wait when there is nothing to do. This is the salon. I am the wife. I am the husband. I am going to have the babies now.

Wife *screaming. Baby is born.*

Wife   Look at our first son! Name him. (*Pause.*) Aghhhh. Aghhhhh.

Father   What. What is it?

Wife   I don't know! But I'm not done. Aghhh. Aghhh.

Father   What do you mean not done?

Wife   Aghghghghghghghg. Look. Your second son.

Father   Second son? How did you do that?

Wife   I don't know. It's a gift from God. Yalla name him.

Father   The first one is Ahmad.

Wife   Pretty ya Abu Ahmad.

Father   And this one is . . . Ummm . . . Ahmadino.

Wife   Ahmadino? (*Curious.*) What kind of name is that?

Father   Modern. Fresh. Different.

Wife   I don't want different. I want like everyone else.

Father   Ahmadino is his name. I have spoken.

Wife   Fine my angel. Who am I to argue with you. Ahmadino is a perfect name. Mabrouk Abu Ahmad Ahmadino.

They each sit by a kid across the wood stage. The kids are babies.

Father   Cuchy, cuchy, chuchy.

Kid One   Are you my babba?

Father   Of course, habibi.

Kid Two   Are you my mother?

Wife   My angel. I am mamma. Say, yammmmma, yammmma.

Kid One   Where did we come from?

Kid Two   Why can't I speak normal?

Kid One (*to* **Kid Two**)   Who are you?

Kid Two (*to* **Kid One**)   I don't know. Who are you? Where are we?

Kid One   It must be where we belong. Are you comfortable?

Kid Two   Yanni. There is something wet happening.

Kid One   Yes, it happened to me.

Kid Two   Is it normal?

Kid One   Yamma: Is it normal? Am I broken? Leaking?

Wife   Shame on you.

Father   They are your sons in these matters.

Wife   Change one of them.

Father   Me????

Wife   We have two of them. One for you and one for me. Yalla change. This is a bammpers. You do this and this and open here and glue here and now he's all wrapped up.

Scene Two

They change clothes and grow a bit. **Kid One** *is neat (mother's work) and* **Kid Two** *a mess (father's work). The changing of clothing, sometimes just by adding a piece, is how they will grow up. After this first diaper change, they are now two–three years old.*

Wife   Look how big they've grown. Take a photo.

Father   Ahmad looks just like me and . . .

Wife   And Ahmadino looks just like Yanni, not exactly. He looks a little lost.

They pose.

Kid One   I don't like this food. I prefer the milk from that lady.

Kid Two   Yeah, why do we have to stop drinking her milk?

Kid One   What is this white stuff?

Kid Two   I heard her say 'rice' . . .

Kid One   And the green?

Kid Two   Spin-Itch.

Kid One   You like it?

Kid Two   I don't know. (*Louder.*) Hey you two, where's the milk?

Kid One   Why are we eating like this? I'm all green.

Kid Two   Where is the milk fountain we always suck from?

Kid One   And why is she getting so fat?

Kid Two And why is he always putting my shirt on backwards?

Kid One Why is the father always shouting? I have a head-ache.

Kid Two Why is everyone always kissing us?

Kid One I want milk. Yaaaaa.

Kid Two Me, too. Yaaaaaaaa.

Wife Now they are crying again. I told you to lower the TV or they would wake up.

Father But it's the news. I have to keep in touch.

Wife It's football. Now go bring me something sour. I feel like eating something sour. Watermelon with lemon. Yallah hurry.

Kid One Yech.

Kid Two Really yech. What's football?

Kid One What's news?

Kid Two What's watermelon?

Kid One Maybe that's what's making her fat. And news?

Kid Two Maybe something sour.

Father Right away, habibti. Whatever you want. Whatever you want I will bring you.

Wife My hero.

Father Just remember, only one this time.

Wife One girl, inshallah. (*Again having a baby.*) Aghghghghghggh.

Kid Two Why is she yelling?

Kid One Do you think she's broken?

Father What? Speak my dear. Is it time?

Kid One Time for what?

Kid Two Why is she yelling?

Kid One What is happening?

Kid Two No idea.

Wife I am having the baby. Be a girl. Be a boy. Be anything. Just come out.

Father What is it?

Mother I don't know. Waaaaaiiiiiiit. It's a girl, Abu Ahmad. It's a girl. (*A wrapped-up baby comes out.*) Name her.

Father Ya my daughter, we will call you Ahmaedah.

Mother Waaaaaiiiiiiittttt.

Father What??????????

Mother It's a girl.

Father You told me that.

Mother Another one!

Father I told you only one!

Mother You want me to give her back?!

And she comes out with another girl package. They have to be made beautifully and shouldn't be store bought. They will be blankets wrapped up. We don't have to see faces. Props. But beautiful.

Father AGAIN. Now what are we going to do?!

Wife Give her a name.

Father I have no more ideas.

Wife Think.

Kid One What are those?

Kid Two Yamma, what are those?

Kid One First friends?

Kid Two They are too small to be friends.

Father Ahmadetta.

Wife Look ya Ahmad, look ya Ahmadino. These are your sisters. This is Ahmaedah and this is Ahmadetta.

Father No, this one is Ahmadetta and that one is Ahmaedah.

Wife Ya Abu Ahmad, name them.

Father Call them what you want.

Wife Hamdalillah. Look boys. This is Ahmaedah and this is Ahmadetta. (*Yelling.*) Go get bammbers. Plenty of them. Enough for everyone.

Girls' voices can play the girl babies or the actors playing **Kid One** *and* **Kid Two** *will be the voices of* **Girl Baby One** *and* **Girl Baby Two**.

Girl Baby One Where are we?

Girl Baby Two No idea. We were warm in the dark and now we're freezing and who are those?

Girl Baby One Are you my mother?

Girl Baby Two Are you my my my, what's the opposite of mother?

Kid One Father, dummy.

Girl Baby Two Who are you?

Kid One Brothers.

Girl Baby One What's that?

Kid Two We say what to do and you do it.

Girl Baby One Not fair. Why am I wet?

Girl Baby Two I also got wet. Is it raining?

Kid One I'm also wet.

Kid Two It must be raining.

Wife Where are the bammpers ya Abu Ahmad. Everyone needs to be changed. Yalla you take these two and I take these two.

Father Me with two? Me? Never! I will make a mistake. Why did you do this . . . Twice??? Can't you be normal like the other mothers, one at a time? Every time you bring me two.

Wife Thank God. Look. We were married two years ago and now we have four. All beautiful. God keep them. God protect them, and you too Abu Ahmad, who brought them up and made them beautiful.

Father They are beautiful because of you. So you change them.

All kids *crying.*

Scene Three

Kid One *and* **Kid Two** *have changed into five to six-year-old kids.* **Kid One** *is neat.* **Kid Two** *is artistic. But they are dressed the same. The* **Father** *is messy. The* **Wife/Mother** *is pregnant.*

Mother No. No. No.

Father Yes. Yes. Yes.

Mother No. No. No.

Father Yes. Yes. Yes.

Mother *and* **Father** *continue as background noise.*

Kid One Who will win?

Kid Two What's the subject?

Kid One School.

Kid Two What is school?

Kid One I don't know. The kids next door go. The bigger ones.

Kid Two What happens in school?

Kid One They make you carry bags.

Kid Two What's in the bags?

Kid One Books.

Kid Two Story books?

Kid One I don't know.

Kid Two I don't want to go to school.

Kid One I want to go to school.

Kid Two Why do we go to school?

Father No. No. No. (*They have switched positions, he says no, so it's another subject.*)

Mother Yes. Yes. Yes.

Father No. No. No.

Mother Yes. Yes. Yes.

Kid Two What will we learn in school?

Kid One Will we do football in school?

Kid Two Will we do news in school? I hope not.

Kid One Who is the leader in school?

Kid Two What's a leader?

Kid One Can I be the leader?

Kid Two Can I be the leader?

Kid One We'll both be the leader.

Kid Two OK.

Mother No. No. No. (*Again, they have switched positions, she says no, so it's another subject.*)

Father Yes. Yes. Yes.

Mother No. No. No.

Father Yes. Yes. Yes.

Kid Two Can I play in school?

Kid One Can I play with numbers in school?

Kid Two Can I play with words in school?

Kid One Can we go to school?

Father   They are old enough.

Mother   No they are just babies.

Father   They are going to school.

Mother   Fine. Then help me dress them.

Scene Four

Again they dress them, the clothes are those of nine to ten-year-olds, everyone gets a little older. But no big costume changes. Just additions. We keep adding pieces from the diapers to the final costume.

Mother   He is stubborn like you. That's why he doesn't learn right.

Father   Me? Stubborn? There is no one more *not* stubborn than me. He doesn't concentrate. That comes from your side of the family. That's why he doesn't learn right.

Mother   Well, my dear, I finished school if you forgot, and you had big problems with my father until he accepted you. It's because of your charm that you got me. Not your education even though you are so very clever, my beloved.

Father   Yes, I could have chosen from among many but there was only you I wanted. Even if you were a bit spoiled with all your diplomas and certificates. Let's have more kids. Bring me two more. But boys this time.

Mother   And it was only you I wanted. So what do we do about the boy who isn't learning?

Father   Let the other one teach him. I don't even know which one is which anymore. Did you have to make them exactly the same?

Mother   This is from God. He wanted two the same. Hamdalillah, all the girls are different. That's because they are girls. Girls are better.

Father   Everyone knows, my sweet, that boys are better.

Mother   What ever you say, dear, as long you remember that I was a girl once. So think on that.

Father   Where are those girls? All studying in a row. Always studying. No one ever sees them.

Mother   Another set of twins, Ahmaderella and Ahmadarinna.

Father   No one has three times twins. Even the doctor said it was strange.

Mother   Are you saying I'm strange. Shall I go back to my father's house?

Father   No, no, no, my sweet. I like strange. Strange is fresh. Don't I always say that? And no one is more strange than you. I will always like you just as you are. The strange woman, my wife.

Mother   BOYS come in here.

Kid One   Why are you shouting? Where is lunch?

Kid Two   I lost my book.

Mother   Where?

Kid Two   In the bag.

Mother   So go get it.

Kid Two   I lost the bag.

Kid One   And the bag is gone forever. Why don't people give things back when they find them?

Kid Two   Why do I keep losing things?

Kid One   What grade did you get on the test?

Kid Two   Was there a test?

Mother   What test?

Father   I have no money for another bag or another book. You solve that problem.

Kid One   Why don't you have money?

Father   Life is hard.

Kid Two   Why is life hard?

Mother   It's none of your business.

Kid One   Why is he strange?

Father   Strange is good.

Mother   Strange has its limits.

Kid Two   I'm not strange. I'm different.

Kid One   You are not.

Kid Two   I am so.

Kid One   Then what grade did you get on the test?

Mother   What test?

Father   Where is lunch, my dear?

Kid Two   Do grades matter? I wrote a poem. Listen.

Mother   I have no time for poems.

Kid Two   Why don't you have time for poems?

Father   What is the poem about?

Kid One   Where is lunch?

Mother It's where it always is.

Kid Two Why is everything where it always is?

Father Don't ask silly questions. Is there a poem?

Kid Two Give me your book and I will learn it all and give it back.

Kid One I want it back before you lose it.

Father Call your sisters.

Mother They ate already. (*Pause.*) Aren't we a lucky family?!

Father Why do you even ask? Look! Bless your hands, ya Im Ahmad for this meal.

All happy. And then they each change clothes and fix the set for start of next scene.

Scene Five

The boys are twelve to thirteen years old. It's a mess. More stuff in the house, things broken, part of the room broken as if something fell into it. Everyone is older and more tired. Something has happened and things have changed.

Kid Two Why did they ruin our house?

Kid One Did we do anything wrong?

Kid Two Yabba, are you in the resistance?

Kid One I bet he is?

Mother We all resist as best we can.

Father Good that the girls were at your mother's house.

Mother Yes, their room is filled with the neighbour's house from upstairs.

Kid Two Why? Why every year?

Mother Is it every year?

Kid One It's every day. Why can't I fight?

Father What do you mean fight? You have to be precise. You want to fight with me or with your brother or with your mother?

Kid One Can I fight the ones who broke our house?

Kid Two Can you fight the ones who broke our house?

Kid One What do you mean?

Kid Two Are you strong?

Kid One Of course I'm strong. And you?

Kid Two   Not as strong as you but I can speak and write and talk.

Father   You can speak and write and talk?

Mother   And you are strong? When did you become strong?

Father   We made wonderful boys, Im Ahmad.

Mother   And girls. But they are always studying and we never see them.

Kid One   Together, can we make this story better.

Kid Two   We have asked a thousand questions since we were born and now we have to stop asking.

Kid One   Asking questions is good!

Kid Two   Is asking questions good?

All laugh.

Scene Six

The boys are older. The parents have aged. Four short epilogues.

Father   I don't know how to answer my children about the life we lead here in Gaza. I can't find the work I want and I can't bring the money they all deserve. I find my wife as wonderful as the day I married her but I see how she struggles with the children. And I see her worry about me. I don't want her to worry. But she does. And I worry about her worrying about me.

Mother   I was lucky. We all lived. We lost a room and part of the garden but it will grow again. And look at my children. I think they asked us a thousand questions. Some are very difficult to answer. Some have no answers. We can't meet the people who broke our houses. They don't want to talk to us. They lock us up and we can't ask a single question. I see my husband hiding his fear. Together we whisper to each other all the things we would do if we could travel. We talk about something called freedom. It's another question we cannot answer.

Kid One   My parents are good parents. They did everything they could. We went to school. They got us what we needed. We know we are poor. We know that we miss so much. We have seen the internet and we have read what people say in the other countries. I went to university. I graduated. But now I can't find work. I look at my father looking at me. I look at my mother seeing life repeating itself. I want to have a country, a job, we want to take a family vacation. For now, I have a fiancée and will marry and keep the family line going. I will work for the country.

Kid Two   I still have a thousand questions. No. I have two thousand questions. Why does the world ignore us? Why can't I go out of Gaza? Where is the rest of my family? Why can't they come visit? Who will publish my poems? Why don't tourists come here? Why is there only one version of this story? Why do they say I'm bad when all I want is a country? Does everyone have a thousand questions? Yes, I believe that everyone has AT LEAST one thousand questions. And I have only one answer. All our sisters got married but you won't see them. Hamdalillah.

End.

Play #2: The Snow Trip

Characters

Older sister, **Adan**, *age fourteen.*
Middle sister, **Siba**, *age ten.*
Younger sister, **Hind**, *age five.*
Voice of Mother
Voice of Father
(or two extra actors)

Gaza. Summer. Three girls are cleaning their messy room. They have finished their exams. The unseen mother wants the entire house cleaned and the unseen father is in and out all day making and receiving phone calls to all sorts of people. The mother is both cleaning and following the news of the husband. The three sisters enter their very messy room. They wonder how to begin. They start by making things worse.

Scene One

Adan I want everything cleaned up the way my mother said and I know exactly how she does it. This mess must go. Everything in the right place. Today our room, tomorrow the boys' room, then the salon. The kitchen will be last.

Siba No one touch my things.

Adan And then we pack because everything has to be ready when we go to Jerusalem.

Siba We have to think very well of what we will bring. We have to buy the presents also. I heard them talking. We have a huge family in Jerusalem. Maybe one hundred people. My mother said we are going shopping tonight. And tomorrow night.

Hind It's snowing in Jerusalem.

Siba No it isn't.

Hind Yes it is.

Adan No it isn't.

Hind IT IS. I saw it on television.

Siba Oh really? When?

Hind Before yesterday. I don't remember exactly but it's snowing. Remember when it snowed and the roof fell down and everyone died. I'm not going to Jerusalem.

Adan That was in the winter. It's the summer now.

Siba There is no snow now. I am going to bring my pocket money with me. Listen. (*She shakes her change purse.*) I saved some. I can buy things in Jerusalem.

Adan We will all go to the mosque in Jerusalem. And the Dome of the Rock.

Siba And the market. It's a big market.

Hind I'm not going. It's snowing. Everyone will die.

Adan It's not snowing. It's August.

Hind August is bad.

Siba Why is August bad? It's summer. We have no school. We have a vacation. We're going to Jerusalem.

Hind I'm not going in August in the snow.

Adan Stop being silly. Father has been working for months to get us a permit to go. You are going . . . but first start cleaning this room.

Hind I'm staying here. Right in this room. I want nothing to do with snow. (*They clean.*) What's a permit?

Adan What do you care? You're not going.

Hind What's a permit?

Adan It's a thing that you need to leave Gaza and go somewhere else.

Hind I don't want it.

Siba You have to have it or you can't go.

Hind I don't want it. I'm not leaving.

Adan Oh no? And what do you think you will do when we are all in Jerusalem and you are here alone? Who will take care of you?

Hind My mother, of course.

Siba She is coming with us.

Hind No she isn't. We are not going. Not her and not me. We will stay here with Selwa and her mother and play with our dolls.

Adan Stop being silly. Father has planned this trip with mother. We are going to a wedding. A big wedding. In Jerusalem. Now clean up your stuff and stop being silly.

Siba You don't even know where Jerusalem is.

Hind Oh yes I do. It's there. (*She points with a moving finger.*) And look. It's snowing. Don't you feel it? Don't you hear it? It's coming. Listen. There it is. Coming, coming, coming. And boom. Snow on our heads. Roof broken.

Siba You don't even know what snow is.

Hind What, are you saying I don't know what snow is? I know exactly what snow is.

Siba Oh yeah, oh yeah, OK, smartie, what is snow?

Pause.

Hind I'm not telling you. I'm not telling you or anyone.

Siba Because you don't know what it is.

Hind I DO. AND I'M NOT TELLING AND I'M NOT GOING TO JERUSALEM.

Adan Stop shouting or I will smack you. Enough.

Hind Yaaaama. Adan is hitting me.

Adan I am not hitting you.

Hind You are thinking about it.

Siba You are so stupid. You're going to ruin it for everyone. You are going to Jerusalem if I have to stuff you in a suitcase.

Hind I know exactly what snow is and it comes and comes and booooom booom boooom and then grrrrrrrrrr and boooom and grrrrrr and the house falls and everyone screams. I'M NOT GOING. I'M NOT GOING.

Scene Two

Adan Sit down you and you. (*To* **Siba**.) Stop provoking her. (*To* **Hind**.) Come sit here on my lap. That is not snow, my little girl. That is something else all together. You remember that booom boooom boooom. That isn't snow.

Hind So what is snow?

Adan It's weather. It's science. It's complicated. Don't you want to talk about Jerusalem? It's our holy city and it's only one hour away in the car.

Hind I know where Jerusalem is. It's there. With the snow!

Siba I'll tell.

Adan (*to* **Siba**) Not one word. Listen. Snow is when it's very cold. If it rains and when it's very cold the rain freezes into little white things called snowflakes. If it stays cold all of the snowflakes cover everything and it's all white and it's very pretty like you saw on television. That's snow. But it never snows in Gaza.

Hind Why not?

Siba (*pause*) Because of the siege . . . nothing comes to Gaza because of THE SIEGE.

Hind WHAT'S A SIEGE?

Siba GAZA.

Hind WHAT'S A SIEGE?

Siba GAZA.

Hind WHAT'S A SIEGE?

Adan WHAT IS WRONG WITH YOU TWO. If my father hears this he will leave us all here and he will go to Jerusalem with my mother and you two will have ruined everything. (*To* **Siba**.) Leave her alone. Why are you provoking her? Why?

Siba (*imitating* **Hind**) What's snow? What's a permit? I'm not going. What's a siege? She's making me crazy with her stupid questions.

Hind I'm not stupid. I got twenty stars from the Miss in school. (*Showing off.*) I got a star from the Miss for being good. And a star from the Miss for my drawing and a star from the Miss for playing and a star from the Miss for sitting still. I have more than any of you.

Adan Good. That's because you do what you're told. Now . . . we are cleaning up this room and we are going to pack and get ready so when the time comes we are all ready.

Hind Ready for what?

Adan To travel.

Hind I'm not travelling.

Adan You are.

Hind I'm not.

Siba You are!

Hind WHAT'S A SIEGE?

Siba (*frustrated*) I don't know what a siege is. BUT everything is blamed on the siege. Every time you ask for something they say no because of the siege. When do we fix the roof? When the siege is over. When will my mother fix her eyes? When the siege is over. When can we have new clothes? When the siege is over. Why are there so many kids in the class? Because of the siege. Why did Abu Ala die? Because of the siege.

Hind I AM NOT GOING TO JERUSALEM.

Adan CLEAN YOUR THINGS. (*Pause.*) A siege is when you are surrounded from all sides and nothing goes out and nothing comes in. That's a siege. But no one needs to worry about the siege because my father has been working on the permits for a year and he says that we can all go to Jerusalem.

Hind Where is it?

Adan What?

Hind The siege.

Siba I told you, it's here and here and here and here and here. And it goes all the way to there and there and there and there . . .

Scene Three

Hind What's a permit?

Siba For leaving the class . . .

Hind Right. I got a permit once. I had to go and the Miss said, 'Hind you have a permit to go.'

Siba I passed all my classes. I got higher grades than you. Stars don't count. You need numbers. Numbers count. You need nine from ten and twenty from twenty.

Hind I have twenty points from twenty. I just told you. (*Pause.*) Why do we need a permit?

Adan To go to Jerusalem.

Hind And the Miss does that?

Adan Clean up your mattress.

Hind (*on her mattress*)   I don't want a permit. I don't need one.

Adan This isn't the same kind of permit. It's a permit to leave Gaza and go to Jerusalem.

Hind But I don't want to leave Gaza and go to Jerusalem. It's snowing in Jerusalem.

Siba *takes a whole big pile of clothing and throws them up in the air and they land on all the girls.*

Hind   AGHGHGH WHY DID YOU DO THAT? YAAAAAMA. . . .!!!

Adan QUIET. (*To* **Siba**.) STOP AND PICK THIS ALL UP AND (*to* **Hind**) YOU GET OFF THAT MATTRESS AND PUT YOUR THINGS AWAY. LOOK AT ALL THESE SOCKS. YALLA, PUT THEM TOGETHER. AND STOP BOTHERING HER AND NO MORE TALKING. QUIET.

Adan We are so messy. But all girls are messy. My friend Hanan told me that. She is also messy. But her mother hits her.

Siba We have a good mother, hamdalillah. I will fold these.

Hind I fold better than you. Watch.

Siba That's not folding. This is folding.

Hind I'm not going to Jerusalem . . .

Adan Of course you're going. We are all going.

Hind   . . . because it's snowing and I don't need a permit and I have a siege. I'm staying here and watching my stars and folding.

Siba That's not folding. Look. This is folding.

Hind And this is UNFOLDING. (*She undoes her arranging.*)

Adan You're coming with us. Stop talking about it.

Siba My father says you already have the permit. So even if you don't want it, you have it.

Hind (*singing*)   Here is a star and here is a car and here is a street and here is a treat. Here is a star and here is the sand and a music band . . .

Scene Four

Adan   Let's take a rest. Who wants a sandwich?

They sit down in the half-cleaned room and have a small bite to eat.

Adan (*to* **Hind**)   So your plan is that you will stay with Selwa while we go to the wedding in Jerusalem?

Hind   Wedding?

Siba   Didn't you know? A huge wedding. A huge, huge, huge, huge, HUGE wedding.

Hind   Who is getting married?

Siba   Our cousin Musa and our cousin Moeen and our cousin Khaled and our cousin Saleem.

Hind   I don't know those names. We don't have those cousins. I never met them.

Adan   No one ever met them but they are our real relatives. And they are all getting married.

Siba   All of them, together. That's what my mother said.

Adan   She's right. We will have four grooms and four brides and a big hall. And we will dance for them and sing for them and bless them.

Hind   Four grooms and four brides?

Adan   Four grooms and four brides!

Siba   And each bride will change her dress many times . . . !!!!

Hind   Each bride will change her dresses?

Adan   That's many beautiful dresses. And you can see them all.

Siba   It's seven times four – it's twenty-eight dresses. We can see twenty-eight dresses.

Adan   I never saw twenty-eight dresses.

Siba   And you know what mother said? She told me they have a cake as high as a house. A white cake as high as a house covered in cream and it has dolls on top, one of a bride and one a groom, it's like a big pile of cream and everyone gets to eat it in the wedding.

Hind   Really?

Siba   Oh yes. Like one giant pile of SNOW . . . !!!!

Hind   Adanaaaaaaaaaaaaa. (*And she throws herself on her mattress crying.*)

Scene Five

Adan   Quiet. Listen, my father is still on the phone. Quiet I said. Stop crying or I will rip up your stars. Shhhhhhhhhh.

Siba And now he's yelling.

Adan It's just nervous tension.

Siba Sometimes he yells and sometimes he says good, good, good. I think the whole story is so complicated and that's why we all have to go this time. This is the only time we will ever go to Jerusalem. It is very difficult to go to Jerusalem.

Hind What's nervous tension?

Siba Your questions are nervous tension. Stop asking questions.

Hind STOP YELLING AT ME.

Siba I'M NOT YELLING. FATHER IS YELLING.

Adan STOP YELLING. Listen. He closed the phone.

Siba He wasn't yelling.

Adan So everything is fine.

Hind Does my father have nervous tension?

Adan Everyone has nervous tension because soon we are going to Jerusalem. (*Pause.*) Listen to me, both of you. All these things need to be looked at carefully. The dirty things will be washed and the clean things will be put away. No more talk of Jerusalem.

Hind I have a lot of nervous tension . . . Four brides? Really four brides?

Adan Yes. Look. We have an invitation.

Adan *produces an invitation that has the announcement of all the four cousins marrying all the four girls.*

Hind Read it to me.

Adan It says here: In the name of God, the family of Doctor and Mrs Khawaldi from Beit Hanina in Holy Jerusalem will marry their sons Musa, Moin, Khaled, and Saleem to the girls Anan, Jumana, Huda, and Hala in the Four Seasons Hall in Al Ram on 15 August 2015 and may you join us in blessing them for a happy life on this day. (*Pause.*) Isn't that beautiful.

Siba I will wear this dress. I am packing it here. No one touch it. We are buying shoes tonight.

Hind Shoes?

Adan Of course. Everyone is getting new shoes. And you are even getting a new dress because the old one is too small for you now. You grew this year.

Hind I'm getting new shoes AND a new dress? I grew this year?

Siba We told you before that we are going shopping tonight. All week we are cleaning and shopping and shopping and cleaning and getting ready to go.

Adan And you don't want to come with us?! We will sit next to the four brides and bring them juice and hold their hands. And take photographs with them.

Hind Photographs? With four brides. (*Pause.*) But . . . the snow . . .

Adan Habibti, I swear on the life of my mother that there is no snow in Jerusalem. We can look at the television and you will see sunshine in Jerusalem.

Siba And not so hot like here. At night, it gets cool. That's what they say. At night you need a sweater.

Hind I don't have a sweater!

Adan We will get you a sweater.

Hind A sweater in summer?!

Adan Let's clean up and finish this room.

Hind I will put these dolls here in case I go to Jerusalem. And here will go the new shoes. And the dress. And the sweater. If I go.

Adan You don't get the dress if you don't go.

Hind WHY NOT?

Siba Because the dress and the shoes and the sweater and the permit is for the wedding.

Hind (*hard thinking*) OK. OK. OK. OK. OK. OK. OK. OK. I'm going to Jerusalem. (*Pause.*) OK I AM GOING TO JERUSALEM. (*Pause.*) Can we take Selwa. I'm sure she wants to go. And her mother. They are sad.

Adan They don't have permits to go.

Hind But they have a sweater.

Adan No. They can't come.

Hind WHY?

Siba Because it's complicated and it takes time and they don't have a permit and I don't know. But they can't come.

Hind We can go to the Miss and get her a permit.

Adan No.

Siba Why are they sad.

Hind Because everyone died.

Adan We are almost done. I'm very happy, ya Hind, that you are coming with us.

Siba We can sleep together in Jerusalem like we sleep together here. It's exactly the same as here.

Scene Six

Voices of **Father** *and* **Mother**.

Father For four months I'm working on these permits. I call every day. We have all the papers . . .

Mother What are they saying?

Father Be quiet, I'm trying to listen. What do they need now? We have all needed papers!!!

Mother We have all needed papers.

Father What do you mean in processing?

Mother What is in processing?

Father DENIED? But they said it was in processing. How can it be DENIED?

Mother Who is DENIED?

Father Stop talking to me while I'm talking to them. Are you sure? You have to call again. We are ready to go. We have all the papers from this side. We are planning this for a year. We told you. We told you. And we told the kids. *(Pause.)* It's not possible. DENIED? Why am I DENIED? I went last year. Last year I'm APPROVED and now I'm DENIED. *(Pause.)* WE DON'T HAVE PERMITS??? *(Pause.)* They won't let us leave.

Hind What?

Adan Wait. (*She listens to the rest of the phone conversation, but nothing.*)

Hind What is DENIED?

Adan I don't know.

Siba I think it's snowing in Jerusalem.

Hind No it's not. It's August.

Adan No. It's the permits.

Hind He was yelling at the Miss?

Adan No.

Siba What now?

Adan I don't think we are going. This is not possible. I don't think we're going.

Hind WHAT?

Adan He said DENIED.

Hind What is DENIED?

Siba   It means no going.

Hind   Why?

Siba   We are DENIED.

Hind   What is DENIED?

Adan   Stop shouting. It means we are not allowed to go.

Hind   WHY? WHAT DID I DO? I GOT TWENTY STARS AND YOU HAVE NUMBERS AND WE ARE GOOD AND THERE IS NO SNOW AND THERE ARE FOUR BRIDES AND TWENTY-EIGHT DRESSES AND A CREAM CAKE AS HIGH AS A HOUSE????

Adan   I don't know.

Siba   It happens to everyone.

Hind   What happens to everyone.

Siba   That they try to get permits and they think they have them and then at the last minute, they are DENIED.

Adan   I thought we had them. We were on the list of approved people. Something must have happened.

Hind   What list? What happened? Now I must go to Jerusalem. You said we could go and see the four brides. You said we could see the biggest market and the holy mosque. You said we have one hundred relatives there. And we would buy one hundred gifts. And now you say we aren't going? (*Shouting.*) Yamma, they are mean, my sisters, they promised me Jerusalem and now they take it back. Yamma. Yamma answer me. Yamma, answer me. Yaaaaaamaaaaaaa.

Adan   QUIET. (*Pause. Silence.*) We will go another time.

Siba   Yes, my father will try again. He said he would try until he dies. One day he said that.

Adan   I was so excited.

Siba   Me too. Do we still have to clean?

Adan   We might as well finish it up.

And now the room is all clean.

Hind   When we come back from shopping we will call the Miss again and my father will fix it.

Adan   We are probably not going shopping tonight.

Hind   Why?

Siba   Because we are not going to Jerusalem.

Hind   Of course we are going to Jerusalem.

Siba　Don't you hear. We are not going!!

Adan　Let's see mother.

Hind　I am going!

Adan　Stop talking, ya Hind. We are not going.

Hind　Yes we are. (*Shouting as they leave.*) Yamma, I am going to Jerusalem tomorrow. Yalla, we are going shopping to buy presents for the brides. (*Pause.*) I am going to Jerusalem. TOMORROW.

End.

Play #3: The Boys in the Mirror

Characters

Ahmad
Mirror Image *of Ahmad.*
Mother, *a small woman.*
Another Mirror of Ahmad. **Mirror Image Two**
Note: because of casting limitations, there is no mirror image of the Mother in this play. There could be if wanted, and an actor were available. The props needed and used by Mirror Image of Ahmad are hidden under the mirror bed and used as needed.

Ahmad *has stopped talking. His* **Mirror Image** *is getting bored. The* **Mother** *is busy chopping onions and crying all the time. (It has to be both real crying and onion tears as needed.)*

Scene One

Ahmad *is laying on his bed. The* **Mirror Image** *is doing the same. What separates them is a frame. At first the* **Mirror Image** *is doing exactly what Ahmad is doing.*

Mother (*crying*)   These are very fresh onions. Look at my tears. I have to be careful with the salt or everything will be salty. (*Pause.*) Ahmad do you want tea? I will make tea. I will make you tea, ya Ahmad, and you can drink it if you want. (*She brings* **Ahmad** *the tea. Same tea appears in the mirror image. She continues with her onions and tears.*) The boy hasn't spoken in three days. How can a person live without talking? Why does a boy stop talking? I talk. His father talks. Him? He doesn't talk.

Ahmad *drinks the tea and the* **Mirror Image** *drinks the tea. But the* **Mirror Image** *watches the* **Mother** *as she moves back to her onions and* **Ahmad** *does not.*

Mother   Oh yes, these are very fresh onions. Look at these tears. And now he doesn't drink. A person gets thirsty in the heat. A person can melt without drinking. (*Pause. Tears.*) Ahmad yamma. Do you want a sandwich of white cheese or turkey? Which one yamma? Hurry with your answer before the bread gets wet. Do you want cheese or turkey? (*No answer.* **Mother** *has more tears.*) Ok dear, I will wait until you answer. Tell me when you're ready. (*Pause.*) It's three days that he doesn't have a sandwich. They tell me 'Leave him alone and soon he will get hungry.' So I leave him. But a boy has to eat. Yamma. Do you want onions? (*Crying.*)

Ahmad *is still laying there thinking about yesterday and tomorrow. He doesn't think about today. The* **Mirror Image** *is thinking about today because he is quite hungry.*

Mirror   Psssst. (**Ahmad** *doesn't react.*) Psssst. Hey. Pssssst.

After no reaction from **Ahmad** *the* **Mirror Image** *throws a small stone at* **Ahmad***.*

Ahmad *looks in the mirror.*

Mirror Image   Hi.

Ahmad (*No answer.*)

Mirror Image   Come on, man, you gotta eat something. I say white cheese. Tell her white cheese. Go on. Say it.

Ahmad *is annoyed with this and turns his back to the mirror. The* **Mirror Image** *also turns with him but the head is still facing* **Ahmad***.*

Mirror Image   Psssst. (*No reaction.*) Pssst. Come on. Hey boy. White cheese.

Mother   Did you say something, Ahmad? Did you say 'white cheese'? (*To herself.*) At your service, yamma . . . I will make you a nice white cheese sandwich. Don't you worry.

Mirror Image   Thank God. We haven't eaten in days. Listen.

Ahmad *and* **Mirror Image**   Stop. Stop talking. I'm not talking. Why are you talking?

Mirror   Because we're hungry.

Ahmad *and* **Mirror**   Shshsh. Why are you talking? Stop talking. You only talk when I talk. That's the rule.

Mirror Image   She's bringing the sandwich. Look, she's bringing the sandwich. Here it comes.

The **Mother** *comes with a sandwich and puts it next to* **Ahmad**. *On the mirror side the sandwich appears as well.* **Ahmad** *puts his sandwich at the end of the bed. The* **Mirror Image** *does not.*

Mirror Image   Come on, boy, we have to eat. My stomach is making noise and so is yours. We have to eat.

Ahmad *and* **Mirror Image**   Shhhhhhhhhhhh. Stop talking. I'm not eating.

They stay watching each other.

Mirror Image   Listen boy, I'm eating. I haven't eaten in three days.

Ahmad   You can't eat. I'm not eating so you can't eat.

Mirror Image   I'm hungry.

Ahmad   I'm also hungry but you don't see me eating.

Mirror Image (*eating but being careful, he is not moving all that differently from* **Ahmad**)   Eat. It's good.

Ahmad   No. I'm on a strike.

Mirror Image   Against who?

Ahmad   Everything. Now stop talking to me.

Mirror Image   Eat your sandwich.

Ahmad *and* **Mirror Image**   No.

Mirror Image   Well I am eating.

Scene Two

The **Mother** *is now trying to thread a needle to sew a ripped sheet. It's big so she gets 'lost' in it. The mother is always struggling and suffering.*

Mother   Yalla, one two three in. Missed it. In the old days, I could just throw the thread and it would go through the eye of the needle. Today I can't see like before. Maybe I need glasses. Everyone gets glasses when they grow old. (To Ahmad) Yamma, I am getting old. Please say something to me, habibi, before I'm too old to hear you, yamma.

Mirror Image That was good. (*The sandwich on* **Ahmad**'s *bed has disappeared.*) Your strike doesn't fit our situation.

Ahmad Where's my bread?

Mirror Image I ate it.

Ahmad Good. Because I'm on strike.

Mirror Image Yeah, yeah, yeah. Against everthing.

Mother Ahmad did you speak? Habibi, I need your eyes, yamma. Come thread this needle. Yamma, I need to fix your sheet. Look how you ripped it from sitting on it all day and all night. Yamma, you have to move. Come thread the needle. I really need eye glasses. I'll try again. One two three . . . AH . . . look yamma, it went in all by itself. (*She can start sewing the sheet.*) Blessing on your hands, ya habibi, I couldn't have done it without you.

Ahmad *and* **Mirror Image** Did you do that? Stop. Stop talking. Stop helping her. I'm on strike. Stop repeating me.

Mirror Image You can't strike on everything. You need to pick a good cause. Is your strike to hurt your mother?

Ahmad No.

Mother If I fix his sheet he will have a nice fixed sheet on his bed. Fixed and washed. (*Tears.*) It must be the smell of the soap that is making these tears. It's very strong soap. That's what the man in the souk told me.

Mirror Image So what's your issue?

Ahmad Issue?

Mirror Image Every strike has an issue. Something you want to change.

Ahmad *and* **Mirror Image** I want to change everything. Everything that ever happened.

Mirror Image Tsk tsk tsk tsk . . .

Ahmad What?

Mirror Image Forget it.

Ahmad WHAT!

Mother Yamma, did you say something? Have you started talking?

Ahmad Look what you did.

Mirror Image You're the one who yelled. Listen, boy, you can't change everything on the same day. You have to start with one thing and change that. And the next day you do another thing. Like that.

Ahmad I don't want to talk about it.

Mirror Image You can't change if you don't talk.

Ahmad *and* **Mirror Image**   You have to stop talking. Leave me alone.

Ahmad   Every time I talk, I say the wrong thing. I talk to my father and he yells and he gets nervous and doesn't realize I need things for school. I talk to my teacher and he is tired and if my answer is wrong he gets nervous and if it's right he also gets nervous. And with all the friends we can't find anything to do because all the places are either forbidden or broken. So we always argue. It's better to just stop with everything. Yes. It's better to stop. So I am stopping. I am never doing another thing. Ever. Ever. I stop. Everything. Everyone.

Mirror Image   Everything everyone everything everyone everything everyone. Slowly slowly ya Ahmad. One by one. One person. One problem. Not everything at once. Now you're not talking and your mother is crying.

Ahmad   It's the onions.

Mirror Image   It's not the onions. Stop acting like your little brother.

Mother   Where are the kids? I'm so busy with this one that I forgot about the others. Ya Mohammed, ya Saleem, ya Abduallah, ya Mahmoud, ya Zeina, ya Amal, ya Imad, ya Susu, ya Soheir, come in and make yourselves tea and a sandwich. I'm busy with Ahmad. (*She takes the finished sheet and goes to* **Ahmad**.) Yalla habibi, get up so I can put this on your bed. Yalla yamma. (*But* **Ahmad** *doesn't want to get up. So the mother puts the sheet on the bed with* **Ahmad** *on it. In the mirror, the* **Mirror Image** *moves around like* **Ahmad** *and a sheet appears on the mirror bed.*) Be comfortable, yamma. And if you want to talk, here I am ready to listen to all of you and to do whatever you ask. (*Pause.*) I'm going to clean the whole house now. I won't bother you.

Scene Three

The **Mother** *brings all the stuff she needs for cleaning: a bucket, a mop, broom, etc. She makes noise with the buckets and knock things together. She drops things. She's funny and noisy.*

Mother   I need the girls to help me but I can't let them see this boy. It doesn't matter. I will clean the whole house by myself. I like to clean and make sure that all is tip top and fresh. (*Crying.*) The smell of the chlorine is making me cry. It must be very good chlorine.

Mirror Image   She's going to turn the house upside down now. Why don't I come to your side.

Ahmad   Can you?

Mirror Image   If you agree.

Ahmad   This is crazy. You're only a mirror. You are me. You aren't you. You and I are one. You cannot do whatever you want. Stay where you are.

Mirror Image   True. (*Pause.*) So who am I talking to?

Ahmad   To myself. I'm talking to myself.

Mirror Image   Don't you want to talk to yourself in quiet without all the noise of your mother cleaning?

Ahmad   OK. But you are me. You can't go running around doing whatever you want. And stop talking so much. You talk too much. I don't want to talk.

Mirror Image   Agreed. But you do talk a lot.

Ahmad *and* **Mirror Image**   I'm not talking.

The boy in the mirror comes through the mirror and sits on the edge of the bed like **Ahmad**. *They sit side by side but mirror each other's movement as* **Ahmad** *makes sure that the* **Mirror Image** *is under his control.*

Ahmad   No one understands me.

Mirror Image   No one understands anyone. You are not alone here. There are two million people who don't understand.

Ahmad   No. It's me. I can't forget what happened and the future isn't coming fast enough.

Mother (*passing by with her broom; she sees* **Mirror Image**)   AGHAHGHGHAH AHGHGHAH. Who is this? A ghost. Out, out, out. (*She chases the* **Mirror Image** *around the house.*) A jinn. God protect us. Out, out, out.

Ahmad   What is happening? Why does she see you?

Mirror Image (*still running from* **Mother**)   I forgot to tell you that when I come out, everyone can see me.

Ahmad   How can you forget to tell me that?

Mother   Who are you? How did you get in here? Ahmad? Are you talking? What did you do to Ahmad? Why is he talking?

Mirror Image   Don't you want him to talk?

The **Mother** *knocks the* **Mirror Image** *over the head and he falls down knocked out.*

Ahmad   What did you do?

Mother   I saved you from the ghost.

Ahmad   What ghost?

Mother   The one who looks like you. Habibi, are you hurt, did he hurt you?

Ahmad   Yamma, you hit me on the head.

Mother   No I didn't. I hit that one on the head. What is that?

Ahmad   It's me.

Mother   No. You are you. I am me. And that is that. Habibi, you are speaking? (*Pause.*) I will make food for you. Come, yamma, I will call your father and tell him you are speaking.

Ahmad No. I am not speaking. Go away. Leave me alone. Go. Go. Leave me alone. You don't understand.

Mother (*crying*) Aghghghg ya Allah, what have we done to Ahmad? First he doesn't speak and doesn't eat and you can barely see him and now he comes as two. Astaghfirullah Al Adheem. I'm going out for air. (*Tears.*) It must be that jinn bringing me tears. All day long tears. Fine. One day these tears will end. I will use them all up and that will be that.

Ahmad (*to* **Mirror Image**) Hey Ahmad, get up. Get up.

Ahmad *puts water on the* **Mirror Image**'s *head and his own head. They both shake their heads as if waking up from the water. The* **Mirror Image** *and* **Ahmad** *see that the* **Mother** *is outside crying and nervous. It appears that she is talking to several people though no one is there but her.*

Mirror Image I think the first change we have to do is to make her feel better.

Ahmad Yes. We have been terrible to her.

Scene Four

Now **Ahmad** *and the* **Mirror Image** *will be in sync. They will move and play exactly the same.*

Ahmad *and* **Mirror Image** Yamma. Yamma come back in. I am OK.

Mother I hear two voices calling me. I must see what is happening.

She enters.

Ahmad *and* **Mirror Image** Mother, I am Ahmad.

Mother *faints. They both pick her up. Put water on her head. And they hold her up. Her feet struggling to stand up. Eventually, she will stand on her own.*

Ahmad *and* **Mirror Image** Mother are you OK? Habibti, I am Ahmad. Don't worry. It's OK.

Mother (*touching them both*) You are Ahmad.

Ahmad *and* **Mirror Image** Yes. And I want to tell you that I am sorry.

Mother (*again she faints, but gets back to herself*) I really need eyeglasses. I am seeing double.

Ahmad *and* **Mirror Image** I am sorry for being so mean to you, habibti, yamma.

Ahmad Yamma, I am the Ahmad who sees everything as impossible.

Mirror Image And I am the Ahmad who sees everything as possible.

Mother (*crying*) And I am the mother who has an ocean of tears in her eyes.

Ahmad (*taking a sandwich*) Look, yamma, I am eating a sandwich.

Mirror Image I ate mine before.

Mother (*to* **Mirror Image**) You have a nice smile, just like Ahmad.

Mirror Image Because I am Ahmad.

Mother (*to* **Ahmad**) But you are still frowning.

Ahmad Because I'm angry . . .

Mother *starts to faint but the boys catch her and* **Ahmad** *continues . . .*

Ahmad But I am not angry at you. I am angry at me.

Mother Why, yamma? What did you do, habibi?

Ahmad Nothing. And that's the problem. For three days I sit here doing nothing.

Mirror Image It's because he's confused.

Mother But we are all confused, yamma. It's normal. Don't tell him I told you, but even your father, God help him, is confused.

Mirror Image We are going to help you clean, yamma.

Mother A boy doesn't clean.

Ahmad *and* **Mirror Image** Oh yes they do. Watch.

Now the three of them will move together and wash the floor together. The **Mother** *will keep falling out of step but the boys help her so they can stay as one group of dancers.*

Ahmad Yamma, tomorrow I will take my little sisters and brothers to the beach so you can rest.

Mirror Image I will watch them like a hawk and teach the small ones to swim.

Ahmad I have to let yesterday go.

Mother What happened yesterday?

Ahmad All the yesterdays.

Mother Which yesterdays?

Mirror Image He means all the sad things that have happened. He has to let go.

Ahmad We can throw them in the sea.

Mother All sad things in the sea? Then we will have sad fish.

All laugh.

Mother Yamma, when you throw your yesterdays, remember to keep your memories. There's a difference, yamma. (*Calling.*) Ya Mohammed, ya Saleem, ya Abduallah, ya Mahmoud, ya Zeina, ya Amal, ya Imad, ya Susu, ya Soheir, your brother Ahmad and your brother Ahmad are talking and dancing and tomorrow you are all going swimming. I will prepare the lunch.

Mother *begins to prepare a big package of lunch while* **Ahmad** *and* **Mirror** *play chess.*

Scene Five

The frame of the mirror is where it was when the play started. **Ahmad** *and* **Mirror Image** *are playing chess on the one bed. A third Ahmad* **Mirror Image Two** *appears on the bed in the mirror.*

Ahmad   Look.

Mirror Image   I see.

Ahmad   What is it?

Mirror Image   Another part of me.

Ahmad   How many parts do we have?

Mirror Image   I only know what you know.

All Three   Hello. You are Ahmad? Yes I am Ahmad. Do you want to come out of there.

Mirror Image Two   Yes. Let's go out.

Ahmad *and* **Mirror Image**   Out? Where do you want to go?

Mirror Image Two   Can I come over? (*He comes without waiting for an answer.*) I say we should go to the march. All of Gaza is walking east, in groups, as families, alone, walking towards the border. Why are we sitting inside when the whole world is walking north?

Ahmad *and* **Mirror Image**   It's only walking. It's a good way to begin again.

The three are now standing like men. The **Mother** *comes in. She stands looking at the three versions of her son. She goes back to her kitchen. She looks at the boys again to make sure they are moving together. The boys are whispering . . . planning. They are very engaged in what they are doing.*

Mother   I will bring him something cool to drink. He must be tired having found so many parts of himself. I worried. I thought I failed. But outside, all the different parts of me told me that he would be fine. (*She goes over to the three boys who all look at her and together smile the same smile.*) Here is something to drink, habibi. What are you doing, yamma?

Ahmad   I am thinking about taking a walk.

Mirror Image   East. Do you want to come with us?

Mirror Image Two   Come. Put on your scarf and walk with us. It's cool outside. It's good for your health.

Mother You want me to go for a walk with you? That's nice. Let me get us some juice.

Mother (*tears*)   I think the juice is making my eyes run tears.

Ahmad *and* **Mirror Image** *and* **Mirror Image Two**   Yes, yamma, we all know that juice makes you cry. Let's go. We will see all the people.

Mother *joins the three boys as they walk off stage, heading east.*

End.

Play #4: The Boys Who Can't Sit Still

Characters

Mustafa, *older brother.*
Noor, *middle brother.*
Ali, *youngest.*
Abu Mustafa, *Father.*
Aunt **Selwa**, *Mother's younger sister, a teacher at the girls' school next door.*
Grandfather
Grandmother Bahiyya
Sounds from a Loudspeaker
(*If one actor plays Father, Selwa, and Grandfather, it is a good joke.*)

A courtyard of a school and a wall. All entrances and exits are ONLY over the wall. There is a pole with an old loudspeaker attached to it.

Scene One

From behind the wall, a boy pops up and looks around, whistles a signal to his brother who also arrives and who signals to the third brother who arrives. Seeing the empty space, the boys begin to run, jump, they find or make a ball and throw it around, maybe a dead ball that they play with anyway. They try all kinds of acrobatic tricks, they fall, they get up, they are monkeys in a cage . . .

Sounds from a Loudspeaker   STOP. All activities in the school yard are to stop immediately. (*Boys freeze and listen scared.*) Anyone who is in the school yard must leave the school yard. This is not a school yard for children. And before you leave CLEAN IT UP. We are watching so do it well or you will be in trouble. You three are always in trouble. We will take care of that.

The boys, angry, begin to clean.

Noor   Who is talking?

Ali   The guy in the loudspeaker.

Mustafa   There is no guy in the loudspeaker.

Noor   Who is talking?

Mustafa   It's the guy in the school who has a thing and the thing is connected to another thing and it comes out here, in that thing up there. (*He throws something at the loudspeaker.*)

Ali   Be careful. They are watching us.

Noor   Where? I don't see anyone. It's a ghost.

Ali   A ghost?

Mustafa   Come on, let's clean up – and there are no ghosts. On three. One, two, threeeee.

And at top speed they clean up the place and combine some of their tricks and games into the cleaning until the courtyard is clean.

Mustafa   I would like to be the guy who talks.

Ali   Yeah me, too. (*Imitating.*) Kids, it's play time . . .

Noor   Kids eat your sandwiches . . .

Mustafa   Kids there is no homework . . .

Noor   Kids you all passed.

Ali   Kids we have books for everyone.

Mustafa Kids the border is open. Go visit your relatives. (*Pause.*) OK, it looks pretty clean. It would be nice to visit our relatives.

Ali We have relatives?

Noor You're really blank.

Mustafa Don't be rude to him. He's young. Habibi, all the cousins we talk to in the West Bank, they are the relatives, and the ones in Jerusalem, they are the relatives, and in Sweden, relatives, and Norway, relatives, and Jordan, relatives, and . . .

Noor And that's why everyone is always on the phone?

Mustafa Smart boy . . . Yalla, everyone up on the wall.

They all jump onto the wall and sit. But slowly they start moving again until they end up in the courtyard as in the beginning, playing and jumping.

Sounds from a Loudspeaker (*The boys again stand still. Teacher on the telephone.*)   This is the headmaster of Boys School B. Is this Abu Mustafa? Please come to the school to collect your sons. They are bothering everyone on the street, the phone is ringing every minute, and they are destroying public property, they are breaking the cement, and making noise and eating all the cookies, and we cannot sleep. They are ruining our break. (*Aside.*) Pass the cola, Abu Khaled.

Scene Two

Sound of Father MUSTAFA! NOOR! ALI! Save me some cookies. (*Enter the father, also over the wall, like a grown-up version of his sons.*) Who is yelling across the neighbourhood for all to hear? (*Into the loudspeaker.*) Hello in there. I am Abu Mustafa. You order – and I am here. I have nowhere else to be. I'm very sorry if my boys are eating your cement but they haven't eaten in a week. (*The boys join him on the wall and make sounds, if possible, that match what the father says.*) Since we cannot build, I have lost my job in the cement factory and all the workers are asking the kids to eat cement so we can go back to work. Very tasty, that cement. Keep those cookies for us. Shall we meet? Shall I come up to your office? Hello? Hello?

Mustafa They went home, I guess.

Noor You don't work in a cement factory.

Father One day I will work in a cement factory. And we will build houses. For now, it's a story that has to be told. Yallah, sit down. I brought you each an apple. Your mother says to eat it and you won't get sick. (*But there are only three apples on the wall, so the three boys and the father share, like juggling, the three apples.*)

Mustafa Let's play.

And again they jump in the way they jumped in, and begin to move and run and do their tricks in the courtyard. They play tag and they do games that require four people, make acrobatics, the father is happy but – as he is getting old and broken in spirit – we see he can't keep up with them. **Mustafa** *notices this.*

Mustafa   Let's carry father out to the taxi.

Father   I have money. Listen. (*And shakes his pockets and we hear strange sounds that might or might not be money.*)

Father   Carry me, my sons, carry me and I will wait for you at home where mother is preparing a feast of rice and eggplants and meat. Ahhh ya pine nuts. Oh where are the days of the pine nuts. When the cement factory opens, we will swim in pine nuts. Don't be late. And don't talk to that loudspeaker.

The boys carry him up the wall and 'throw' him over the wall.

Sound of Father (*cheerfully*)   Bye bye boys. Have fun and don't be late. Beautiful boys. Hamdalillah, they all look like me.

Scene Three

Again the boys are sitting on the wall. They spontaneously look at the loudspeaker and decide to open their bags and take out books. Almost like choreography, they read a page, turn a page, read a page, turn a page, cross a leg over a leg, uncross it, lean to one side, and slowly, movement by movement end up reading the books in all positions, upside down, laying down, hanging, all around the wall and loudspeaker. But they are still reading. In the end of this study time, they are, again, all like monkeys, in every possible crazy position they can make. An image. They say the below text while sitting still.

Mustafa   I'm done. Bring on the test, ya teacher, bring on the test. I studied all the formulas and I can pass the test.

Noor   P A C I F I C – Pacific – an ocean in the eastern hemisphere and the biggest ocean on our planet earth. Around the ocean is the circle of fire that often causes dangerous weather such as hurricanes and tsunamis. Bring on the geography test. I learned the whole book.

Ali   Red and blue make purple and purple is the colour of the sky in the night on a summer day. Red and yellow make orange and orange is the colour of the sea when the sun is going down. Yellow and blue make green and green is the colour of oil. Hamdalillah bring on my test. I know all the colours I need to know.

Sounds from a Loudspeaker   Abu Khaled, turn off the loudspeaker so we can go home. The courtyard is quiet. Everyone has gone home. Bye. Bye.

Slowly, and as before, the boys start to move until they are running through the courtyard, playing and throwing in school words in all crazy orders, borrowing from each other words and subjects as they like.

Scene Four

We need **Ali** *to end up on the wall during this running part. From up there he sees his aunt* **Selwa**.

Ali (*shouting, and really shouting, very excited*)   Ya auntie Salwa, ya Salwa, up here, on the wall. Look up. (*To the boys.*) It's our aunt Selwa. (*All boys jump up on the wall.*)

All   My aunt . . . we are here. Come. Come.

Appearing by the top of the wall, the wonderfully charming aunt **Selwa** *in her red dress and her beautiful smile. A teacher in the Girls School D, right next door. (Consider a ladder or two to help the actor go over the wall but she does it like a lady.)*

Selwa   Why are you not home?

Mustafa   Nothing to do at home. Mother is complaining that we are in her way. She is busy with the new twins . . .

Ali   And I'm afraid to break them.

Noor   And they are girls and we don't really know what to do with them.

Ali   Look, I cut my finger. It really hurts.

Selwa   I might have a bandage in this bag. What happened to this finger?

Ali   It got stuck . . .

Noor   Between my teeth . . .

Ali   No, no, no, not between his teeth, it's a real cut, I cut it on the loudspeaker. The loudspeaker bit me.

Selwa   Oh really? Yes the loudspeaker in our school also bites. (*She puts a bandaid on his finger.*) How's that now with a plaster on it.

Ali   Healed.

Mustafa   Watch, ya Salwa. (**Mustafa** *does a trick and tumbles and bangs his head.*)

Selwa   Yeeeee, your head!!! Don't move. Let me see. Maybe you have a concussion? (*She holds his head but knows he is not hurt. She rubs his head and is gentle with him. The other brothers hug her or stay close to her. They love her and find ways to show it.*)

Then **Mustafa**, *stands up, walks around, and starts to dance.*

Selwa   Ahhhh, you play tricks on your Aunt Selwa. Now show me a real trick so I can see how good you are. Stand on your head, do a tumble, jump from the wall. Show me what you have. (**Mustafa** *does a funny trick or nice dance for her.*) Ya hero. Ya artist. You should go on television. Or maybe not. Shall we walk home together?

Noor We can't go home yet. And we have nowhere to go. So we stay in the courtyard and we study and that loudspeaker keeps biting us. But I have a pain.

Selwa A pain? Tell me about it.

Noor It's here, and it hurts until here. (*From one end of his body to the other.*) It feels yellow. Maybe I have the yellow sickness. Or the sugar sickness. We ate sweets. What if I have the sugar sickness. Feel. It hurts from here all the way to here. What is it? Feel.

Selwa *plays the role of a nurse and feels* **Noor** *and checks his knees and arms almost like playing with a standing doll. She turns him upside down and shakes him and twists him.*

Selwa Ah ha! Just as I thought.

Noor WHAT? What do I have???

Selwa You have the 'boys can't sit still' sickness.

Mustafa What is that? There is no such thing.

Selwa Oh yes there is. And I have the cure.

Selwa *opens her bags and takes out white paper and markers.*

Selwa (*to* **Mustafa**) You, draw a lion. (*To* **Noor**.) And you make me a tiger. (*To* **Ali**.) And you draw a dragon.

The boys start drawing. They make these masks. During the drawing . . .

Mustafa This is the best lion.

Noor I don't know how to do it really.

Ali Just think like a big animal and make lines. It will come.

Mustafa Done.

Ali Done.

Noor Wait. Wait. Wait. Done.

Selwa Now, first we do this and then we do this and then a little of this and now this. (*From her bag, she has the materials to turn the drawings into masks and puts a mask onto each boy.*) GO. Make me a circus.

With this, the boys start to behave like lions and tigers and dragons. It's short, noisy, and with a lot of movement. As they are playing wildly, **Selwa** *pretends to be afraid of them.*

Selwa Lions and tigers and dragons, I must go home to cook. Don't stay here too long. I will pass by your mother and tell her you are fine. Don't be late.

And the wonderful aunt **Selwa** *leaves over the wall and the boys, still animals, laugh and growl saying goodbye.*

Scene Five

The masks have fallen off their faces. They are all laying down resting from the hard playing. Slowly they start to sit up and climb up back onto the wall. Again, as before, they slowly start to move.

Mustafa   You had to break the football!

Noor   I didn't break it. It just exploded.

Mustafa   Nothing just explodes.

Mustafa   We need another football.

Ali   Let's have a race. One, two, three. (*He jumps down, runs around, jumps back up and . . .*) I won!

Noor   I need new socks.

Mustafa   Me, too.

Ali   Everyone needs new socks.

They are moving more and more, getting restless.

Noor   I can make a football

Mustafa   Yeh. (*They jump down.*)

Ali   I'll get a bag.

Mustafa   I'm not collecting garbage.

Noor   We'll find clean garbage. It works. Come on.

Noor *has a plastic bag in his pocket.* **Ali** *starts collecting 'clean garbage' and they stuff the plastic bag. They make one ball, kick it, and it explodes all over.*

Ali   Let's make another one.

From over the wall, enter the **Grandfather**. *He is old. He is grumbling, complaining, and carrying a big bag that has the contents of all he has left. He has lost his house and is looking for a place to put himself. But he is also forgetful and a little nuts. He speaks in an unclear voice.*

Grandfather (*grumbling*)   We never did it right. I never should have left. Nothing is left. Everything is changed. First it was empty, then it was full, now it's all broken. Never looked at the situation. We never understood. What a world. One day nothing. The next day nothing. It's hot. And then it's cold. I've come a long road that leads to nowhere. Where is my wife? She was behind me the whole way. Maybe someone took her also. (*Sees his grandsons.*) BOYS. What are you doing here?

Mustafa   Ya sidi, this is the school yard.

Ali   We are studying.

Noor   To stay smart.

Grandfather Good. Good. Stay smart. Or else you'll end up with your house on your back. Help me with this.

Mustafa What is it, ya sidi.

Grandfather It's the house.

Mustafa That's not the house.

Grandfather It's the house. Where is your grandmother? See if she is in this bag. Yalla, open it.

They open the bag. It is full of useless things except for cardboards that they will use to set up the 'house'. Each cardboard can be a different funny shape as if they were crazy mattresses and this will let the sleeping scene be funnier. These cardboards have to be made to fold with tape and fit in the big bag of the grandfather.

Mustafa What is this?

Grandfather That's my bed. Put it there.

Noor And what is this, ya sidi?

Grandfather That's your grandmother's bed. See if your grandmother isn't in the bag. I don't know where I put her. I never did anything right. I never knew what was going on. And now we lost the country and your grandmother. Look. Look in the bag.

Ali She is not in the bag, ya sidi.

Grandfather Put her bed next to mine and you take this one for you and there . . . this is for you two. Your father will sleep on this paper. Where is your father? See if he is in the bag.

Ali He was here but now he's gone. He went to look for work.

Grandfather He'll never find it. He's like your grandmother. When you want it, you don't find it. Call him. Tell him to come to sleep on that mattress.

Grandfather Everyone go to bed.

Noor But it's not night yet.

Grandfather But we are all tired. Yalla. Listen to me. I am the grandfather here. I decide for the family. Like my grandfather decided for my father and like I decided for – I decided for no one. Life happened one day. Hamdalillah. Did you find my wife? Ya Bahiyya, where are you? Come. You have to make the food.

Mustafa Ya sidi . . .

Grandfather What, ya sidi . . . lay down on your mattress and I will tell you stories about when I was a fisherman.

Each boy and the grandfather lay down on the strangely shaped cardboard mattresses.

Mustafa Look, I have to sleep like this. (*He is making a strange shape to fit on the cardboard.*)

Noor And me, look, I have to do this? How does one sleep like this?

Ali Mine is in two parts. I have to sleep standing up.

Mustafa Grandfather, how are you sleeping like that?

Grandfather I do well with whatever I get. Hamdalillah. Bahiyya, come and fix my pillow.

Ali She isn't here, ya sidi. You left her at home.

Grandfather You sleep. I will go get her. She has to make you tea with biscuits. She forgets everything. Yalla. Wake up. Wake up. It's time to go to school.

Mustafa Sidi, shall I help you with your things.

Grandfather Don't touch a thing. You have to be careful with the merchandise.

Noor We are careful. You raised us well.

Grandfather Yes. I raised all my boys well. Hamdalillah. Everyone is well. Everyone lives. We did it all right. And we are fine. Yalla, give me that piece. And that piece. I have to get your grandmother. She is going to a wedding. I will drive her.

They pack the grandfather's bag. And he leaves grumbling.

Grandfather Every time there is a wedding we have to give a present. Do you have the present, ya Bahiyya? Is it enough? Good. We want to be generous. We did everything wrong. But we can start over again and this time we will do everything right. Yalla, my sister. I will carry you over this wall like a prince.

He goes up and over the wall carrying the bag as if it's his wife.

Scene Six

All of a sudden they start to play tag.

Ali You're it.

Mustafa You're it.

Noor Find your grandmother in the bag.

Ali You sleep like this and I sleep like that. You're it.

Mustafa He fell on his head. You're it.

Noor We did everything wrong. You.

Ali We did everything right. You.

Mustafa Got ya.

Ali I'm a fisherman. You're it.

Noor I'm a Bedouin. You.

Mustafa It's day. Got ya.

Ali It's night. You.

Mustafa Everything is upside down. You.

Noor We are boys who can't sit still. You.

Mustafa I can't sit still another second. You.

Ali I am going to fly away. You.

And they are running, running, running. From over the wall we see the head of **Bahiyya**. *She is wearing a colourful funny veil and a long, coloured dress. She was once beautiful and modern and she remembers those days of youth and love. Now she is very old and large and a true grandmother.*

Bahiyya Boys, come, come, help me over this wall. Ohhh you are all so handsome. Look at you. You are like your father. And you are like your mother and you, you are just like your grandfather. He was so handsome.

Mustafa Ya sitti, what are you doing here at the school yard.

Bahiyya I heard shouts of You, You, You, You, Got ya, You. I thought it was your grandfather. Did you see him? He left to go shopping and he hasn't come home yet.

Mustafa He was just here, sitti, but he wasn't shopping. He is a little lost.

Bahiyya Yes. He is very tired. We are all very tired but we have to go on. Look how handsome you are. Who is getting married first? Which one wants me to find his bride. There are many. All pretty. I know them all. You, you are Mustafa right?

Mustafa Yes sitti. How are you?

Bahiyya Old. (*She opens her purse and takes out her large mirror.*) Look in here with me. (*All the boys try to look in the mirror together with her.*) You see all these faces. I can see the whole of our family in these faces. Look. This one looks exactly like my brother. The one in Khan Yunis. That's his face when he was a boy. And this one here. That's your mother only with short hair. You see her face here, her cheek, look, the smile, that's your mother. And here, this face is like my mother. That's what my mother looked like, rest in peace, yamma, habibti. You, you also look like my brother who looked like my father. And this face here also looks like my brother and my sister who also looked like my uncle. You see all the faces here? That's what we look like. Everyone smile now. Now we look like my wedding photo. Everyone was smiling when I married your grandfather. When I first saw him my heart went thump thump thump. You boys, it's time to get married and make more of us. (*Pause.*) Who is first?

Ali But sitti, I am only eight.

Bahiyya It's never too soon to start looking. Like life. You have to live it from the minute you are born. First you cry and shout for food. And you stay crying and fighting until you finally rest. In between . . . in between . . . you have the moments.

Mustafa   Moments?

Noor   What are the moments?

Ali   I never heard of the moments.

Bahiyya   Those are the special times. They are the days when we are happy. The moments are the special days we will all get to live when our hearts are jumping around inside us like little children.

Ali   I don't understand.

Bahiyya   On the day your father was born, that was a moment. Happiness raining down on us. And on the days that you were all born, you mother had the same moments. Great happiness.

Mustafa   But nothing turned out right, ya sitti.

Noor   Everything is broken.

Ali   Our grandfather . . . he has no moments . . . he forgot them . . . but his heart jumps when I talk to him.

Mustafa   We don't have moments.

Ali   I never had a moment.

Noor   I don't know of a moment in my life.

Bahiyya   No moments, ya sitti. Come sit and put your heads here.

As she is already sitting in the middle, each boy puts his head on her lap.

Bahiyya   Here is a moment. (*Again she opens her large bag and takes out a fruit and a knife and she cuts this and feeds this to the open mouths on her lap.*) Your grandfather brought me these this morning. That was nice of him to bring me fruit. And your father passed by to play with you. You were all laughing and playing together. That's what I heard. And then your aunt Selwa came by and played the lion game with you. We heard you making noises all the way on the roof. And now we are eating fruit together. You had many moments today. Think how many you had and how many more wait for you.

Mustafa   But sitti, what about everything else?

Bahiyaa   What else?

Noor   Everything else.

Ali   I can't sit still.

Noor   Me either.

Bahiyya   Well look at you now. The three of you are just about to fall asleep.

Mustafa (*now relaxed*)   Is this a moment?

Bahiyya   What do you think?

Noor I stopped moving.

Bahiyya Swallow or you'll choke.

Ali I'm having a moment, ya sitti. I'm having a moment.

End.

Afterword

By Jan Willems

To a director, Jackie's plays are a true delight because of the infectious optimism and joy of her characters. Her protagonists communicate thirst for life and energy despite the darkness they are confronted with in the conflict-ridden Middle East, in Palestine. At the same time, her texts are challenging. They require profound preparation when considered for theatrical productions. While her dialogues are to the point regarding content, they are written with a light pen and lots of comic relief. They are also surprisingly short and extremely dense. The director must pick up the subtle and casually written signals related to character development and societal context. In short performances of forty minutes, an entire world of Gaza youngsters' lives is brought to the stage. She usually depicts a situation of emergency, painted with the writer's colorful brush and showing characters who find strength, resilience, and optimism. The Gaza Strip is the always present context of her plays, whether they are based in harsh reality or hilarious imagination.

Thinking about Gaza, you might picture children and young people as victims, which is quite logical considering the media images of misery, war, deprivation, oppression, poverty, violence, and fear. Jackie's plays open up to another reality, picturing kids and adolescents as the agents of change they often are. Her characters are not only regular and simple heroes of daily resistance, but they are also role models for youngsters in the entire world.

Written for a school-aged young audience, the texts always provide valuable themes for dramatic work in class, and discussion before or after a performance. These themes vary from early marriage of girls to the neglect and abuse of young boys in families at risk; from overcoming pain after loss of loved ones in war or conflict to the joy and feelings of safety that come with solidarity and new friendships; from the problem of patriarchy ruling the life of a girl – older brother, father, clan leader or boss – to the creativity found by children to save themselves from pain; and in Jackie's plays 'A Human Writes' from the traditional control of a stupid Wazir to the bright and funny young King, a boy almost, who loves the inventiveness and humor of his people.

In the compact nature and content of the plays, this author demands that actors accept the fictionalized reality of their characters as a matter of life and death. A physical approach, using dance and movement, is often a good choice for a director to find appropriate expression for the challenges the young characters are facing. In the play *The School*, the main character Jaber tells us about yesterday, a long monologue of wonder, pain, surprise, oppression, and almost painful humor, all lived on that day. He reports on his responsibilities for his family as a young boy, on oppression by brothers and neighbors, on an Israeli bombardment while doing errands, running between rubble, and collapsed walls; on efforts to earn a sandwich for his hungry stomach by moving cardboard boxes for a shop keeper, no food at home . . .; and on the tears in his eyes at night while desperately trying to do his homework for class the next day. Reading this text, one feels how his body is beaten by life, physically and psychologically mugged. How can this day, and Jaber's abuse, be expressed in acting on stage? How could an audience become aware of the painful sensations in Jaber's body? Here, the director's challenge is to find imagery – dance, movement and other physical interpretation, or audiovisual support – for the acting work. Jaber's own acceptance of this day as a simple fact of life causes dry and comic relief. The more Jaber's abuse is visualized, the more his acceptance is comic and hopeful, as well as deeply tragic.

In some plays, the writer herself has provided the visual expression and physical action as part of the text and stage directions. In *The Boys Who Can't Sit Still*, boys are running, running, and running even more. They want to live every second they can, to search, act, find questions, and look for answers. Their fervor and over-the-top actions reflect the insecurity of life in Gaza, but also shows their will to live intensely as long as they can. The play portrays the energy and resilience of youngsters, as opposed to the common western media images of defeat, nihilism, and drug addiction. Resilience remains after decades of warfare! In *The Brothers*, two small gangs of boys interact in a choreographed fight to control a small playground in their refugee camp. They find a common goal and peace; their dance confrontation reminds us of the good old Manhattan Sharks and Jets.

For dramaturgy. The emotional impact of most plays in this collection becomes evident when a striking experience in the past of one of the characters is revealed. In *The White Play*, one of the four girls appears to have lost her brother in recent political violence. In the moment this is revealed in the text, the previous seemingly unintentional dialogue of the girls about typical teenage concerns is given a new, intensified and hitherto unexpected charge to the text. It is a wake-up call for the play's director and actors: the unintentional dialogues have an important emotional context and provide important subtext for the actors. The three other girls are well-aware of their friend's trauma, but none had the courage or opportunity to address her loss. Using this structure, Jackie presents readers and theatre makers with a 'late point of attack,' a postponed release of emotional depth. She gives the actors foundational secrets and layers of subtext for their roles. Especially for young beginning actors these are interesting dramatic details for performing and character study.

For context. Gaza has always shown another picture than the dark, gloomy, sometimes aggressive images of misery in the mass-media. Gaza's people know how to connect to hope. Their creativity sometimes strikes you with disbelief. In the years 2007 to 2009, when Israel allowed no import beyond the strict elementary goods for survival, the shortage of gasoline prevented all cars from driving; but old Mercedes taxis were adjusted for driving on cooking oil as fuel (an elementary product for food and a necessary part of emergency humanitarian imports). Soon people could move between cities again. Watching these cars from the sidewalk, was quite an experience; they smelled as if a fish and chips market was passing by.

Jackie's plays generated many discussions in Gaza, especially during the years after the wars of 2009, 2012, and 2014. Are these plays educational? Are they giving children the proper example? Could plays about trauma and conflict have a negative effect and maybe push children back into trauma? Jackie's texts take children and youngsters seriously as full partners in dialogue, as people who can teach adults, as much as adults can teach them. They live a life full of valuable experiences, conflicts, and contradictions. It would be belittling to give children only 'good' examples, to only show them the obligatory rosy or utopian side of life. It is exactly this belittling attitude and lack of trust that alienates kids from schools and general education. Art, especially drama, can make children and youngsters feel at home in school because it allows their real lives, the depth of their problems and conflicts to exist, to be shared and discussed, and to be given a place for development, maybe even for resolution.

In the difficult years of wars on Gaza, Jackie's plays allowed children and youngsters to give their feelings of loss and desolation a place in their lives, by sharing stories, or even by mourning together with classmates, triggered by the content of the plays that had fictionalized the reality they experienced. In the end, the story of each play always brought them 'home' to a safe place of solidarity, new friendships, and family.

The performances by Theatre Day productions in Gaza, the plays in this anthology, and the personal stories of the school students in our drama workshops, made storytelling events that functioned as remedy and antidote against trauma and despair.

Sarah in '*The Room*'

Sarah And the balcony flew away. I am 100 per cent certain that someone found our balcony and sewed it onto their house. And our bedroom just fell off the house. Kablonggggg. Lucky I wasn't in it or kablongggg on me and I wouldn't be here anymore. I would be with God and that's better than being here. I have nothing anymore. Nothing nothing nothing. I hate it here. Our house is scattered all over the city. Where are my clothes? Also scattered. Maybe I will see someone wearing my things and then what? Fight her in the street for finding flying clothing and socks. And where are my shoes? I have no shoes. Only my shib-shib. Like the Nakba. My grandmother said, 'We all left in our shib-shib because we were going to come back.' It's the Nakba all over again. That's what grandmother said. I lost my boots. The ones with the fur. From Wahdeh Street. The good ones. Where are we? Whose house is this?

Vernacular glossary

Abaya: Loose over-garment or cloak.
Abu: Father of…
Alhamdulillah: Praise be to God or thank God.
Askadinya: A loquat tree.
Assalamu Alaykum: Peace be upon you.
Astaghfirullah Al Adheem: A prayer to God for forgiveness: I seek forgiveness from Allah.
Aza: Funeral.
Bamia: Okra.
Bammpers: Pampers. Sometimes, Arabs mix the letters P and B.
Bismillah Al-Rahman Al-Raheem: In the name of God, the most gracious and the most merciful.
Dabkeh: A traditional Palestinian dance style.
Diwan: A traditional sitting area for hosting. It also refers to a site or gathering used for official state governance.
Habibi: My beloved (male).
Habibti: My beloved (female).
Haj: Refers to a pilgrim. It is sometimes used as a sign of respect for the elderly. The Haj is also the sacred Muslim pilgrimage to Mecca.
Hattah and Agal: Traditional Palestinian head-wear worn by men.
Im: Mother of…
Inshallah: God willing!
Jalabia: Traditional loose-fitting Arab garment worn by men or women.
Khair Inshallah: All good, God willing.
Khair: Good.
Khalas: Enough. Sometimes it can mean 'please' or 'stop it.'
Khishkhash: Bitter oranges for marmalade.
Kufiyah: A black and white scarf that is symbolic of the Palestinian struggle.
Labtob: Laptop. Sometimes, Arabs mix the letters P and B.
Mabrouk: Congratulations!
Mandeel: Hijab or veil.
Mashallah: What Allah willed. Also means, 'how wonderful!'
Mowwal: A traditional form of Palestinian music. Usually, it is sad.
Mukhtar: Village chief or representative leader.
Nakba: The historic catastrophe of 1948.
Qumbaz: Traditional Palestinian attire worn by men.
Sahtayn: Literally means 'double health' and the equivalent of 'bon appétit'
Salam: Salutation. Greetings!
Shekel: Israeli currency, which Palestinians under occupation must use.
Sheshbesh: The Palestinian version of backgammon, known also as Tawlet Zaher.
Shibshib: Flip flops.
Sidi: My grandfather.

Sitti: Grandmother.
Souk: Market. Souk Ez-Zawyeh is a market in old Gaza.
Tfadal: Welcome. Come on in.
Wallah: By God!
Wawa: A childish reference to an injury that is similar to the American 'bobo.'
Ya Allah: Oh my God!
Yaba: The equivalent of calling one's father 'baba'. Can be seen as short for 'ya baba'.
Ya Haram: An expression of sympathy meaning 'how sad' or 'poor thing.'
Yamma: The equivalent of calling one's mother 'mama'. Can be seen as short for 'ya mama'.
Yallah Ya Shabab: Let's go, young men!
Ya'ni: The equivalent of 'I mean...' or 'you know...' 'Shoo Ya'ni' asks 'what do you mean?' or 'what if?'
Ya Sheikha: 'Old lady' or can mean sarcastically, 'fancy lady,' or simply, 'woman.'
Ya'tik El-Afieh: May God give you health. 'Ya'tikum' for plural use.
Ya Zalameh: A way to refer to a man in casual conversation, like 'dude' or 'man!'

www.ingramcontent.com/pod-product-compliance
Ingram Content Group UK Ltd.
Pitfield, Milton Keynes, MK11 3LW, UK
UKHW021933290525
459105UK00007B/149